13.2.25

R. O. BUCHANAN
AND
ECONOMIC GEOGRAPHY

BELL'S ADVANCED ECONOMIC GEOGRAPHIES

General Editor
PROFESSOR R. O. BUCHANAN
M.A.(N.Z.), B.Sc.(Econ.), Ph.D.(London)
Professor Emeritus, University of London

A. *Systematic Studies*

PLANTATION AGRICULTURE
P. P. Courtenay, B.A., Ph.D.

NEW ENGLAND: A STUDY IN INDUSTRIAL ADJUSTMENT
R. C. Estall, B.Sc.(Econ.), Ph.D.

GREATER LONDON: AN INDUSTRIAL GEOGRAPHY
J. E. Martin, B.Sc.(Econ.), Ph.D.

GEOGRAPHY AND ECONOMICS
Michael Chisholm, M.A.

AGRICULTURAL GEOGRAPHY
Leslie Symons, B.Sc.(Econ.) Ph.D.

REGIONAL ANALYSIS AND ECONOMIC GEOGRAPHY
John N. H. Britton, M.A., Ph.D.

THE FISHERIES OF EUROPE: AN ECONOMIC GEOGRAPHY
James R. Coull, M.A., Ph.D.

A GEOGRAPHY OF TRADE AND DEVELOPMENT IN MALAYA
P. P. Courtenay, B.A., Ph.D.

R. O. BUCHANAN AND ECONOMIC GEOGRAPHY
Ed. M. J. Wise, M.C., B.A., Ph.D., & E. M. Rawstron, M.A.

B. *Regional Studies*

AN ECONOMIC GEOGRAPHY OF EAST AFRICA
A. M. O'Connor, B.A., Ph.D.

AN ECONOMIC GEOGRAPHY OF WEST AFRICA
H. P. White, M.A., & M. B. Gleave, M.A.

YUGOSLAVIA: PATTERNS OF ECONOMIC ACTIVITY
F. E. Ian Hamilton, B.Sc.(Econ.), Ph.D.

RUSSIAN AGRICULTURE: A GEOGRAPHIC SURVEY
Leslie Symons, B.Sc.(Econ.) Ph.D.

AN AGRICULTURAL GEOGRAPHY OF GREAT BRITAIN
J. T. Coppock. M.A., Ph.D.

AN HISTORICAL INTRODUCTION TO THE ECONOMIC GEOGRAPHY
OF GREAT BRITAIN
Wilfred Smith, M.A.

THE BRITISH IRON & STEEL SHEET INDUSTRY SINCE 1840
Kenneth Warren, M.A., Ph.D.

Robert Ogilvie Buchanan

R. O. BUCHANAN AND ECONOMIC GEOGRAPHY

Edited by

M. J. WISE

Professor of Geography, University of London,
London School of Economics & Political Science

&

E. M. RAWSTRON

Professor of Geography, University of London,
Queen Mary College

LONDON
G. BELL & SONS LTD
1973

Copyright © 1973 by
G. BELL AND SONS, LTD
York House, Portugal Street
London, W.C.2

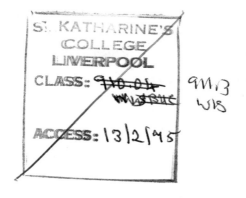

ISBN 0 7135 1766 2

Printed in Great Britain by
Redwood Press Limited, Trowbridge, Wiltshire

I.B.M. Computer Typesetting by
Print Origination, Liverpool.

Preface

There has been for some time a feeling among friends, former students and colleagues of Professor R. Ogilvie Buchanan that a suitable way should be found to mark the success of his work, especially as a teacher of economic geography. Various means of achieving this aim have been suggested from time to time and, after consulting some of those who know him well, it seemed to the editors that by far the most suitable way would be to bring together in one volume a number of Buchanan's papers. While providing a permanent record of his work, this volume should also make readily available to present and future students several relatively inaccessible papers which might otherwise be overlooked notwithstanding their importance in the evolution of economic geography.

For an appreciation of Professor Buchanan's work as a teacher at University College, London, and of his contribution to the founding and growth of the Institute of British Geographers, the editors turned immediately to Professor A. E. Smailes, one of Buchanan's first students at University College and his successor as Honorary Secretary of the Institute: they express their gratitude to Professor Smailes.

The editors are grateful to G. Bell and Sons Ltd, for the readiness with which their proposal for this volume was accepted and for their sympathetic interest at all stages of preparation and publication.

The editors wish also to acknowledge with thanks the assistance of the following societies and individuals who generously gave permission for publication of the papers:
The Royal Geographical Society and the Editor of *The Geographical Journal* (Paper 8)

The Royal Scottish Geographical Society (Paper 2)
The British Association for the Advancement of Science (Paper 9)
The Geographical Association and the Editor of *Geography* (Papers 3, 4 and 6)
The Institute of British Geographers and the Editor of the *Transactions and Papers* (Paper 11)
The Indian Geographical Society (Paper 1)
Clark University and the Editor of *Economic Geography* (Paper 7)
The Hong Kong University Press (Paper 12)
The London School of Economics and Political Science (Paper 10)

The editors are also indebted to Dr. Mark Abrams for his agreement as editor to the re-printing of Professor Buchanan's contribution to *Britain and her Export Trade* (Paper 5)

The maps have been skilfully redrawn for this volume by Mrs. Jeanne-Marie Stanton: the photograph of Professor Buchanan was taken specially by Brian Lessware and Derek Summers. Gail Cockwill, Wendy Greenwood, Jane Fleming, John Ockenden and Carl Pearson all gave helpful assistance in the preparation of the volume. Finally, the editors wish to express their thanks to the many friends to whom they have at one time or another turned for advice.

October 1972

M. J. W.
E. M. R.

Contents

List of Tables

List of Maps and Diagrams

R. Ogilvie Buchanan : Economic Geographer

by M. J. Wise & E. M. Rawstron

Few men have contributed more to the study and teaching of economic geography than Professor R. O. Buchanan. Not the least of his contributions has been made as editor of the series of books on economic geography in which, to his surprise, this volume will find a place. It seemed to the editors of this book, and to the publishers of the series of Advanced Economic Geography books, which he has edited with such success, that no more fitting way could be found to express the appreciation of his friends, colleagues and students than to reprint a selection from his papers on economic geography and related subjects. These have appeared in journals in many countries since his first publication in 1930: many are no longer easily available to students. Their re-appearance, at a time when their author is still active in academic affairs, will, we are sure, be warmly welcomed.

Robert Ogilvie Buchanan was born at Maheno, near Oamaru, in the province of Otago in the South Island, New Zealand, on 12th September 1894. The movement of his mother's family from Roxburghshire in the Scottish Border country had started in the 1860s, when his mother's eldest brother had sailed for New Zealand in charge of a consignment of pedigree sheep. Two other uncles followed him, in charge of further consignments. In the early 1870s, probably in 1873, his mother with her remaining two brothers sailed from Glasgow on an unbroken four months' voyage. Buchanan's father, one of two sons of a ship's captain who was lost at sea, leaving the boys to be brought up by relatives, gave up a place at the University of Glasgow and the prospect of a career as a minister of the Free Church of Scotland to follow the sea, but eventually, seduced by the attractions of New Zealand, decided to settle there.

At the time of his mother's arrival in the South Island, Otago was still in the full flush of the exploitation of its alluvial gold and was very much the hub of New Zealand life. But his parents' interests were in farming, and eighteen months after his birth the family moved to the Tapanui Valley in West Otago. Here Buchanan spent his boyhood. Today, the Tapanui Valley, overlooked from the east by the Blue Mountains, presents a smiling and prosperous farming landscape. The names at the farm gates suggest the Scottish origins of many of the early settlers. The introduction of refrigeration in the 1880s had given an impetus to the pastoral industries and Buchanan's parents played their part in the transformation of the landscape and the building of a new economy. Across country with yet poorly developed transport facilities Buchanan walked, or rode on horseback, many miles daily to school. In retrospect it may not be altogether fanciful to suggest that it was these early experiences that aroused his curiosity into the ways in which agricultural patterns were shaped and agricultural regions emerged.

His early studies in the University of Otago before the First World War were in history and economics: geography was not yet known in New Zealand as a university, or indeed as a High School, subject. After two years at the University he answered the call for volunteers, joined the 2nd Otago Regiment and, with so many of his generation, sailed for service in the Middle East and in the trenches of the Western Front. He was wounded and in hospital for some months but returned to the front in time for the final campaign. He returned to New Zealand in 1919 and completed his B.A. degree. A year as assistant master and housemaster at Whangarei enabled him to save enough money to return to the University of Otago to take his M.A. with Honours in 1921. Economics was his honours subject.

Buchanan was then appointed to a teaching post at Mount Albert Grammar School, Auckland, to teach mainly History. We imagine him throwing himself as enthusiastically into training the Rugby Football XV as into the academic work.

He was undoubtedly successful in both. At this time came a major turning point in his career. His headmaster, a man of progressive views, induced him to take charge of a new subject, geography, which he wanted to introduce into the school. His was probably the first appointment in New Zealand of a specialist geography master. Few books were available. Buchanan has told how a search of the second-hand bookshops yielded, among other books, Marion Newbigin's *Commercial Geography*, which gave him a first glimpse of a worthwhile intellectual discipline.

His interest in this new subject quickly grew, and the links with his earlier studies in history and economics became apparent. If the new subject was to be taken up it was first to be studied and where better than the London School of Economics, where H. J. Mackinder and Ll. Rodwell Jones had established a strong school. L.S.E. was then a much smaller institution than it is now. The majority of the undergraduates were part-time students and many of the lectures were given in the evening. From 1925 to 1927 he read there for the B.Sc. Econ. degree, with geography as his special subject. But only three final papers out of ten were taken in geography and Buchanan's first class degree (he was second in order of merit on the list) says much for his ability to compete on their own ground with specialist economists, historians and political scientists. No doubt his achievement owed much to the clarity with which he was able to identify and apply essential principles, a characteristic later to become evident in his writings and lectures.

A year as a research student under the guidance of Professor Rodwell Jones was followed by his appointment in 1928 as an assistant lecturer in geography at University College, London, to work under Professor C. B. Fawcett, and for almost a quarter of a century he was closely identified with the life of the College. This part of the story we leave to Professor Smailes (pages 17-21) who was one of Buchanan's first students at University College.

With the Second World War in prospect, Buchanan volunteered again; this time for service with the Royal Air Force. He served for some time on, and in charge of, balloon barrage posts in the London area. Fortunately, his geographical skills were recognised and put to profitable employment. He was the first R.A.F. officer to serve in the Air Ministry maps branch of G.S.G.S., which became in 1942 part of the newly organised Directorate of Military Survey. In 1943 he returned to the Air Ministry as Maps Officer in charge of a maps service designed to meet the special needs of the Air Ministry and the R.A.F. His rank by then was Squadron Leader.

In 1938 he had been appointed to a Readership in Economic Geography at University College and he returned to this post at the end of the war. When in 1949 the London School of Economics was seeking a professor to take charge of its geography department, at a time when Dudley Stamp was translated from the Chair of Geography to a new post as Professor of Social Geography, thoughts turned naturally to Buchanan and he was persuaded to move. He was already well known to his new colleagues at L.S.E. through his service on university committees such as the Board of Studies in Economics and respected by them for his grasp of economics and for his ability to trace the operation of economics in geographical patterns. It was not surprising, therefore, that following his appointment economic geography took a new enhanced status in the School of Economics. His teaching attracted and inspired able undergraduates: he built around him a like-minded group of younger teachers and laid the foundations for the growth of the graduate school in geography at L.S.E.

Buchanan has always seen himself as a servant of the community. In addition to his service on L.S.E. committees, he was a member of the Senate of the University of London from 1951 to 1967, Chairman of the Academic Council of the University from 1958 to 1962 and Deputy Vice-Chancellor in the year of his retirement. His interests in Commonwealth affairs led him to the work of the Association of Commonwealth Universities, of which he was Honorary Treasurer from 1961 to 1967. His services to the geographical societies of Britain have been recognised by his election as President of Section E of the British Association for the Advancement of Science in 1952, of the Institute of British Geographers in 1953 and of the Geographical Association in

1958. He was made Honorary Fellow of the Royal Geographical Society in 1966. The London School of Economics elected him to Honorary Fellowship in 1970. Outside the universities he worked as a member of the Nature Conservancy from 1955 to 1970, as Chairman of the Executive Committee of the Association of Agriculture from 1964 to 1972, as a member of the Council and the Committee of Management of the Institute of Education from 1955, and of the governing bodies of several colleges of education. But probably his greatest pleasures have come from the frequent visits of his old students now working in universities all over the world, who regularly call to visit him in his tiny office on the fifth floor of the St. Clement's Building at L.S.E.

II

Buchanan's writings on economic geography fall readily into three groups, namely, those that demonstrate his approach to the subject and his view of its content; those that deal especially with New Zealand; and those that indicate some applications of the subject to problems of public concern.

His attitude to economic geography was expressed simply but effectively in the opening words of his book *An Economic Geography of the British Empire*, published in 1935: 'Human geography is the study of how man's life is influenced by the world in which he lives. It follows that if we are to try to relate man's work to the natural or geographical conditions in which he works, we must know not only the natural conditions, but also the sort of equipment he has to work with. This equipment includes both his stock of material goods, like tools, and his accumulated knowledge and organisation'.

His interests have lain particularly in the study of commercial economies and of the ways in which through the accumulation of capital, the application of skill, the gathering of economies of scale and the development of transport, specialised economies became associated with areas. In his own words again: 'The beginnings of this specialisation of areas are due to the fact that when all the conditions are weighed it is found that the areas in question are more

suitable for the production of particular commodities than
they are for the production of other commodities, or perhaps
than other areas are for the production of the same commodities. This means that the favoured commodities can be
placed on the market from these areas at less cost than other
commodities from the same areas, or the same commodities
from other areas, and is nearly always due in origin to some
geographical factor such as climate or soil, or proximity to
power sources or to markets. But once such specialisation of
an area has been established it tends to stay. The invested
capital, the developed organisation, the presence of a large
supply of skilled workers, the reputation that has been gained
for the quality of product, all tend to cause an area to retain
its special production, even though other areas may later be
recognised to have geographical conditions equal to or better
than its own.'[2]

So Buchanan placed his studies clearly in the field of the
localisation of industries, a field which in economics may be
traced back in English writing certainly to Alfred Marshall
and to which Alfred Weber had made the first major
theoretical contribution. Before Buchanan there had been
relatively little activity in this field by British geographers:
the work of G. G. Chisholm is the outstanding exception.
Buchanan and his contemporary Wilfred Smith, whose work
in this same series may instructively be compared with that
of Buchanan, were the two leading workers and teachers in
this field in Britain in the period between the two world wars
and immediately after the second. Whereas most of Smith's
studies concerned the economic geography of Great Britain,
Buchanan was interested to draw a clear picture 'of world
economic activities organised for production for the world
market'. To aid him there were well developed economic theories and principles, of the division of labour, of
comparative advantage, of economies of scale, of transport
costs; there were studies of human organisation and its
evolution. The geographer's work, however, was distinguished
from that of the economist or economic historian by its
reference not merely to *where* the various kinds of production were carried on but to *how* the conditions in those areas
and the development of communications between them

favoured the kind and amount of production that was under-taken.

With these points in mind, attention should now be given to Buchanan's paper 'Approach to Economic Geography,' reprinted in this volume. Against a background summary of the development of economic geography, he clearly brings out the tasks of explaining the existence and changing nature of the economic landscapes that offer the visible expressions of economic specialisation of area. Man's work was not haphazard or capricious. Geographical patterns of economic activity reflected considered evaluations of natural conditions made in the context of assessed opportunities for producing and marketing particular commodities. Producers in any one area were tied into a wider economic system and explanations for regional specialisation had to be sought not only within the region but in the operation of the wider system of exchange and marketing, a point he stressed again in 'Some Reflections on Agricultural Geography'. In this paper, as generally in his writing, Buchanan did not waste words: the argument is concise. Three of his observations deserve special mention since they refer to ideas that recur in his work. First is his observation that 'it is precisely the areal investigation of comparative costs that gives the economic geographer his peculiar opportunity and gives his contribution real substance'. Second is his interest in the application in geography of the marginal concept of the economist. Third, is his emphasis not merely on the conditions of physical geography but on what men have thought those conditions to mean for them in the light of their own resources and opportunities: in short, on changing geographical values.

No paper more clearly indicates Buchanan's interest in the first two of these ideas than that on 'Some Features of World Wheat Production', undoubtedly one of the most thoughtful papers in economic geography of its period. It may well be argued, indeed, that his greatest contribution to economic geography lies in his emphasis upon the central role of a geography of costs and prices. The paper attempts to test the proposition that movements of the price/costs ratio for a particular commodity find expression in the movement of the general geographical margin of production. The tests applied gave some support to the association of a rapid positive movement of the geographical margins of world wheat cultivation with high prices for wheat in the open world market. But the conclusions were less decisive than the author may have hoped for, partly, as he pointed out, because of the intervention of social and political factors, especially at times of low prices, and partly because of the problem in economic geography of the 'time lag'. Economic changes do not always find immediate expression in economic landscapes: it takes time for information to disseminate through the system and for new appreciations to be made by the men on the ground. Even when the need for change has been accepted, further time is needed to adapt farming and industrial systems. Economic landscapes may thus quite often reflect adaptions to economic conditions that have now ceased to exist.

It is a matter for some regret that the ideas and tests in 'Some Features of World Wheat Production' were not directly followed up. But it was a time when war was on the horizon and patterns of world trade were being heavily distorted by political considerations. But, happily, in more recent work in economic geography, especially in application to changes in industrial regions, it is possible to discern the underlying influence of the arguments expounded in 'World Wheat'. It is undoubtedly a classic in the field.

The paper 'A Note on Labour Requirements in Plantation Agriculture' has been much used by students of economic geography for its definition of plantation agriculture. Perhaps of more interest, in the context of Buchanan's approach to economic geography, is its concern with the organisation of a farming type, and especially the influence of labour requirements on the development of the system. The crux of the problem remained, as it had been since the 17th century, 'the provision of an adequate supply of the right kind of labour in areas where the population is scanty, or for any reason unable or unwilling to meet the needs of the planters'. In what circumstances could capital be substituted for labour? What was the relation between climatic conditions and the problems of plantation organisation? In his answers to these and other questions one notes Buchanan's ability to draw on a wide range of examples, a reflection of an interest in comparative studies that will be referred to later.

One or two sentences from 'Some Reflections on Agricultural Geography', which is the next paper to be included, well illustrate Buchanan's handling of the economic background to the establishment of specialised farming systems:

'Not surprisingly the longest strides to extreme specialisation of agricultural areas were taken in the earlier nineteenth century in some of the areas of new colonization overseas. The plantations and the Australian sheep runs have already been mentioned . . . The essence of their economic position lay in the fact that land was normally plentiful and cheap, while extreme scarcity of labour was reflected in very high rates of wages. Efficient use of labour demanded systems of farming that would spread labour thinly over much land and give a high return per unit of labour, though normally this would be accompanied by a low yield per unit of area'. Generally the paper is concerned with approaches to the study of agricultural regions: it was the precise analysis of economic conditions that made such a study an exercise in economic rather than in regional geography.

The final paper in the first section is, we are sure, one of Buchanan's favourites. It was contributed to a volume entitled *Britain and her Export Trade*, published in 1947 under the editorship of his old fellow student and friend, Mark Abrams. The paper retains value not only for the analysis of the characteristics of the trade of an Empire with dissimilar parts but also for the historical summary. In the analysis lie many of the answers to those who have recently questioned why Britain should enter the European Economic Community and apparently 'abandon' the Commonwealth. The optimum development of the economies of the various parts of the Empire required, Buchanan argued, a trading area and system much wider than the Empire, 'wide enough indeed to include the whole world'. And that is an objective still far from achievement.

III

The second section of papers reflects, in the first place,

Buchanan's interest in the economic geography of his own country. His attachment to his native land is clear: it provided him with type examples for his studies of the emergence of specialised agricultural regions in relation to far distant markets. Comment on them would be superfluous: it is more useful to refer at this stage to his monograph, *The Pastoral Industries of New Zealand* which appeared in 1935. The monograph deserves reprinting for its own sake; unfortunately it is too long to be included in this volume and the decision not to include passages from it, or an abstract, was taken, partly at least, in a desire not to preclude the possibility of future re-publication in full. Significantly, the monograph was published in the volume which records the events that led to the foundation of the Institute of British Geographers in 1933, events in which Buchanan had himself played an influential part. The monograph was based on his Ph.D. thesis. Distinct from many geographical studies of his time, the monograph opened with an account of the economic and historical background: the physical setting was placed second. Buchanan's view, as explained in his Preface, was of an economic geography that was truly a study of the *inter-action* of geographical and economic conditions. 'In industries organised on a commercial, as distinct from a purely subsistence basis, geographical conditions express themselves, if at all, in economic, mainly monetary, terms; . . . the nature and extent of the influence of the geographical conditions are themselves dependent on the precise nature of the economic conditions. That will be recognised as merely specifying one type of instance of the generally accepted view that geographical values depend on the cultural stage achieved by the human actors.'

His first task was to determine as precisely as possible the distributions of cattle and sheep in New Zealand. His explanation of those distributions took account of the circumstances in which the country had been settled and of the agricultural practices that had been followed. It was informed by an understanding of the colonists and of their animals. Turn, for example, to pages 44 to 45 of the monograph for a description of the colonists in Canterbury, their merino sheep and their adaptation of methods of management already pioneered in Australia. Note also the assessment of the effect of the climatic differences, especially the abundance and reliability of spring rainfall, which enabled New Zealand to dominate its rivals in the southern hemisphere in the production of meat from sheep. Here in Chapter V is a balancing of natural conditions, human initiative, economic possibilities that remains a model to the economic geographer: here may be found an interweaving of the many aspects of the problem into a coherent pattern. While a general picture is drawn for New Zealand as a whole, regional and local variations are not overlooked: the influences of local changes in the physical environment or of the particular circumstances of settlement locally are clearly traced and woven into the pattern. The New Zealand farmer was shown 'to have evolved an agricultural system, which, pivoted on grass, takes maximum advantage of the peculiar character of the New Zealand climate, with its combination of mildness of temperature in the winter and general adequacy of rainfall in the summer, to the end of maximising economy of the most expensive factor in production, labour'.

Fully to understand the agriculture of a country, it was necessary also to study the processing of the products. The freezing works, butter and cheese factories were an essential part of the farming system: their establishment had brought New Zealand produce within the sphere of influence of world prices, and so contributed to the rise in land values and emphasized the need for high net productivity on the farm. In the dairying industry co-operation had been an important influence; the role of government had also to be assessed.

In his appreciation of all the factors that had been at work in the making of New Zealand agriculture and in the areal differentiation of activity within the country it is Buchanan's success in highlighting the geographical aspect of the story that commands most admiration. Let us take one example in which he discusses the difference between the importance of co-operation in the development of the dairying industries and its absence in meat freezing:

'In this difference between the dairying and the meat-freezing industries, geography was an important factor. It was the institution of the dairy factory that established dairy farming, and dairy farming took root in districts in which dense forest had long delayed the settlement. New settlement, dairy farming and the establishment of factories went together in much of Auckland, Taranaki, Manawatu and the Bush Districts, and the problem of raising capital was naturally acute. Sheep rearing had been long established on the open grasslands of the South Island before meat freezing was introduced. Large runholders and prosperous farmers were available to provide capital for the industry. The location of the works near the cities and ports brought them to the notice of the urban business communities. It was inevitable that the limited liability company was the form adopted for the new organisation.' [4]

The state of the pastoral industries in 1935 was viewed as a stage emerging from the past and merging into the future. The position in 1935 was a serious one: the onset of the great depression had brought a disastrous fall in prices for primary products. Wool prices in 1931 had been only one-third of those in 1913. Protective policies had closed many markets for agricultural products and New Zealand had come to depend even more upon the United Kingdom market. Buchanan himself held the view that if a study in economic geography had been efficiently performed, a reasonably accurate forecast of the direction of future trends should be possible. The circumstances of the depression made forecasting doubly difficult, but some possibilities were indicated. While, on a short term view, wool seemed to hold a strong position, for substitutes were not then technically possible, on a longer term view it was in dairy products and meat that he foresaw the major developments. He also forecast the steady, if not rapid, growth of beef production. The geographical patterns of production were not permanent. They reflected fairly stable price relationships between sheep products and dairy products in which slight differences in the geographical environment had produced distinct areal specialisations. But alterations in the geography of production would follow from changes in the world market and from the resulting adjustments made by farmers.

It is probable that in writing *The Pastoral Industries of New Zealand*, Buchanan was absorbed by the academic task:

by the requirement of describing exactly the geographical distributions and of providing the best possible explanations. The result is certainly a fine example of the craft of the economic geographer. It has provided a model, an example of method, for his students and colleagues: it has inspired others, especially in New Zealand, to take up and test his propositions. It has taught many of the ways in which regional specialisation of agriculture develops in relation to a wider market: has revealed the value of human endeavour in creating a new society and a new landscape in a fresh land. The result is thus a notable contribution to the understanding of an important aspect of man's relationship with his environment. We surmise, but it would probably be Buchanan's view, that it is through such precisely articulated studies, rather than through polemics, that the more lasting contributions to the age-old problem of the relations between societies and environments are likely to be made. He would, in any event, almost certainly under-estimate the practical value of his study to the continued success of the agricultural economy of his native country, for the lessons of such studies in various ways have a pervasive influence in public and commercial life.

IV

We have termed the concluding section of essays, 'Geography and the Community'. The section includes four widely differing contributions. The first 'Some Aspects of Settlement in the Overseas Dominions' reflects Buchanan's interest in the occupance of land: he is concerned to show how the characteristics of settlement patterns in the dominions reflect the nature of the occupying communities with their own value systems, conditioned by the circumstances of the time as well as by the nature of the terrain occupied. It is a study of the processes of occupance and of adjustment in many lands: it reveals Buchanan's breadth of grasp, his ability to paint a wide canvas and to leave clear brush strokes. For many years he was one of the most successful teachers of that most difficult of subjects in the old geography syllabus of the University of London, Comparative Regional Geography.

This paper, more than any other, reveals the secret of that success.

'Air Transport: Some Preliminary Considerations' was written for the volume of essays published in honour of his teacher, Professor Ll. Rodwell Jones, who had died in 1947. It is probably the first attempt by a British geographer to lay a foundation for the geographical study of air transport, a field that has subsequently been developed notably by one of his former graduate students, now a colleague at the London School of Economics. Buchanan's knowledge of the technical aspects of aircraft and airports must undoubtedly have owed much to his wartime service in the Royal Air Force, for he was responsible for providing maps for air force operations in many parts of the world. But the effects of technical changes in industry and transport in altering the values of locations had long interested him and his work on air transport may thus be seen also as a logical outcome of his earlier studies in economic geography.

Mention has been made earlier of his role in the founding of the Institute of British Geographers and his work for the Institute as Honorary Secretary from 1939-1950. Professor Smailes also refers to Buchanan's contribution. The academic community of geographers had formed the Institute and Buchanan derived obvious enjoyment from serving it, as indeed, in various ways, he served other geographical societies too.

The lecture 'Geography and the Community', given in 1958 in the University of Hong Kong, during a visit there as external examiner in geography, records the emergence in Britain, during the period of his own career, of applied geography; the use of geographical methods in application to problems of the national community both in peace and in war. It attests his faith in the geographer as a valuable and valued servant of the community.

Certainly, no more valuable and valued servant of the geographical community in Great Britain lives today than R. Ogilvie Buchanan. He is respected also as a master, a respect earned by the integrity of his scholarship in economic geography and by admiration for his technique. Undergraduate students of many generations have recognised the clarity of his exposition of the principles of his subject. In delivering a lecture his notes were almost never used; but the lectures had always been carefully considered beforehand. The arguments were logically developed and delivered in a clear voice and in measured tones. He never found difficulty in holding attention: students sensed that his lectures were truly original. There was always something new; some new angle to provoke thought and prompt further inquiry. Graduate students, of whom he had very many, found him critical in discussing their plans for research, and profited from his skill in helping them to focus on essential questions and from his training in how to select. He was patient and conscientious in reading drafts, firm in insisting on concise and economical writing, quick to eliminate the irrelevant.

R. O. Buchanan, with his eager step and quick eye, is a man on whom all have been able to rely for support in times of depression and difficulty. Never himself a man to seek sympathy, he has been quick to recognise the need of others for re-assurance. We are indebted to him for his energy and cheerfulness, his skill in opening opportunities for younger colleagues and students, the encouragement to research and publication that has been given so generously. Above all, it is the steadfastness of his own academic purpose that will stand for a long time to come and may be seen from his teaching and from his writing.

At the age of 78, R. O. Buchanan remains happy and active. Each day he comes to the London School of Economics and carries on with his work, much of it now concerned with editing and arranging the publication of books in this series, and of books still to appear. He has had since his marriage in 1931 the devoted support of his wife, Kay. To them both, as also to their three children and seven grandchildren, this book carries the message that R. O. Buchanan's work has been appreciated by his students, colleagues and friends, and the hope and expectation that he will continue to contribute, and to help others to contribute, to economic geography, for many years to come.

REFERENCES

[1] R. O. Buchanan, *An Economic Geography of the British Empire*, London, University of London Press, 1935, p.3

[2] *Ibid*, p.6

[3] R. O. Buchanan, *The Pastoral Industries of New Zealand*, Institute of British Geographers, Publication no.2, London 1935, p. xv

[4] *Ibid*, pp. 66-67

R. Ogilvie Buchanan

A Personal Appreciation by A.E. Smailes

When C. B. Fawcett came to University College, London, in 1928, on the retirement of Professor L. W. Lyde, he recruited two new assistants—R. O. Buchanan and R. E. Dickinson. They joined Margaret Shackleton, the only continuing member of Lyde's team. These four composed the entire staff of the Geography Department, although it was already a flourishing Honours school, however small by the standards of the 1970s.

Already a man of 34 and experienced beyond his years, Buchanan only then embarked upon his career as a University teacher. For the next twenty-one years, with the interruption of the Second World War period, when he was not with the College in evacuation at Aberystwyth but back in the armed forces (although a veteran of the First World War), Buchanan was successively lecturer and then Reader at University College.

As a mature student his outlook had been most profoundly shaped at L.S.E., especially under the influence of Rodwell Jones, than whom he held none of his teachers in greater respect. And he belonged to the ethos of L.S.E., rightly regarding his translation to a Chair there in 1949 as a return home. Yet the long spell at University College covered the main part of his career as an academic geographer. It was during these years that most of his own original work was produced and his influence as a teacher was exercised most profoundly. In the small and intimate circle of the pre-war Department of Geography, occupying an annexe of the College in a converted Georgian town-house in Bloomsbury, at 24 Gordon Square, which was shared with the young

Department of Economics, he found a milieu that suited him admirably. Here he lectured on economic geography and on the regional geography of the Southern Continents to small classes of undergraduates preparing together for the B.A. and B.Sc. degrees in Geography or for the B.Sc.(Econ.) degree.

Under the benevolent authority of Fawcett and with the active co-operation of his Economics colleagues, notably Noel Hall and Hugh Gaitskell, he built up the geography teaching for the B.Sc.(Econ.) degree. For these students, and also for the Arts and Science students with whom the prevailing course structure of the University degrees provided considerably greater teaching contacts, he brought an original conceptual approach to economic geography, which up to that time had tended to be a compendious but undisciplined array of facts relating to the geographical distribution of products and trade. His training in economics, still an unusual equipment for a geographer, appealed to his logical mind, and was applied rigorously to the courses he was assigned to teach. During this period he developed, along with Wilfred Smith at Liverpool and a few others, including some of his own pupils, an approach to economic geography that was securely integrated with economics and economic history, and conceptualised and forged into a respectable academic discipline. In an age of course-texts, it is deserving of emphasis that there was in those years no text-book that in any sense matched the lecture-courses in economic geography that were being given by Buchanan at University College, stimulating successive groups of students. They pre-date the emergence of economic geography as it has been developed conceptually as a systematic branch of modern geography. It is as a contribution to this that some of the accompanying papers, illustrative of those lectures, are so significant.

It is no exaggeration to claim that, over this period of two decades, his influence as a teacher of geography in the University of London was second only to that of S. W. Wooldridge, one of his closest friends. The two men, so different in temperament, were complementary in their approach to geography. Wooldridge, grounded in the natural sciences, was an inductive scientist and field geographer *par excellence*; Buchanan, trained in economic theory, had a more abstract and deductive approach. Outside the lecture rooms, over innumerable cups of coffee, Buchanan's young colleagues sharpened their wits in the arguments the 'old man' so loved to pursue (and to win!) and learned a respect for logic, a critical sense of relevance, abhorrence of woolliness, and an appreciation of terseness that was likewise imparted in small, elegant calligraphy to all who had essays, examination scripts, or thesis drafts returned to them from 'R.O.B.'. In the intimacy of day to day contacts in college, as well as in the evenings that were interludes during the vacation field classes in which Buchanan dutifully played his part as member of a small staff, though he was never a field expositor with an 'eye for country' the like of Wooldridge, Buchanan exerted a profound influence upon younger colleagues, as well as upon the students he came to know so well. At the same time they learned to appreciate not only the strength and firmness, the lack of humbug and the incisiveness that are immediately apparent in the man, but also the underlying warmth and humanity, his essential friendliness and his tolerance of personal attitudes and characteristics often very different from his own. Himself so rational, unemotional, well adjusted and set in his ways, though in repeated references to himself as 'the old man' and to others as 'laddie' he no doubt often tended to exaggerate a generation gap, he yet attracted in peculiar degree the confidence of young colleagues and students. They sensed his patience and readiness to listen, his human interest in their personal problems and development and his willingness to advise when asked, as well as his tolerant understanding in not assuming that the advice would necessarily be followed.

Throughout these years he worked in close association with Fawcett. Different as were the two men, both in their approach to geography and in their personalities, their mutual respect for each other's qualities grew with the years, and their innate integrity, rationality and tolerance made their leadership in the Department immensely productive. It was a happy Department in which to train, to teach and research, for both Fawcett and Buchanan were men possessed of that rare combination of qualities of maturity which is summed up as wisdom. Already, before his services were sought, in 1949, by his *alma mater*, to assume a major role in organising the flourishing Joint School of geography that had been built up by Rodwell Jones and Dudley Stamp at L.S.E. in association with Wooldridge at King's College, his soundness of judgment, ability to work with the most diverse colleagues, and his technical expertise in committee were being increasingly recognised outside his own Department in the wider circles of University College and the University Board of Studies in Geography, as well as among British geographers, especially in the Institute of British Geographers, in the post-war resuscitation of which Buchanan took his place naturally as an elder statesman. His sound judgment and other qualities in committee, where he brought his own incisive grasp of the crux of any issue and ability to expound it with measured clarity in rare combination with a remarkable patience in listening to and then elucidating the woolliness of others, were soon to be realized in the highest councils of the University. He relinquished the office of Honorary Secretary-Treasurer of the Institute of British Geographers at the end of 1950, a year after moving to the Chair at L.S.E. In 1951 he was elected to the Senate of the University and there began another phase of his career, that as a University administrator, in which the quality of his statesmanship emerged and was duly recognised.

Although Buchanan himself, when President of the Institute of British Geographers in 1953, put on record an account of the birth and first twenty-one years of the Institute,[1] it is fitting that the magnitude of his contribution to British geography through his work for the Institute should be emphasised here. The bare facts as he has recounted them indicate that the I.B.G. was the brainchild of Buchanan and his London colleagues, Wooldridge and H. A. Matthews. How much his own personal qualities of tact and patient steadfastness of purpose contributed to its birth and survival can only be estimated. What is clear in retrospect is that Buchanan especially combined the ability to win the confidence of established and conservative senior personnel in the subject, who saw in him anything but an iconoclast and 'angry young man', with an equal ability to secure the confidence of colleagues in London and elsewhere in Britain to the extent that they were willing to be persuaded to subscribe for years an appreciable levy from their modest pre-war salaries to the cause of academic geography. That the Institute owes an immeasurable debt to a very few men, among them Buchanan, who prepared the way for its inception, nourished and guided it in infancy in the pre-war years, then re-established it and set its course after the war in readiness for the post-war expansion is undoubted. The modest account of its foundation and of those minority years given by Buchanan himself, set alongside the publications of the period, as the background for the subsequent growth in membership and burgeoning of the range and scale of activities of the Institute and its output of publications, attest the role of Buchanan, Wooldridge, J. N. L. Baker and a few others, who were the trusted and inspiring leaders of some 60 founder members who joined with faith in their vision and ability to achieve it. The statesmanship that was to find its consummation in Buchanan's career after 1951 in the University of London was already apparent, as it was no doubt further developed, during the decades that saw the birth and guidance to maturity of the Institute of British Geographers. When he handed over office as Honorary Secretary-Treasurer in 1951 it was at once clear that the time was ripe for the financial and editorial administration to be separated from the secretaryship and thenceforth they have been separately represented by Council officers. That the Institute was so soundly established and well-poised to embark upon its remarkable expansion in the '50s and '60s is attributable in large measure to the policy conceived with foresight and carried out with such prudence and competence by Buchanan and his close associates in the years before and after the War. Its senior living ex-President may well take pride in the present-day size, and especially the status, of the Institute among world geographical institutions.

REFERENCE

[1] The I.B.G.: Retrospect and Prospect, *Transactions and Papers of the Institute of British Geographers*, 20 (1954), pp. 1-14, reprinted as paper 11 in this volume.

APPROACH TO ECONOMIC GEOGRAPHY

I

Approach to Economic Geography*

The term Economic Geography is among the newer of the descriptive labels that the subject has accumulated in its modern development. True, Gotz used it in Germany as far back as 1882, and it may possibly have been coined earlier. He used it to distinguish between Commercial Geography, concerned with the accumulation of facts for utilitarian purposes, and the scientific investigation of 'the nature of world areas in their direct influence on the production of goods,' which was Economic Geography. There is a very modern ring about that definition, but the new term made headway only very slowly. In Britain even the older term, Commercial Geography, was in Gotz's day something of a newcomer, struggling for recognition against the still older name, Political Geography, whose roots lay in the Mercantilist concepts that had also produced the corresponding term, Political Economy. There was apparently little difference in denotation between Political Geography and Commercial Geography. Both alike focussed on trade, emphasising such aspects of production as provided a surplus for export and such ancillary elements as trade routes, ports and transport. This was no doubt a very understandable bias in Victorian England, for which foreign trade was of such peculiar importance, but the term Commercial Geography better reflected the laissez-faire spirit of late Victorian times, when Britain had become the world's shop-keeper and the world's best customer. The highlight of Commercial Geography in Britain was Chisholm's Handbook, a monument to

*Reprinted from the *Indian Geographical Journal,* Silver Jubilee Souvenir Volume and N. Subrahmanyam Memorial Volume, 1951

its author's industry and orderliness, though doing less than justice to the constructive originality he showed in his shorter research papers. In Germany Andree's 'Geographie des Welthandels' was an even more imposing opus, but characteristically enough contemporary French geography produced nothing of quite this type. By 1914 Commercial Geography was already dying as a fashionable label, and the inter-war period saw the general adoption of Economic Geography.

The spread of the new term indicates some shift of concept, or at any rate of emphasis. Geography in its human aspects had come to be regarded in Britain as concerned with the relationship between man and his environment, with the region as the accepted unit of study. Against this background Economic Geography fell easily into place as concerned with the economic life of the region. Some interesting consequences followed. In the first place since man's economic activities are overwhelmingly preponderant among his total activities, the economic aspects of the region tended to pre-empt the attention of the regional geographer and to monopolise much of the space devoted to allegedly regional geography. Such treatment was often very superficial, and almost inevitably so, since the trained ability to analyse the economic environment was often, even generally, not at the command of the geographer. A genuine endeavour was indeed made to base conclusions on firm data, but the technique seldom advanced beyond the mapping of relevant phenomena and the noting of areal correlations. The logical problems of whether the correlations were significant, and, if so, in what way and to what extent they were significant were largely overlooked. This pre-occupation with regional description of the economic life of communities would seem to imply a corresponding neglect of the opportunities to develop economic geography as one of the essential systematic branches of the subject, and it cannot be denied that a coherent and developing body of doctrine, comparable for example to that available in geomorphology, has been slow to affect geographical thought in general.

In the second place trade, and particularly international trade, loomed less large as the criterion of profitable study. All production (in the narrower sense of the word) was seen to come within the sphere of the geographer, whose particular task was to study the influence of the physical environment on the nature and methods of production. Given the concept of relationship between the human and the physical elements of the environment, this task was clearly legitimate, but, since a relationship, if it exists, must of necessity be mutual, half of the logically implied problem, the reverse influence of economic organisation and economic activities on the physical environment, was ignored. Even so, there was room for useful work, and one of the by-products was the idea of the economic region as distinct from the natural region. Localisations of highly developed manufacturing industries had of course long been familiar and had come to be accepted as the power-house areas, increasingly interconnected by commercial and financial links, of the world production plant. Elementary economic texts normally made reference to their productive advantages, and geography texts attempted with limited success to find reasons in the physical make-up of the immediate environment for their establishment in the particular areas they occupied. The special advance of the 'twenties lay in the recognition that the old localisation of industry was merely one kind of instance of the world-wide tendency to specialisation of area, which was seen to be true in all essentials of agriculture as well as of industry in the narrower sense. A great impetus to systematic study was given by O. E. Baker's work on the agricultural regions of North America, which was quickly followed by applications of his methods to other continents, and later by the elaboration by Jones and Whittlesey of a set of criteria that could be applied to the world as a whole. The world picture of a patchwork, but a surprisingly continuous patchwork, of distinctive areal productive units, was acquiring some sharpness of definition. Whatever the criteria used by different workers, they had in common the fact that the data were economic and not physical, a dominant crop, a crop or crop-and-livestock association, sources of farm income and so on, statistically determined and cartographically applied, and that they portrayed and summarised differences that existed on the ground and could be checked by observation.

This mention of what is visible on the ground brings us to

the latest stage of thought on the nature and methods of geography, the 'cultural landscape' concept. The term in its English form was first adopted in America, which in the inter-war period was much more intimately and vigorously influenced by German work than was Britain. It is a translation, perhaps not a very happy translation, of *Kulturlandschaft*, which itself in its somewhat abstract form and implication is apt to conceal the fact that a *Landschaft* was originally a specific area of distinctive character, analogous to the French *pays*, and it may well be that the plural form, 'landscapes', would better have preserved the concrete reality involved, and have prevented some of the cruder fatuities that have been perpetrated in the name of cultural landscape.

The essence of cultural landscape geography can be put very simply. A landscape, as one sees it, consists of a complex of natural and human elements so intimately associated that they form a recognisable, and therefore logically a definable, whole. Both sets of elements are subject to continuous change, which is in general gradual, though the changes made by man are commonly much more rapid than those made by nature. On balance, a considerable, though varying, degree of stability is characteristic. The task of the geographer is to 'describe and interpret' the landscape, which might be paraphrased by saying 'to understand the landscape through the study of the landscape', and many would add that the study is particularly aimed at the appreciation of those characteristics of the landscape that differentiate it from other landscapes. It will readily be seen that the differentiation of area here postulated as the prime duty of geography is at bottom the same aim as that of the older regional geography, and the individual landscape in its finite areal extent is indeed a region, though not necessarily, nor even probably, a 'natural' region in the older sense of the term. The cultural landscape concept, however, does make direct observation on the ground the starting point of geographical work, and does emphasise the position of man as a contributor to and a fashioner of the material environment in which he lives, instead of merely a creature of that environment. Its proponents claim, too, that it gives the geographer for the first time a defined, concrete field of study, free from the unsatisfactory subjectiveness of the 'relations between man and his environment'.

That broadly, and perhaps not too inaccurately, is the frame-work within which American geographers have been working for a generation and German geographers for almost two generations. French geography, too, though still fortunately innocent of most of the jargon that has accrued in Germany and the United States, bears a strong family likeness in its devotion to delineating the portrait and in its insistence on the activity and the significance of the human agent. In Britain on the other hand, apart from Dickinson and Bryan, geographers have done little explicit work in cultural landscape, but it is perhaps a fair summary to say that British geography to-day, tacitly and somewhat unenthusiastically, accepts the soundness of the cultural landscape concept in its less extreme manifestations. It remains, therefore, to consider how a working scheme of economic geography fits, or can be fitted, into this background.

A priori, economic geography in this context should be a study of economic landscape, whether or not it is directed specifically to those features that differentiate the particular landscape from others. Let it be admitted at once that an economic landscape is a visible reality, and that just as economic activities are the dominant activities of mankind, so the economic landscape is usually the major part of the total cultural landscape, sometimes indeed the whole of it. It is a patent fact, too, that economic landscapes differ strikingly with differences in kind or intensity of production, in density of population or in standards of technological achievement. Consider, for example, two simple cases, the Taranaki dairy-farming area of New Zealand and the alfalfa-cattle-wheat belt of the Argentine pampa. In this part of Taranaki the observer notes the succession of small farms, typically some 75-100 acres in size, each one marked by its neat little single-storey, iron-roofed, timber house, with garden and small patch of exotic shelter trees; the milking shed, equipped with electrically driven milking plant; the central runway, giving convenient access to every one of the small fields, each with its hedge to provide shelter for the dairy herd of visibly dominant Jersey blood; the permanent

pastures of rye-grass, timothy, and cocksfoot, with an ad-
mixture of one or more of the clovers. Off the farm itself will
be noted the close net of good roads, the ubiquitous
overhead power lines, the recurrence of cheese factories every
few miles, and the almost equal frequency of the small, busy
country towns. All this, you will observe, forms a hollow ring
around the majestic volcanic cone of Egmont, whose very
gently rolling lowest slopes it occupies. On our selected
pampa belt on the other hand the eye sees for miles over the
dead flat plain. Hedges are conspicuously missing, though
occasional, widely separated plantations of exotic trees may
break the view, and wire fences sparingly subdivide great
holdings into enormous fields, most of them deep in alfalfa,
on which graze herds of fine cattle of Hereford or Aberdeen
Angus type, but some few of them under cultivation for
wheat. Equipment includes at least one set of substantial
drafting yards per holding, and, strikingly, a greater or
smaller number of wind-pumps. A homestead of mansion
proportions, often adorned with beautiful plantations and
spacious gardens, a few huts for the small permanent labour
force and some scattered temporary hovels for the nomadic-
tenant wheat growers complete the tally of buildings. Dirt
roads, deep in dust in dry weather and in gluey mud in wet
weather, lead to the nearest railway. A town or a village is a
rarity.

It is clear that the mere enumeration of the common
objects in sight has given some indication of the nature of the
productive specialisation and some impression at any rate of
the methods employed, and indeed it is part of the landscape
purist's case that the landscape carries within itself the
answers to the questions it asks. True, these are the simplest
of cases but, even so, if that is all there is to economic
geography there can be small ground for ambitious claims for
the subject. In fact of course the recognising of particular
signposts in an economic landscape or any other landscape is
far from being the same thing as understanding the landscape,
though Hartshorne seems to come perilously near to asserting
just that when he says, ' . . . though geography must know
where things are, the study of the 'where' is not geography,
nor an integral part of geography, and it is therefore not the

function of geography to explain the 'where'—that is to give the full explanation of why a phenomenon is found where it is found'. Hartshorne was thinking strictly in terms of differentiation of area, and no doubt, if that limitation of objective be accepted, his conclusion is defensible. If, however, the aim be the understanding of the landscape, a wider and more satisfying field is opened up. The economic landscape is the material framework or skeleton of the economic activities of the area. It conditions those activities, and therefore its own consequential modification, but in large part it is itself crystallised out of activities in the past, in some areas and at some times out of the very distant human past. Two conclusions seem to be inescapable. The first is that understanding of an existing economic landscape demands an understanding of how it came to be like that. The study is one of a process of change, so incomplete at any one stage that inliers from the past continue to be to a greater or smaller degree contributors to the existing character, and any analysis confined to current conditions must necessarily miss significant elements. The second is that since an economic landscape at any one moment is an end product up to that moment of human activities modifying a basal natural landscape, it is via the activities that the study should proceed. The economic landscape poses the initial questions, and it provides some of the necessary checks on the accuracy of the findings, but the investigation itself must be focussed primarily on the working activities of which the landscape is the consequence. So economic geography proves to be the geography of man's work—and in making that point explicit we have come nearly full circle to a position not so very much different from that occupied by Chisholm half a century and more ago. More fully it is concerned with the conditions, the methods and the effects of man's work in its spatial extension.

That brings us to the central point of the argument. Man's work is not haphazard or capricious. In any given area he works in and on a relatively fixed physical milieu, with a certain material and organizational equipment, in a commonly pretty stable human environment of conventions, laws and institutions; and in a commercial economy he works to

produce goods and services for sale. His individual aberrations
are over-ridden by the statistical regularities that provide the
basis and the justification for the economists' special study,
and these regularities of action and their concomitant institu-
tional facilities far transcend the local area. So far as the
tendency to a world market is effective, no region or
landscape lives to itself or of itself alone. Indeed, the whole
stimulus to production and the means for carrying it through
may come from far outside and the resulting consumption be
equally distant. In any case the individual area is tied into a
widespread economic system, which nevertheless shows
regional as well as functional differentiation. Herein lies the
secret of the worldwide spread of specialisation of area in the
last century or so, but just what is the particular specialisation in a particular area and just how it was established and
works depends both upon the territorial position and the
inherent physical character of the area and also upon the
economic mechanisms for the satisfying of demand by
appropriate supply. Clearly any geographical study of production requires competence in the economic field as much
as it does a trained ability in the analysis of the physical
milieu. Economic geography in short lies, systematically, in
the field of applied economics, economics applied to the
realistic study of production in area to the end of understanding the area (landscape or region) in its productive
aspect.

A somewhat sharper point can perhaps be given to that
argument by a little more attention to just one facet. To the
extent that we can postulate an economic world in which
specialised areas take their place as functioning parts of a
whole, any specialised area, unless it has a complete monopoly of its kind of production, is in a state of competition
with other areas. According to its degree of success its
specialisation may increase or decrease its local dominance
and may extend or retract its areal borders. Here is pre-
eminently a field for the geographer, since even on a
stringently purist view it affects the character of the visible
landscape and results in differentiating the area more decisively from other areas. But such developments are clearly a
matter of the kind, richness and situation of the natural

resources, of the availability of capital, of the availability and character of the labour supply, and of the efficiency of management in utilising the agents in the most appropriate combinations. Here, then, we meet the doctrine of comparative costs, and it is precisely the areal investigation of comparative costs that gives the economic geographer his peculiar opportunity and gives his contribution real substance. If we may assume that price sets a top limit to the costs that can be carried, then a disadvantage in any aspect of one producing area must be offset by an advantage in some other aspect, if production is to continue and the character of the area to remain, and these advantages and disadvantages reflect essential differences in the areas concerned, while the differential use made of them creates further differences.

It will be clear, too, that such a study of comparative costs brings one directly to the marginal concept of the economist. Here we shall touch on only one aspect of the margin, an aspect of peculiar concern to the geographer but of so little interest to the economist that he has ignored it altogether. A hypothetical case will best illustrate the point. Imagine an area in which all the physical conditions, except one, say rainfall, are pretty uniform, but that rainfall decreases regularly and gradually in one direction. Where the rainfall is heaviest, the conditions are excellent for the growth of a particular crop, say spring wheat of high quality, but with decreasing rainfall they become progressively less favourable. A rainfall is sooner or later reached at which the yield is only just sufficient to repay the cost, and that on the assumption of perfect efficiency of production. Beyond that rainfall line wheat is not grown. Geographers have commonly thought of that as a rainfall limit to crop production, but surely it is a margin in the strict economic sense. A new breed of wheat better adapted to low moisture conditions, a new technique that lowers costs and permits a smaller physical yield to cover costs or alternatively a rise in price will permit the margin to be pushed further out, while increased costs or lowered prices should cause it to contract. This margin, be it noted, can be recognised on the ground and can be mapped, and is geographical not only in that sense but also in its complete independence of the particular weaknesses of individual producers. The character and the extent, therefore, of a specialised area may seem to represent a somewhat precarious local equilibrium, at the mercy of the disruption of equilibrium elsewhere, and certainly one must not think of the present pattern of productive regions as in any strict sense permanent. The individual regions, however, and consequently the pattern as a whole, do show a considerable measure of stability, and catastrophic change is not to be expected except where complete social upheaval succeeds in destroying the existing organisation and in insulating the area concerned from the rest of the economic world. Even then something of the original pattern is likely to remain.

So far little except passing reference has been made to the physical aspects of economic geography. The omission must now be remedied. The physical milieu is the site of man's work, and much of his basic work is done with direct reference to that milieu. True it has been mainly by a process of trial and error, often costly and wasteful, that he has selected for exploitation those elements he could most effectively use with the material equipment and the organisation he had available. He has not normally made any scientific surveys of his physical environment before using it (modern prospecting for minerals is an obvious exception to the general rule) any more than he has deferred productive activity until he had produced a valid theory of value, but the economic geographer is not thereby absolved from the necessity of applying his knowledge of earth structure and processes to an analysis of the terrain on which the productive energy is employed. Two very elementary examples will serve to illustrate the point. The exploitation of coal is not merely a matter of the presence of coal and of capital and labour and a market. It is intimately 'conditioned by the character of the coal, the depth, thickness, dip and continuity of the seams, the prevalence of faulting and the direction and amount of the throw of the individual faults. Compare, for example, the massive differences in organisation and productivity of the coal industry of the Appalachian fields of the United States on the one hand and those of Great Britain and adjacent north west Europe on the other, and reflect that even complete Americanisation of the European fields in equipment, labour and management would still leave coal yields here much less in man-shift-tons and much greater in pithead-ton-cost than those achieved in the upper Ohio basin. Or return for a moment to those two agricultural landscapes we glanced at earlier, the Taranaki dairy farming area of New Zealand and the alfalfa belt of the Argentine pampa. Their character as landscapes no less than their economic functioning is missed unless one penetrates below the surface of their physical make up. On the one hand is a plain of windborne deposits, rising imperceptibly to the west towards the Andes, with drainage wholly sub surface and a water-table whose depth below the surface increases very gradually to the west. The sediments themselves are only loosely consolidated, and are eminently penetrable by plant roots. The soil that caps them has been developed under a grass cover in an area of very moderate rainfall. Both the fertility and the penetrability extend far beyond the range of the alfalfa, which has in fact been established only in the belt that lies between two critical water-table depths, an upper one in the east that is just not high enough to smother the plants, and a lower one in the west that is just not deep enough to be beyond the reach of the very long roots of the alfalfa. The key to the beef fattening specialisation lies in the alfalfa, the wheat is an incidental to the establishment and maintenance of the alfalfa, and the alfalfa is rooted, metaphorically as well as literally, in the sub-soil. That is still far from being the whole story of the alfalfa-cattle-wheat belt but it is an essential element in the story. In Taranaki on the other hand the basic volcanic flows from Egmont provided the parent material for a deep, rich, if somewhat light, soil developed under a dense, evergreen forest cover, in an area of mild temperatures and abundant, all-season rainfall. The forest was still in its primeval state when white settlement first commenced, and its laborious elimination was the necessary prelude to successful settlement, but soil, rainfall and temperature conditions combined, once the forest had gone, to promote vigorous growth of European grasses practically all the year round. The forest extended far beyond the volcanic area into the heavily dissected country of Tertiary sedimentaries to the east, but the dairying landscape did not follow there. The junction of the volcanic and the sedimentary rocks marks not merely a structural boundary, but a remarkably abrupt change in relief and in soils, and sheep displace dairy cows as the animals round which a very different economic landscape has been created.

The general case is, then, that the physical milieu is relevant, and indeed central, but that in its economic context it is to be evalued in economic terms, mainly indeed in monetary terms. General principles there are, and valid methods of analysis, both on the human side and on the earth side, and a real understanding of an area in its economic structure, economic functioning or economic landscape demands the effective application of both sets of techniques. In the course of that work the investigator will be aware that what John Neville Keynes called the relativity of economic doctrines has its parallel in the geographical significance of the facts of the world of nature. Within the time span with which we are concerned the facts of the physical world change comparatively little, but their significance to man at work may change decisively. The rainfall line, the frost-free season, the soil boundary or the geological outcrop, useful signposts to-day to economic distributions, may tomorrow have to carry amended or even cancelled notices. It nevertheless remains true that with every improvement in man's equipment and organisation the power of even slight differences in the character of the physical milieu to induce differentiation of economic character becomes not less but greater, and the tendency, in spite of human conservatism and man-made obstacles, is progressively towards the specialisation of every area to that type of production for which its advantages are at a maximum.

II

Some features of World Wheat Production*

This paper is an attempt to make a broad survey of the major shifts of world wheat production since the last pre-war quinquennium, and at the same time to essay a preliminary test of the geographical applicability of the concept of marginal production.

The argument, in short, is that price sets an upper limit to costs in the commercial production of any article, and that where costs equal price, we find the margin of production. To the geographer this means that as he works outward from an area of optimum geographical conditions for the growth of a crop the physical yield becomes poorer in quantity or quality or both, and/or costs per unit of output increase. Sooner or later he comes to the point where costs equal price and the margin has been reached. This margin is regional in that it is independent of the peculiarities of individual producers, and will exist as a feature of the landscape on the assumption of the most efficient application of the most appropriate methods of cultivation. Its position can normally be indicated by a geographical or 'natural' boundary (a climatic isopleth, for example), but the only validity of such a boundary is relative to a given state of prices and costs. A rise in the effective price or a fall in the necessary costs will bring previously submarginal land above the margin: a fall in the effective price or a rise in the necessary costs will depress below the margin land that was previously above it. Normally, therefore, a persistent movement of the price-costs ratio should be followed by a corresponding movement of the

*Contributed to *The Scottish Geographical Magazine*, 52, 1936

geographical margin, and the necessity for a new geographical index to it.

The application of this concept has been somewhat simplified in two ways. In the first place costs have been ignored, since, owing to the habitual lag of costs behind prices, farmers themselves use price movements as the index to the direction of movement of the price-costs (profit) ratio. In the second place the geographical margin has been classified into two types, general and local, the former indicating, for instance, the outer edge of a crop belt, the latter demarcating local areas of less favourable geographical conditions within the belt. The general geographical margin is quite commonly, though not necessarily, a function of one or more climatic elements and has its position marked by a climatic isopleth—a somewhat rough index. It is only this general geographical margin that is considered in this paper.

The difficulties that remain, however, are very serious. In the first place the open world market price for a commodity is only a rough guide to effective local price. The *direction* of movement of local price may usually be assumed to be the same as that of the open world price, but the *rate* of movement may be very different. Secondly, the time lag between movements of price and consequential movements of production may be considerable, and may vary from one area to another. Finally, there is a conspicuous lack of precise knowledge as to the location of the margin at any given time, a lack that can be remedied only by large-scale mapping by workers on the spot. For these reasons the conclusions deduced in this paper must be regarded as no more than tentative.

Wheat is one of the major crops of the world, and one of the most widely produced, but the main producing countries stand out fairly clearly, and readily permit of a degree of convenient grouping. Group A consists of Western Europe, including the British Isles and Italy, but excluding Spain and Portugal. It forms a fairly compact area, supplying large quantities of wheat, chiefly autumn-sown soft wheat, with a high average yield per acre, but a large aggregate deficiency. Group B includes the great producing belt of Hungary, Bulgaria, Rumania and the Soviet territories, together with

India. India is placed in this group because, like the majority
of countries in this group, it had a large surplus for export
before the War, but has since ceased to be really significant as
an exporter. Total production in Group B is usually about 75
per cent. greater than that of Group A; it consists almost
entirely of hard wheat, and, except in India, is mainly
spring-sown. Group C, consisting of the United States,
Canada, Argentina and Australia, is even less homogeneous
than Group B, but the countries included all had a surplus of
hard wheat for export before the War and have almost
monopolised the world export of wheat since. Table I
summarises the production position of these areas for three
quinquennial periods: the graphs show the position year by
year. (See Figure 1, a, b and c.)

TABLE I

PRODUCTION OF WHEAT BY GROUPS OF PRODUCERS

	000 Hectares.			000 Quintals.		
	1909-13.	1921-25.	1929-33.	1909-13.	1921-25.	1929-33.
Group A .	14,342	12,640	13,422	204,350	174,631	224,941
,, B .	44,210	31,811	52,478	331,904	259,384	392,092*
,, C .	32,658	43,267	47,237	306,121	408,301	421,879
Total .	91,210	87,718	113,137	842,375	842,316	1,038,912

*   Four-year average, omitting the year 1931

These figures account for well over 80 per cent. of world
acreage and production in the pre-War quinquennium, and, as
implied above, they include every area that took at that time
a significant share in the exporting or importing of wheat.
The only considerable producing country that has been
omitted is China, for which reliable statistics are lacking, but
which was before the War virtually self-supporting in wheat.
Group A had 13 per cent. of world acreage and 20 per cent.
of world production. Group B had 41 per cent. of world
acreage and 32 per cent. of world production. Of this India
contributed 11 per cent. of world acreage and 9 per cent. of
world production, Russia being responsible for the bulk of
the remainder. Group C contributed the same acreage as the
Russian, Rumanian, Bulgarian, and Hungarian belt, 30 per

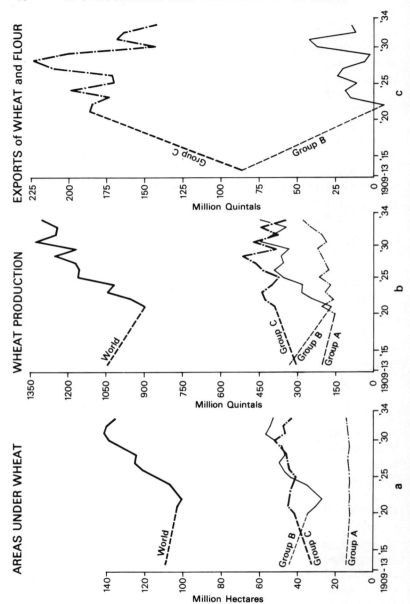

Figure 1. Areas under wheat; wheat production and exports, 1909-34

cent. of the world total, but surpassed it in production, which amounted also to 30 per cent. of the world total.

Trade in wheat was even more widespread than production; there was indeed no single country that did not have either some export or some import. The major part of the world market, however, was exceedingly concentrated. Three-quarters of all imports went to Western Europe (as defined above), and of that amount almost half (36 per cent. of all world imports) was taken by the United Kingdom. The United Kingdom, too, was one of the few countries (Denmark and Holland were others) where wheat was subjected to no customs duties or other import restrictions, and it is for this reason that prices quoted in the wheat exchanges of this country may be accepted as typifying the open world market price.

TABLE II

NET EXPORTS OF WHEAT AND FLOUR IN TERMS OF WHEAT

	000 Quintals.		
	1909-13.	1921-25.	1929-33.
U.S.S.R. . .	42,758	+ 862	12,647
Rumania . .	14,351	1,096	3,008
Bulgaria . .	2,703	696	1,147
Hungary . .	11,442	2,374	5,513
India . .	13,849	4,679	+ 1,105
GROUP B . .	85,103	7,983	21,210
Canada . .	24,473	68,059	64,048
U.S.A. . .	26,519	55,783	25,434
Argentina. .	22,866	34,733	40,964
Australia . .	13,450	25,047	33,968
GROUP C . .	87,308	183,622	164,414
World . .	172,411	191,605	185,624

+ = net import.

World exports of wheat were not nearly so concentrated as world imports. The countries included in Groups B and C, listed in Table II, divided total exports pretty evenly between the groups, but individual countries, especially in Group B, showed wide differences. Half the total of the group came from Russian territories alone, which thus accounted for almost one-quarter of total world exports. The whole group, with the omission of India, contributed two-fifths of all wheat handled in international trade. The differences in the contribution of the individual countries comprising Group C are much less noticeable; no one country provided more than three-fifths as much as the Russian Empire, but the group as a whole was responsible for just over half the aggregate of world exports.

The immediate effect of the outbreak of the War was to dislocate the connections between supplying areas and the world market. The closing of the Baltic and Black Sea exits from Eastern Europe eliminated at a stroke some 40 per cent. of the usual sea-borne amount of export. This does not mean that world market supplies were cut down by 40 per cent. : the Central Powers could from the very beginning draw supplies by land from Hungary, and later from Bulgaria and Rumania as well. They were, it is true, in turn completely cut off from sea-borne supplies from any other producing area, but, as they represented a very minor portion of the world market for imported wheat, the net result was an unparalleled shortage in the remainder of the European area. Steps were taken, too, to ration consumption, so that in point of quantity of wheat the needs of the Allied and the neutral importing countries were considerably reduced. The effect of this unprecedented restriction of supplies on wheat prices was consequently not quite so overwhelming as it might have been, but the gap was never completely bridged and the rise in price was sufficiently spectacular. The mean monthly spot price at Liverpool per 100 lb. of good red wheat had been 7s. 9d. for the 1909-13 quinquennium, and for the first seven months of 1914 it was 7s. 4d. By December 1914 it had risen to 10s. 1d., and it continued to rise almost without interruption till after the end of the War. In 1917 it was 16s. 9½d., in 1919 17s. 3d., and in 1920 it reached its maximum at 19s. 3d.

Such soaring prices constituted a very strong incentive to increase production wherever possible. The area most immediately concerned was Western Europe, but the scope for increase of production there was obviously very limited. A not inconsiderable area in the war zone was necessarily out of cultivation. Elsewhere in the belligerent countries the mobilising of man power to the fighting forces seriously reduced the efficiency of cultivation, while the widespread efforts to bring under wheat cultivation land that had previously been utilised for other purposes resulted naturally enough in yields per acre much below the pre-War average. The net result by 1920 was an actual decrease of 17 per cent. in the area under wheat, and in the aggregate crop of 26 per cent. South-eastern Europe was still isolated, the Russian section most effectively, and there also wheat-growing had declined. Acreage had shrunk by 36 per cent. from the pre-War level, and the aggregate crop by 58 per cent. Not unnaturally the great bulk of this decline was accounted for by Russian deficiencies. Tables I and III do not show the full amount of these decreases owing to the additions to acreage and production which began to take effect before the end of the 1921-25 quinquennium, but the position is made clear by the graphs.

TABLE III

WHEAT PRODUCTION OF SOME IMPORTANT PRODUCERS

	000 Hectares.			000 Quintals.		
	1909-13.	1921-25.	1929-33.	1909-13.	1921-25.	1929-33.
U.S.S.R. .	28,011	16,299	33,472*	186,053	118,877	234,447*
U.S.A. .	19,060	23,557	23,326	187,820	218,283	215,219
India .	11,826	11,966	13,160	95,976	91,343	95,165
Canada .	4,025	8,939	10,483	53,648	99,742	96,426
Argentina .	6,496	6,722	7,065	40,023	55,312	62,137
Australia .	3,077	4,052	6,363	24,630	35,024	50,099
France .	6,787	5,466	5,326	88,627	79,136	82,080
Italy . .	4,744	4,677	4,833	49,896	53,904	70,196
Germany .	1,677	1,462	2,029	40,431	26,867	43,958

*Four year average, omitting the year 1931.

It was, then, the remaining overseas exporting areas that might be expected to feel the whole effect of the price stimulus to increased production. Even these, however, were not equally affected. India, Australia and Argentina suffered from their remoteness from Western Europe, and in the conditions of the Great War it was not merely the differentially high cash costs of transport involved. It was a question of the most efficient use of reduced shipping tonnage, faced with the enormous extra task of moving numbers of troops and quantities of munitions as well as of commercial cargo. Comparatively little shipping space was worth sparing for the transport of wheat from these distant countries, since the same shipping tonnage could move almost four times as much wheat from Canada or the United States in the same time. The stimulus to increased production, therefore, was concentrated in Canada and the United States until the era of diversion of shipping from ordinary commercial to extraordinary governmental transport ended about 1920.

Increased production in these two countries was achieved wholly by increase of acreage: indeed production rose to a smaller degree than did acreage. By 1920 the areal increase amounted to practically 30 per cent. in the United States (see Figure 2, a), and to 90 per cent. in Canada (see Figure 2, e). This was especially a period of outward movement of the geographical margin of wheat-growing to include new areas, sub-marginal in pre-War conditions, on the semi-arid edge of the Hard Winter Wheat and Spring Wheat Belts, and on the northern, short-growing-season edge of the Canadian section of the Spring Wheat Belt. Though some extension would have taken place in any case, the actual *amount* of this extension was conditioned by the adoption of new varieties of wheat, especially on the northern edge of the Canadian Spring Wheat Belt. The smaller yield even in good years and the greater frequency of serious crop damage by frost, dust storms or inadequate rain in these new areas did, owing to the very high prices obtaining, permit a financial return adequate to cover inflated costs. In Canada the increase in the aggregate crop amounted to over 33 per cent. and in the United States to 27 per cent.

India, Argentina and Australia in the period to 1920 show the contrast that we should expect from consideration of the transport position. They all witness a slight increase of acreage and production, but in India (see Figure 2, b) and Australia (see Figure 2, c) the whole of the increase was achieved in the last year of the period, acreage and production having been considerably less in 1919 than during the 1909-13 quinquennium. For Australia this summary statement conceals a good deal of fluctuation in the War period,

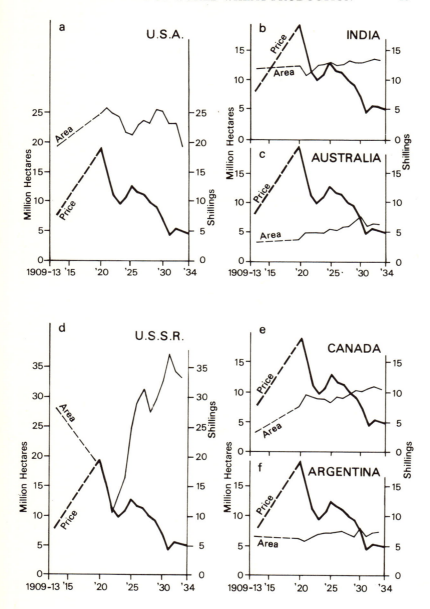

Figure 2. Areas under wheat production and wheat prices, 1909-34

but there was no definite upward tendency. In Argentina (Figure 2, f) the position remained fairly stable.

The effect of these developments on the international trade in wheat was spectacular. South-eastern Europe, even as late as 1921, was contributing only 4 per cent. of its average for the 1909-13 quinquennium, and this wheat came wholly from the Danubian countries. U.S.S.R., indeed, was to a small extent a net importer. India likewise had practically disappeared from the export trade. It exported in 1921 less than one-seventh of its 1909-13 average, and was a net importer in 1922. The check to export during the War had given a fillip to the development of the home market, which was potentially capable of absorbing all the wheat that India could produce. This period of apprenticeship to the wheat-eating habit, short though it was, sufficed to bring into play the inelasticity of demand for wheat, and so to allow continued absorption by the home market of far greater quantities than before the War, even at the much higher prices. Indian acreage has since increased to about 11 per cent. more than the 1909-13 average, but total production has rarely been as great as in the earlier period. Since 1925 there has not been one year in which exports rose to as much as a quarter of the 1909-13 average, and in several years there have been net imports.

The disappearance of these countries in Group B from effective contribution to world exports was compensated by the increase of exports from the remaining wheat-exporting lands, and by 1921 world exports of wheat were already 10 per cent. greater than in the 1909-13 period. Naturally the increase had been greatest in Canada and the United States; and these two countries together accounted in 1921 for 72 per cent. of world exports of wheat. Australia, however, had more than doubled her exports, and actually contributed more in 1921 than Argentina. It is easy now to see that the position, even then, was essentially unstable. It was made possible by the abnormal price situation, and its maintenance depended on the continuation of high prices. That in turn depended on the persistence in the U.S.S.R. and the Danubian countries of political and social conditions militating against the reappearance of significant exports, and also, since the possibility of any effective increase in world consumption was very remote, on the cessation of further expansion in these exporting countries themselves.

Actually prices dropped very sharply in 1921 and 1922, with a further, but smaller decline in 1923. This, the first post-War slump, was short, for there was a fair measure of price recovery in 1924 and 1925, and a widespread belief existed that wheat prices would stabilise themselves somewhere in the neighbourhood of the 1925 level. A corresponding decrease in acreage, with a normal time lag, took place in North America, slight in Canada, but substantial in the United States. This decrease, however, gave way to a renewal of expansion of acreage and crop under the influence of the upward price trend in 1924 and 1925, and the general belief that the slump was over.

In Australia and Argentina, as indicated above, the stimulus to increased production had been largely ineffective until the end of the War, when shipping was released by degrees for ordinary commercial transport. Australia was particularly favoured by the facilities of returning troopships for the conveyance of wheat, but in both countries the year 1920 saw expansion in full swing, and in both it continued uninterruptedly through the short slump of 1921-23. There was an interesting difference, however, between the two. In Argentina increase of acreage was severely limited by the social and economic conditions prevailing in the Alfalfa-Wheat Belt, and so increase of crop was achieved by improved cultivation and accompanying higher yield per acre. By the 1929-33 quinquennium the Argentine crop was 55 per cent. greater than for the 1909-13 quinquennium, but it was obtained from an acreage less than 9 per cent. greater. In Australia, subject to no such social and economic restrictions, expansion was carried out mainly by increase of acreage, and there was a distinct outward movement of the margin of cultivation. These increases were more than sufficient to offset the decline of North American production following the 1921-23 slump, and so even in 1925 there was a world crop and a world export greater than the average for 1909-13. The resumption of increase in North America accentuated this trend towards an ever-growing world export, and by 1928 world exports were 34 per cent. above the average for 1909-13.

Meantime acreage in the U.S.S.R. (Figure 2, d), after reaching its nadir in 1922, had rapidly increased. By 1926 pre-War acreage had been slightly exceeded, and by 1931 it had been raised by 33 per cent. In general, too, the average yield per acre was somewhat greater than the 1909-13 average, with the result that from 1926 to 1933 there was not a single year in which the total crop was not substantially greater than the pre-War crop. A large part of this increase was necessary to bring domestic consumption up to even a low level of adequacy, as judged by Western European standards, and the greater freedom of the peasants to manage their own land and crops in the earlier stages of the Soviet regime allowed of increase in consumption. The later stages of the post-War period, however, were dominated by the official campaign to promote the Five Year Plan. The central purpose of the Plan was the rapid industrialisation of the country, and the large imports of plant and machinery necessary for this purpose required largely increased exports to finance them. The measures taken to augment the export of wheat were designed to increase at once the amount produced and the share collected by the Government, and included the collectivisation of existing farms in the wheat belt, and the establishment of the new 'giant farms' on the practically empty lands on its semi-arid edge. The existing wheat belt was to have a larger proportion of its area under wheat and was to be more efficiently cultivated, but in addition there was to be a southward extension of the margin over what had been sub-marginal lands. This was achieved by a reduction of costs through applying very large-scale methods of production needing only a skeleton labour force. These measures had a considerable degree of success, and in 1930 and again in 1931 the U.S.S.R. exported a quantity of wheat equal to 60 per cent. of its 1909-13 average.

This new export from the Soviet lands reached a world market adjusted to an absence of Russian supplies, and already burdened by the large production and surpluses of the four great exporting countries. The year 1928 in particular had been one of bumper harvests in practically all producing areas (India was an exception), and had inaugurated a period of an abnormally heavy carry-over of surplus wheat. The effect on prices, which had already been falling every year since 1925, was decisive. In 1930 the Liverpool mean monthly price at 7s. 2d. per 100 lb. was below the 1913 level, and a further fall of 34.3 per cent. reduced it to 4s. 6½d. in 1931.

A fall of this magnitude might confidently be expected to lead to a sharp diminution of acreage everywhere, and to a noticeable recession of the geographical margins of cultivation. In reality little of the kind happened. The producing world was divided among nations and individuals, all keenly conscious of their own difficulties and of the pressure of competition. In exporting countries there was at first a general effort by producers to compensate for declining prices by increased production. This would in any case have depressed prices still further, but the effect was heightened by the measures taken by importing countries, notably Germany, France and Italy, to protect their own producers. By means of quotas and of heightened tariffs the domestic price level was kept artificially high to allow of the continued activity of marginal producers. Acreage and production actually increased significantly between 1929 and 1933 in Germany, Italy and Belgium, and imports were correspondingly reduced.

In 1931 the price level was indeed so low that it is very doubtful whether farmers even in optimum geographical conditions in the exporting countries could bring their costs within reasonable reach of it. Governments were forced to come to their assistance to prevent wholesale bankruptcy, and Government assistance by its very nature has to be impartially bestowed. The result is that, while diminution of acreage has been fairly general in the exporting countries since 1932, it seems to represent for the most part a reduction of production in areas away from the margin rather than a retreat of the margin itself. Such a retreat is easy to observe only when the margin is associated with monoculture, and apparently the only area where it has as yet taken place is along the semi-arid edge of the Spring Wheat Belt of the United States and Canada. Here the movement is in fact not due to the unaided influence of price conditions. The price fall was reinforced by the arrival of a succession of dry years, accompanied by dust storms of great severity, and large-scale abandonment of farms resulted. In Canada those farmers who have left the semi-arid margin in southern Saskatchewan and south-eastern Alberta seem largely to have gone to the northern edge of the cultivated area, where wheat will still be almost the only cash crop they can grow, but where the prospects of bare survival on a plan of mixed subsistence agriculture are at any rate better than on the arid edge.

There for the moment the matter must be left, inconclusive though it may seem. We have seen some reason for associating a rapid positive movement of the general geographical margin of wheat cultivation with high prices for wheat in the open world market. At the same time, however, we note that economic, social or political factors may now and then prevent the equal diffusion of the stimulus over all the actual or immediately potential areas of production. Similarly there seems to be some justification for expecting a period of low prices to witness a movement of recession of the general geographical margin, but difficulties associated particularly with the time lag (much more pronounced than in periods of rising prices) and with the lack of adequate local information prevent us as yet from reaching any very precise conclusions. If, however, the argument put forward in this paper is valid, we may hazard the opinion that much land cultivated for wheat in Canada, the United States and Australia in the pre-depression years was not merely submarginal in the depths of the depression but will remain so at any probable post-depression price level for wheat, and that the areal extent reached by the wheat belts of those countries in the late 'twenties is a maximum that will not again be attained for many years to come.

REFERENCE

[1] All statistics except those of wheat prices are based on those in the *International Year Books of Agricultural Statistics*. The wheat prices quoted are the mean monthly spot prices at Liverpool for 100 lb. of good red wheat. (Cf. the *Corn Trade Annual*.)

III

A Note on Labour Requirements In Plantation Agriculture*

It is perhaps advisable to begin this paper with some definition of terms, since 'plantation agriculture', though it is in common use among geographers and others, has normally a rather vague connotation. Here it will be explicitly limited to a system of agriculture characterised by the following features:

(1) Large-scale operation—'large-scale' having no necessary implication of large quantity or high value of output, but meaning solely that the area per unit holding is large.

(2) The direct employment of a labour force that is large, even in proportion to the large area that is being worked.

(3) Specialisation on *one* cash crop per holding. Such specialisation, it should be noted, does not necessarily prevent the growing of food crops for consumption on the plantation or of green crops as fertiliser for the cash crop.

(4) Production primarily for export. The home market, however, is not necessarily negligible.

(5) Production of crops that require planting, and not merely sowing.

(6) Financial and executive control of the holding by foreigners. There are some exceptions to this condition, but it is the general rule, nevertheless.

It is, then, with only this particular type of large-scale, specialised agriculture, and with only a very limited aspect of

*Contributed to *Geography*, 23, 1938

it, that this paper will deal. The essential theme is the influence of labour requirements on the development of the system and on its distribution both geographically and as between crops. It is no part of the purpose to give an exposé of areas as areas; and such areas as are cited have been selected solely because their plantations illustrate most readily or strikingly the immediate points of the argument. Omissions are, therefore, numerous and include the Philippines, inter-tropical Africa, Mexico, Central America and Argentina, all of which have (or until recently have had) some true plantation agriculture.

Plantation agriculture is the oldest of the modern types of large-scale specialised agriculture, dating as it does from the beginnings of colonisation in the warmer parts of the new world. Indeed, the world 'plantation' meant 'colony': it was the colony that was planted. The use of 'plantation' and 'colonial,' therefore, as interchangeable adjectives applied to the distinctive crops (tobacco, sugar and cotton) of the oversea settlements was entirely natural, and from that to the application of the term 'plantation' to describe the agricultural system that was evolved was a short and easy step. It might as easily have been 'colonial' that was applied to the system,[1] just as it was, in fact, applied to the crops, but once 'plantation' had been adopted it had the advantage of stressing one of the characteristics mentioned above—the crops have to be planted and not merely sown.

The nature of the agricultural system evolved was intimately associated with the kind of colonists and the conditions of the regions into which they went. Commonly, free grants of large areas of land were made to men of some standing at home, as, for example, younger sons of noble English families. These took with them into the wilderness a tradition of privilege, a habit of command, and a cultivated taste for the amenities of contemporary civilisation. All this pointed to the establishment overseas of an organising and governing caste, divorced from manual labour, but compelled, as the price of the maintenance of an acceptable spaciousness of life, to undertake the production of appropriate commodities for the market of the homeland.

In these circumstances the land itself could have little, if any, value unless it were cultivated, and cultivation of large areas in pre-power times implied a large labour force. Here was the dilemma that faced the early plantation owners: if the indigenous population was scanty enough to permit the large estate to have most of its area available for commercial cultivation by the owner, it was too scanty to furnish the labour supplies necessary. This was certainly the case in the Old South of North America, and apparently also on the coastlands of Brazil. In some of the West Indian islands, on the other hand, the indigenous population seems to have achieved a fairly considerable density, and did at the outset provide under compulsion a good deal of labour; but European exploitation rapidly reduced it practically to vanishing point. The problem was solved by importation of unpaid labour, first European convicts, later black slaves from Africa, and slavery became universal on plantation holdings. One may note, incidentally, that this gave a curious foreshadowing of the economic organisation of a present-day type of temperate-zone large-scale specialised agriculture, best exemplified by the 'Giant' grain farms of the U.S.S.R.: the investment of almost all the capital of the holding in the instruments of work. This feature assisted the plantation in its day and generation to be a marvel of efficiency, the first application since the days of the Roman *latifundia* of the principles of mass production to agriculture.

Modern plantation agriculture shows a fundamental similarity to its forerunner of the 17th. and 18th. centuries, but has had to adapt itself to different technical, economic and social conditions. The results of this adaptation are to be found in the detail of the methods employed, but are visible also in the choice of crops to be grown under this system, and in a tendency towards a closer geographical limitation of the area covered.

Typically, the scale of the agriculture is still large. That does not, of course, mean that every plantation covers a large area. State initiative, co-operation, and the application of the contract system to the use of machinery have all permitted small holdings to secure some, at any rate, of the advantages formerly enjoyed only by the large estates. Further, apart altogether from the range of size of holding to be found for any one crop, the optimum size of holding will certainly vary from crop to crop: a sugar-cane plantation will, on average, be smaller than a rubber or a banana plantation, and a tea plantation smaller than a coconut plantation. Normally, however, where plantation agriculture in the full sense of the word is practised, the size of the individual holding is measured in thousands, sometimes many thousands, of acres. The following samples, selected at random, may be regarded as not unfair:- A cotton estate of 7,000 acres in the irrigated Peruvian coastlands;[2] the Oahu Sugar-Cane plantation of 12,260 acres in Hawaii;[3] the Fazenda Chapadão of 4,000 acres in the Campinas district of the São Paulo coffee belt;[4] the United Fruit Co.'s banana plantation of 100,000 acres in Columbia.[5]

Methods, as would be expected, show a considerable amount of change since the pre-power era. This is to be associated, on the one hand, with the availability of power-driven machine implements and transport media, and, on the other hand, with the changed conditions of labour supply. It is, in fact, the labour position that is the crux of the whole matter. The problem remains essentially the same, the provision of an adequate supply of the right kind of labour in areas where population is scanty, or for any reason unable or unwilling to meet the needs of the planters. The abolition of the slave trade was followed by the institution of indentured labour. This system, not without its merits, was notoriously liable to abuse; at its worst, it differed very little from slavery, and came to an end in 1917, when India, the only really significant source of this class of labour, prohibited the emigration of indentured workers. Broadly, there is now no legal method of attaching labourers to particular plantations unless the labourer himself is willing to remain. True, in Latin America the operation of the peonage system on large estates may result in an economic serfdom of the workers, but in general it is now the case that, while immigrant labour still remains necessary, immigration must be tempted by attractive conditions of pay and work and living.

With the abolition of the slave trade and the introduction of the system of indenturing, India supplanted West Africa and the slave-breeding establishments of the New World as the great source of plantation labour—a position which it still holds. The sugar plantations of Mauritius, Natal, Fiji, and British Guiana, for example, drew their labour from India. The tea plantations of Ceylon and the rubber plantations of British Malaya depend almost exclusively on Tamils, while emigrants from Bengal and the Chota Nagpur plateau man the tea plantations of Assam. Chinese come locally into the picture as in Borneo and Samoa, while in the Hawaiian Islands, Filipinos and Japanese are numerically preponderant. In passing, then, we may note that the system is still a potent instrument in the migration of coloured peoples, in consequential race mixture and in the piling up of associated social problems. For our present purpose, however, it is the economic aspect that is the chief concern.

Attracting and employing immigrant labour on a large scale implies expenditure for the recruiting and sometimes for the transport of the workers, and almost invariably for housing and for medical and other services on the plantations themselves. These expenses form a significant addition to the cash wages that are paid, and are a significant element, therefore, in true labour costs of production. Cheap[6] as the labour may be, even when full allowance has been made for these extras, if the marginal cost for any particular job can be reduced by having it performed by machinery, sooner or later the machine is adopted.[7] Quite normally, the preparatory cultivation before the planting of the crop, some of the inter-row cultivating after planting, and much of the work involved in the transport of the harvest are done by power-driven machinery, but that still leaves the actual planting, much of the weeding (around the plants) and all the harvesting to be done necessarily by hand. No machine has yet been invented that will satisfactorily pick cotton or tea, harvest coffee, cut sugar-cane, or tap rubber trees. Within those fields labour is in a monopoly position, all large holdings must employ much labour, and labour costs may amount to as much as 70-80 per cent.[8] of total production costs.

Despite the considerable amount of mechanisation, then, it is labour that is the critical factor, chronic shortage of labour seems to be characteristic of the plantation agriculture industry as a whole, and the success whether of the industry as a whole or of the individual undertakings depends on the solution of the labour problem. In view of the predominance of immigrant labour and the location of the plantations in areas of scanty population, it is scarcely surprising that it is the extra labour demand for differential seasonal work that is most difficult to satisfy and that has acted as the most powerful limiting factor. The twin sources of extra labour demand of a seasonal character are planting and harvesting, and it is through their requirements with respect to these operations that the different crops exercise their different influence on the system and indicate their relative appropriateness to it.

Planting becomes a serious labour difficulty only when it must be frequently repeated, and that applies only to certain crops, and then normally only when they are grown near their geographical limits. Two of the traditional plantation crops, cotton and sugar, are of this kind. Where climatic conditions are easy enough, they may be ratooned (that is, grown as perennials) for several years, but for cotton that excludes the whole of the United States Cotton Belt, practically the whole of the Indian and Chinese, and part of the Egyptian cotton-growing areas, or about 90 per cent. of the world crop. For sugar-cane there is no such sharp distinction between ratooning and non-ratooning climatic conditions; so far as climate is concerned, if sugar-cane can be grown at all, it can be ratooned. Ratooning, however, is normally accompanied by progressive decline in the yield and quality of the crop and by increasingly serious trouble with pests, a state of affairs which may much more than counterbalance the economy of seasonal labour that ratooning permits. For these reasons ratooning is little practised in the majority of producing regions.[9] Exceptions are found in the irrigated areas of Hawaii (sugar) and of the coastlands of Peru (both sugar and cotton), where ratooning on balance proves worth while.

This differential seasonal demand for labour for planting purposes is obviously a handicap to the application of the plantation system to the short-lived crops, and in fact the world crops of tobacco, cotton and sugar-cane are now produced mainly by non-plantation methods. The plantation organisation remains in the irrigated lands of Hawaii for sugar-cane and of the Peruvian coast for both sugar-cane and cotton; in the eastern sugar-producing area of Cuba (largely dominated by American capital); and in a curiously modified form in the sugar areas of Java. Elsewhere these crops are characteristically produced on small holdings by peasant cultivators, or, as in Mauritius, Fiji, and the United States Cotton Belt, by tenants. It is, of course, not suggested that this seasonal demand for labour for planting is a sufficient sole cause for the movement of these crops away from the plantation system, but it is one element in that movement, and it is surely significant that, where they remain as plantation crops, the areas concerned are precisely those in which ratooning can be practised (Hawaii and Peru) or which have easiest access to outside supplies of seasonal labour. Peru draws seasonal labour for the coast from the high Andes, Cuba from other West Indian islands, while Java is in the unique position of having her sugar lands in the midst of a dense population of skilful and diligent cultivators. (We may note in passing that the labour demand in Java is exceptionally intense, since the planting and the harvesting seasons overlap). In general, however, the truly perennial crops, by avoiding this particular source of irregularity of demand for labour have a distinct advantage, and the plantation system is tending more and more to limit itself to crops of this kind.

As with planting, so with harvesting, but to a greater extent, the seasonal demand for labour varies in kind and intensity from crop to crop. The difficulty is most acute where the yield fluctuates violently from year to year. For an example which is valuable just because it is an extreme case, and therefore best exemplifies how serious such fluctuations can be, we may select Brazilian coffee. With the trees in good heart, a combination of better-than-average temperature and precipitation conditions produces a bumper crop, and this so exhausts the trees that the crop of the following year is very small, generally less than half the bumper crop. Another two or three years may be required to bring the trees back to full vigour, but once that has happened they are ready for the next bumper crop, which the first good year will assuredly produce. So the coffee crop characteristically moves through a cycle, more or less regular, from bumper crop through short crop and gradual improvement to bumper crop. In normal conditions the coffee market need not be unduly disturbed by these fluctuations, as the surplus of the bumper year is required to make good the deficiencies of the succeeding year or two, but such compensatory action does not apply to the labour requirements on the plantations. This illustrates a disadvantage of tree crops as compared with annual crops; to the possibility of soil exhaustion, which may be produced by any crop, is added with tree crops the further possibility of exhaustion of the plant, a condition which, when it occurs, no measures will immediately remedy. The difficulty, however, is normally much less acute than this Brazilian coffee example indicates, and is not sufficient to offset other advantages of tree crops for plantation agriculture.

Apart from such periodic differences in the amount of the crop, there are permanent differences among different crops in the nature and amount of the harvesting work to be done. The harvesting of such crops as tea, coffee and cotton may demand some skill and a good deal of care, but the work is not heavy, and women and children can undertake it. The problem is, therefore, eased when the permanent labour force consists of married men with large families. Thus the coffee plantations of Brazil, the tea plantations of Assam and Ceylon, and the tea and coffee plantations of Java have on the spot the nucleus at least of the extra labour required for harvesting. Sugar-cane forms an effective contrast. The cutting of the cane is a job for adult male labour, and it is very difficult indeed, if not impossible, even to begin to meet the needs of the situation from the resources of the estate itself. Practically the only exception to this is where climatic conditions are such as to permit harvesting (and planting) all the year round, and these conditions are found only in the irrigated areas, Peru being the best example. Where the harvesting season is confined by climatic conditions to a short period of the year, the difficulty becomes in most cases very great indeed, and the lack of flexibility in this respect is one of the important reasons for the abandonment of the plantation system for sugar-growing in so many areas. Here again the exceptional position of Java and, to a less marked degree, of Cuba is striking.

Among methods of trying to meet the difficulty of shortage of labour for harvesting, the use of the women and children dependants of the regular male labour force, and the importing of seasonal labour have already been mentioned. If it were always possible to import adequate supplies of seasonal labour, practically the whole of the labour difficulty would disappear. As things are, the plantation owner or manager must frequently try other measures. One rather widespread plan is to maintain on the estate a permanent labour force larger than the continuous requirements warrant, so as to have some surplus available for the rush season. Perhaps the best illustration of this is to be found in the coffee plantations of Brazil. There the usual practice on the larger estates is to allot to each colono about five acres of trees for maintenance. The cash wage can be small, for the real wage is considerably increased by rights of cultivation. Such rights of cultivation between the rows of coffee trees seem to be invariable until the coffee trees come into bearing at five years old. After that stage the colono more commonly has an allotment, where he may produce the great bulk of his food requirements. Neither of these concessions, valuable as they are to the labourers, costs the plantation anything: characteristically, only a fraction of any plantation is really good coffee land, and only a fraction of the coffee land is actually under coffee.[10] But obviously, such a plan is less applicable to crops like sugar and cotton, especially where, as in Hawaii and Peru, practically the whole of the plantation is under the cash crop.

The best method of meeting the difficulty, however, and the only one that can be trusted to be permanently effective, is the elimination as far as possible of seasonal fluctuations in the amount of work to be done. Mechanisation of those processes that can be mechanised contributes something to this end, and the choice of tree crops by eliminating frequent planting adds something more. But the process goes further— the longer the period over which the harvesting can be spread, the less the differential labour demand. The two harvesting seasons for coffee is one advantage which Colombia enjoys over Brazil, with its single, short, intense harvest period per year. The greater length of picking period for tea in Assam constitutes one of the advantages of that area over most of the tea-growing area of China, and one of the reasons why tea-growing in Assam was amenable to plantation methods. Ceylon and Java show the same advantage to a higher degree, and the picking of tea on the plantations of those countries is almost a continuous process. The same thing applies to the harvesting of the fruit of the oil-palm in Sumatra, and most completely of all to the tapping of the rubber trees in British Malaya and the Dutch East Indies. In this extreme case the harvesting forms a principal element in the *permanent* demand for labour, and, to the degree that controlled forestry methods replace more formal agricultural methods in the maintenance of the plantations, labour for harvesting will form a progressively increasing proportion of the continuous labour demand.

The argument of the previous paragraph implies crops that are able to produce their harvest all the year round, and we may note that the tree crops that fulfil this condition have the further advantage that the repressive effect on weeds of their own vigorous growth reduces the amount of the periodical cultivation that must be done. It implies also climatic conditions that permit the crops to produce a harvest all the year round, and that means the absence of any rest period. In effect, these conditions are practically confined to the Equatorial Belt. Plantation agriculture is, of course, found outside the Equatorial Belt, and is not entirely limited to tree crops, but the general trend of the last century or so has been a recession equatorwards of the latitudinal margins of the system, accompanied by an increasing preference for tree crops. Near and beyond the edges of the hot belt, and especially for the cultivation of tobacco, cotton and sugar-cane, disappearance of the system in favour of small holdings has been characteristic. Small holdings, for instance, frequently tenancies, are typical of the Cotton Belt of the United States and of most of the cane-sugar producing areas. They are even becoming increasingly common in the Coffee Belt of Brazil. In 1927, 94 per cent. of the holdings in the state of São Paulo, accounting for 51.75 per cent of the total coffee trees of the state, had fewer than 100,000 trees (say, 250 planted acres) each, while just over one-third of the total holdings had fewer than 5,000 trees (say, 12 planted acres) each.[11]

In so far as these facts indicate a distinct trend, it would seem that plantation agriculture in the future is likely to be more and more closely associated with the Equatorial Belt. That is not to say that small holdings will play no part there. In fact, about two-thirds of the rubber acreage of Malaya is in small holdings of not more than 100 acres, owned by Malays, Chinese and Indians, while native small holdings produce almost the whole of the rubber output of Sumatra. (For the Sumatra natives rubber is essentially a sideline to the growth of food crops for direct consumption, and is vigorously exploited only when prices are tempting.) But given the appropriate crops in equatorial climatic conditions, the large plantations by virtue of being able to reduce their agricultural operations to a smooth and continuous routine, and by their command of research organisations (especially for the breeding of more prolific strains) have advantages which should permit them to meet successfully the competition of small holdings.

REFERENCES

[1] The term 'colonial system' became specialised to the political, and in particular to the fiscal, aspects of the control of the colonies by the mother country.

[2] Rosenfeld, A. H. 'The Cotton Industry of Peru.' *Econ. Geog.*, vol. 3 (1927), No.4 (October). pp. 507-523

[3] Coulter, J. W. 'The Oahu Sugar Cane Plantation.' *Econ. Geog.*, vol. 9 (1933), No.1 (January). pp. 60-71

[4] Platt, R. S. 'The Coffee Plantations of Brazil. A comparison of Occupance Patterns in Established and Frontier Areas.' *Geog. Review*, vol. 25 (1935), No.2 (April). pp. 231-9

[5] Jones, C. F. 'Agricultural Regions of South America. Instalment VI, The Banana Region.' *Econ. Geog.*, vol. 5 (1929), No.4 (October), pp. 390-421

[6] Cash wages are in fact not always low: *cf.*, for example, Freeman's figure for the Oahu Sugar Cane Plantation of $1.10 a day. Freeman O. W. 'Economic Geography of the Hawaiian Is.' *Econ. Geog.*, vol. 5 (1929). No. 3 (July). pp. 260-276. Fay's figures for wages on tea plantations in India and Ceylon are, however, more typical. Fay, C. R. 'Plantation Agriculture.' Presid. Address, 1936, to Section F, British Assoc. for the Advancement of Science.

[7] Exceptionally, geographical difficulties like the numerous drainage canals of the British Guiana coast-lands or the irrigation ditches of the Peruvian coast-lands prevent full advantage being taken of mechanised cultivation. The British Guiana canals, however, cheapen the transport of cane to the mills.

[8] cf. Rowe, J. W. F. 'Studies in the Artificial Control of Raw Materials: No. 3. Brazilian Coffee.' *R. Econ. Soc. Memorandum No.* 34, Feb., 1932.

[9] The success of plant-breeding efforts in the development of the Uba cane opens up possibilities of considerable extension of cane ratooning, and may give sugar cane a new lease of life as a plantation crop.

[10] cf. Platt, R. S. 'The Coffee Plantations of Brazil. A Comparison of Occupance Patterns in Established and Frontier Areas.' *Geog. Rev.*, vol. 25 (1935), No. 2 (April). pp. 231-9

[11] *cf.* Rowe, J. W. F. *op. cit.*

IV

Some Reflections on Agricultural Geography *

The adoption of a ruling theme that will give character and continuity to the Conference, so happily exemplified by the contributions in 1956 to the geography of London, and in 1958 to urban geography, proved so successful that I welcomed the Honorary Organizer's suggestion that the theme this year should be agricultural geography and that the presidential address should be an introduction to that theme. I hasten to confess that I was moved not only by the appropriateness of the subject to a Conference such as this, but also by my own professional interest, which, no doubt reflecting a youth spent in close touch with practical farming, has acquired a somewhat pronounced bias to this aspect of our subject.

The task, however, is by no means easy. Agriculture is something of a portmanteau word, including within its denotation a wide range, from very simple to highly complex, of systems of utilizing the soil for the production of food stuffs or raw materials for human use. Clearly any comprehensive treatment of the geography of agriculture is beyond the scope of an address of this kind, and I intend, and have indicated my intention in the title, to be selective both in the material to be treated and in the method of treatment.

The first limitation, then, to be imposed upon the scope of the term 'agriculture' for my present purpose is that implied in the well-worn descriptive tags, 'agriculture as a way of getting a living' and 'agriculture as a way of life'. 'A way of

*Professor Buchanan delivered this Presidential address at the London School of Economics on 30th December 1958 during the Annual Conference of the Association. It was printed in *Geography*, 44, 1959

life' clearly implies that agriculture is something more than merely an industry. It does not, and cannot, cease to be an economic phenomenon, but it extends far beyond the merely economic into the wider social aspects and organization of life. So intimate indeed is the relationship between the agriculture and the character of social institutions and customs that it becomes virtually impossible to decide which is cause and which is effect. With only local and temporary exceptions, agriculture of this kind has been universal until very recent times, is still characteristic of areas of subsistence production, and is far from negligible in areas of small peasant agriculture that are not wholly subsistence agriculture areas.

In passing, one may note that it is precisely because the agricultural system was so closely tied into the wider social activities and values of the peasant communities in Russia and eastern Europe that the resistance to collectivization of farming in these areas was so bitter and so prolonged. The economic incentive to resistance was strongly reinforced by the social objections of the villagers.

So long as agriculture remains at this stage, where the strength of custom and its matching social institutions in a community prevent the free play of purely economic considerations, the geography of agriculture is properly an exercise in social geography. Geographical studies of agriculture of this kind have attracted geographers only to a minor degree. Much good work has been done by social anthropologists, but their interest has naturally been focused usually on the more primitive communities and on the techniques and processes of agriculture in the setting of the social organization of the group. I should be far from suggesting that the influence of, for instance, religious beliefs and practices or other aspects of the social organization of primitive communities on their agricultural methods and the reflex effects of the agricultural conditions and methods on their beliefs and institutions are not properly to be called geography. All that I am suggesting is that they do not exhaust the job of the geographer in studying the agriculture of such communities, and that, broadly speaking, the geographer has perhaps contributed less to the advancement of this sector of his subject than has the social anthropologist.

At this point I hasten to exclaim '*Mea culpa!*', to confess that I have myself done nothing to forward our knowledge of this part of our subject, and that for the rest of this address I shall be devoting my attention to some aspects of the other broad division, agriculture as a way of getting a living. By way of preliminary precaution let me hope that you will not regard my distinction too rigidly. To the extent that it is true that there are areas and systems of agriculture in which the farmer, the farm worker and society in general do in fact regard farming simply as a way of getting a living, farming becomes purely an industry like any other—coal-mining, steel-making, light engineering or what not—but such complete conversion of farming to a purely economic facies is still far from universal, and over much of the modern commercial world and in most of its agricultural systems some lingering elements of the social traditions of a bygone age still survive. There is nevertheless a sufficiently widespread and sufficiently close approximation to a fully commercialized agriculture to justify its examination as a modern industry, or, more accurately, as a pretty considerable group of industries.

The first point to make, then, about this modern agriculture is that it *is* modern, modern in origin as well as in character. True, there were forerunners, some of them in the very distant past, as, for instance, the Roman *latifundia*, which were highly commercialized units. In England the Tudor enclosures for sheep-rearing, capitalizing on the demand for wool from the Continent and from England's own rising woollen manufacturing industry, and compensating for the decline in manpower brought about by the Black Death and still not made good, produced working units which were in all essentials prototypes of the Australian sheep runs of the early nineteenth century. Perhaps most immediately relevant to our present purpose was the overseas plantation unit, a form of organization invented in the sixteenth century and developed in the seventeenth, which, modified in various ways, is still a live and vigorous element of contemporary large-scale commercial agriculture. Nevertheless, despite these and other examples of earlier com-

mercial organization, we may with some confidence date the
beginnings of the present systems of commercial agriculture
to the eighteenth century, when the agricultural and the
industrial revolutions of that century initiated changes that
have gone on at an accelerating rate ever since.

Perhaps the key element in the new agriculture, as in the
new industry, is to be found in specialization. Not only did
agriculture as a whole become more sharply differentiated
from manufacturing industry, with the increasing dominance
of the factory and the mine, but new specializations of
function or personnel (Adam Smith's 'division of labour')
arose within agriculture itself. This process, in agriculture as in
industry, when carried to its logical conclusion results in
specialization of area, a term which expresses the geography
of what the economist has in mind when he says 'localization
of industry'. In this connection it should perhaps be emphasized that specialization of area in agriculture is no more to
be confused with monoculture than, for instance, the specialist cotton-manufacturing area of southeast Lancashire is to be
thought of as manufacturing cotton textiles and nothing else.
The Australian sheep area, the New Zealand specialist dairy-
farming regions, the coffee belt of Brazil, the rubber areas of
Malaya may well exemplify extreme concentration on a
single product, but the Corn Belt of the United States, still
more the mixed farming area of East Anglia, have no such
limitation, while in Denmark we find a most beautifully
designed pattern of an intensive long-rotation arable agriculture focused primarily on the support of dairy cows for milk,
and through them on the production of bacon and eggs.
There is no more highly specialized commercial agricultural
area on earth, though it is by the system rather than by the
product that it is characterized.

Not surprisingly the longest strides to extreme specialization of agricultural areas were taken in the earlier nineteenth
century in some of the areas of new colonization overseas.
The plantations and the Australian sheep runs have already
been mentioned and the examples need not be multiplied.
The essence of their economic position lay in the fact that
land was normally plentiful and cheap, while extreme scarcity of labour was reflected in very high rates of wages.

Efficient use of labour demanded systems of farming that would spread labour thinly over much land and give a high return per unit of labour, though normally this would be accompanied by a low yield per unit of area. This, by the way, is irrespective of whether the labour is hired or is that of independent working owners or tenants. Clearly this is most easily realized where both the land and the labour are severely specialized and a monoculture holds sway. The late nineteenth- and early twentieth-century character of the Spring Wheat Belt of North America illustrates this very well. In recognizing this influence of some of the overseas areas as leaders towards specialization of area, however, one must guard against the danger of under-estimating how much such specialization of area, though not always of product, was concurrently being achieved in Britain and northwest Europe, where much larger labour supplies with lower wages rates and a long-established tradition both acted as something of a brake on the progress to specialization. As in our Danish example, it is easier to gain a relatively accurate idea of just how much has been accomplished if we think of systems of farming rather than of single products.

The world pattern was pretty well established by 1900, though it is true that new settlement has expanded somewhat since then and new areas of specialist production have come into existence. That pattern can best be described as a mosaic, not always completely continuous, of areas of specialist agricultural production. Such a mosaic implies a world market that is effective both over the total area in question and over a considerable range of demand. The great development of powered transport media (rail, marine, road, air), which geographers seldom forget, was instrumental in bringing the far ends of the earth into effective touch with one another, and in permitting the essential and constant outflow of products and inflow of requirements. What is more commonly overlooked is that the commercial and financial aids, the product markets, futures markets, convertibility of currencies, the bill on London, discount and insurance facilities, low tariff walls and so on, were just as essential as the physical aids to movement of goods. The system works much less smoothly now in an era of nonconvertible currencies and of much more pronounced economic nationalism than it did pre-1914, but the continued vigour of world trade originating and terminating in such specialized regions gives evidence of powers of survival of the pattern, reflecting its efficiency as a productive system.

If this picture is even approximately accurate and adequate, it will follow that the task of the economic geographer is to establish the pattern and to interpret it. Establishing the pattern means finding the most precise boundaries possible to the individual regions, and interpreting it means assessing the effect of the various local physical, economic and historical conditions in the context of the world market, including physical and economic access to the world market. To a newcomer to the work it might well seem that interpreting an area in that sense might be very difficult, but that establishing it should be easy. In fact both problems may be very difficult, and in general a study of the published work suggests that the logical problems involved are seldom well understood, or at any rate demonstrably solved.

Establishing the pattern of agricultural regions, as we have just said, involves finding the best possible boundaries to the individual regions, which in turn implies both definition and delimitation. My first proposition is that definition must be in agricultural terms—a crop, a crop association, a crop-and-livestock association, a system of organization of farm processes will serve as convenient examples. It is, unfortunately, necessary to stress this point. It is a curious fact that geographers at large have a quite clear understanding in their studies of climate of the difference between 'elements' and 'factors', but the exactly corresponding difference between the nature of a region and the factors that go to the creating of that nature is quite often not appreciated. So, for the Spring Wheat Belt of the United States and the Canadian Prairie Provinces the criterion is spring wheat, just that and nothing else. For the Cotton Belt it is cotton, for the Wheat-Alfalfa-Cattle Crescent of the Argentine Pampa it is wheat, alfalfa and cattle as an association. All of these, taken from the agricultural field, are simply examples of the wider rule that economic regions are defined in terms of economic criteria, and of the over-riding general rule that definition seeks to express the irreducible minimum of the inherent character of the phenomenon to be defined, so that all other attributes can be derived from it.

Delimitation, the actual fixing of a boundary, implies that the criterion or criteria must be capable of being mapped. On the large scale this means capable of being observed on the ground and recorded on a map of appropriate scale. Where, however, a considerable area, too great for direct field mapping, is being brought under review, it implies that the criteria can be expressed in quantitative, essentially numerical, form and recorded on small-scale maps. Such statistical mapping is of course open to sample field checking, and its final acceptability depends upon its ability to face such field checking, allowance being made for the degree of generalization necessary to fit the scale.

A long step forward in mapping and studying agricultural regions was taken by O. E. Baker in his work 'The Agricultural Regions of North America', published as a series of articles in *Economic Geography* from 1926 onwards for several years. This was in the strict sense a small-scale investigation of a whole continent and of regions some of which were already recognized under specific names in lay usage. His materials for mapping were the county statistics. The counties themselves were sufficiently small and the statistics sufficiently detailed and reliable to be adequate to the scale of the work. His task was to give a degree of precision, previously lacking, to the boundaries of the various belts so established. I propose to look more critically at part of his work in a moment or two, but before doing so I should like to make one or two general comments. In the first place, presumably through the initiative of the editor of *Economic Geography*, then the late Professor Elmer Ekblaw, the journal published further series of studies of agricultural regions, covering all the other continents. It is no disparagement of the authors, Olaf Jonasson, Clarence F. Jones, Samuel van Valkenburg and Griffith Taylor, to say that not one of those series was as successful as Baker's; neither the continents themselves nor the statistical data available lent themselves as readily to the work. Nevertheless this very considerable body of published studies of agricultural regions, covering the whole world, was a very significant addition to the literature of agricultural geography, and may well be seen in retrospect as the greatest contribution of *Economic Geography* to our subject.

In the second place, the criticism put forward by Derwent Whittlesey[1] that Baker's system, however useful it might be in the study of North American agriculture, was merely an *ad hoc* method that could not be used for the world as a whole or for a comparative study of North America with any other continent should not be over-emphasized. It is true so far as it goes, and Whittlesley himself evolved a somewhat complex method of dealing with agricultural regions on a world basis. In so far, however, as Baker's method and his system of agricultural regions materially aided in appreciating the regional character of American agriculture it was of inestimable value to students of the subject.

From the point of view of an economic geographer, however, there would seem to be some methodological weaknesses, or at any rate some lack of logical rigour in Baker's work. He is on quite firm ground in his delimitations where the problem is to find the outer boundaries beyond which a particular crop is not cultivated at all. The northern boundary of his Cotton Belt and the south-western (semi-arid) boundary of his Spring Wheat Belt are instances in point. In such cases the problem is simple and the method cannot fail to be fully objective. Wheat or no wheat, cotton or no cotton, is all that has to be observed and mapped, and a boundary, firm for any particular point of time, though subject no doubt to advance or retreat over a period of time, can be fixed.

The Corn Belt presented a different problem. Corn is the most widely grown crop in the continent, extending from Canada to the Gulf of Mexico, from Kansas and Nebraska to the Atlantic coast, and even, by special methods, far into the dry south-west; and what was required was a valid method of accurately distinguishing the area of corn-growing par excellence, *the* Corn Belt. For this task Baker's basic definition and his consequential criterion for delimitation are either unsatisfactory in themselves, or, if not, are quite inadequately explained. 'This region', he says, 'includes that portion of the east central United States in which corn (maize) is produced in great quantities and is more important than any other crop.' If he had stuck strictly to that definition, he would surely have had to include in his Corn Belt much, if not all, of his Corn and Winter Wheat Belt, where corn in point of acreage and yield is quite generally more important than any other single crop. If, as has been suggested, what he really meant was the area within which corn was the dominant[2] crop, in the sense that the whole farm organization focused on corn and that other crops were grown not so much directly for their own sake as to provide a suitable rotation, he would have had a formula sufficiently rigorous to enable him to separate out that part of the corn-growing area in which corn occupies a different position from what it does anywhere else. It was probably something of this kind that Baker did mean—but he did not say so.

His next problem was to find a quantitative measure of relative importance of corn that could be mapped. On this he says, 'In all counties of the region, except those along the semi-arid western margin, the average annual production of corn per square mile exceeds 1000 bushels, and in a few counties reaches 10,000 bushels and more. The yearly average production along the southern margin is 3000 bushels per square mile and this is generally true also along the northern and eastern margins. On the average the Corn Belt produces 5000 bushels of corn per square mile . . .'

Here we face a logical problem of method that Baker gives us no help in solving. We are not told by what process he arrived at the figure of 3000 bushels, and in view of the fact that he says 'this is generally true also along the eastern and northern margins', we are even left in doubt whether, having decided on that figure, he applied it strictly. It is, I think a not unfair inference from the statement, 'the average production along the southern margin is 3000 bushels per square mile', that Baker may have drawn his southern boundary on some other basis, and then noted the correspondence with the 3000 bushels per square mile yield. And this deduction draws more than a little support from the footnote to Baker's first article 'The Basis of Classification'.[3] If that were so, and we have no means of knowing whether it were so or not, his correlation of the southern boundary with certain features would be logically valueless, being based on reasoning in a circle.

At this stage it may be well to indicate how an appropriate boundary to the Corn Belt may be validly found. On the criterion of dominance of corn in the sense already defined, what has to be done is to find whether that concept can be translated into terms of bushels per square mile, and, if it can, to find the proper number of bushels for the limiting case. Now the Corn Belt as a fact and the name 'Corn Belt' had been in existence for years before Baker began his work.[4] No one previously had attempted to give any precise extent to it, and the kind of general idea that was prevalent is shown very well by an extract from the 1911 Yearbook of the United States Department of Agriculture, quoted by Warntz: 'For the purposes of this paper the Corn Belt will be considered as including the States of Ohio, Indiana, Illinois, Iowa, Missouri, Kansas and Nebraska, together with southern portions of Michigan, Wisconsin, and Minnesota, the south-eastern portion of South Dakota, and the western half of Kentucky.'

Vague as this description is, it does give some indication of approximate boundaries, and a rigorous procedure would have been to do a farm-by-farm investigation along a series of transects from well outside the approximate boundary to well inside it. Such an investigation would have permitted the establishment on each transect of the point at which corn ceased to be the focus of the farm organization and became only another, even if a very important, crop. If the number of transects were impossibly numerous, there would be no need for any statistical evaluation: the points could be simply joined up to give a firm boundary. Within the practical possibilities the transects would be no more than samples, but the position of the points would permit an evaluation of the number of bushels per unit area that would serve as a statistical index. It might or might not be found that the actual value varied from one part of the belt to another, as, for instance, from the southern boundary to the northern.

Once such a numerical evaluation has been made, it must be mapped on a map which contains nothing at all except the county boundaries to which the statistics relate, in practice a tracing overlay. It is then possible by the ordinary procedure of superposition to relate it to a range of maps showing, for instance, isohyets (annual, seasonal or monthly), isotherms, relief, soil boundaries, geological outcrops, drift deposits and so on. Here one might interpolate that the process need not stop there. Maps showing population distribution and density, types of land tenure and other human distributions may also be relevant and important. By such a process the correspondences noted by Baker of the southern boundary of his belt with the southern edge of the Wisconsin glaciation east of the Mississippi and with the northern foot of the Ozark Plateau west of the Mississippi; of the eastern boundary with the westward-facing bluffs that mark the western edge of the Appalachian Plateau; of the northern boundary with the line of 70° F. mean summer temperature east of the Missouri and 69° F. west of that river would have validity as firm correlations, established *after* the extent of the belt had been fixed. At the risk of tedious repetition I stress the general point that no correlation can have any value at all unless the variables it relates are completely independent. The accuracy and validity of Baker's correlations are not at the moment in question: they may be thoroughly sound. All that is argued is that he has given us no means of knowing whether they are sound or not, and that he leaves us with something of an uneasy suspicion that his method was not sound.

This matter of correlation leads me to a further point of what I may call the scientific method of the problem. Having established his correlations (if, that is to say, they *are* correlations, and the belt has not been delimited by mapping the physical elements, the Wisconsin glaciation and so on), Baker has no difficulty in showing that in this belt corn finds better conditions for growth and yield than in any other part of north America. Soils change progressively from forest brown earths in the east through black prairie earths and then chernozems to chocolate and lighter-coloured grassland soils in the west, but are everywhere good and on the grassland area outstandingly good. Length of growing season decreases pretty regularly from south to north, but along the northern boundary the mean summer temperatures indicated as good signposts correspond pretty closely to a frost-free period of

140 days, and that was long enough for the types of corn grown in Baker's day. Rainfall decreases progressively westward and becomes the critical element in the west. Up to that point, however, it is both adequate in mean annual amount and most conveniently distributed seasonally, with a relatively large amount in July and August, just when it is most required by the plant for a good yield. The smoothness of the surface greatly aids ease of cultivation, and the winters are severe enough to constitute a useful check on the multiplication and spread of pests. All that is true, but it still falls a good deal short of explaining why corn becomes dominant in the belt. This great area of country is also the best area in North America for the growing of various other crops, but not one of them achieved supremacy.

In this context it is illuminating to contrast the experience of the Spring Wheat Belt, at any rate in its northern part, including the Canadian portion of the Red River valley. In the early stages of settlement only a small fraction of the present Canadian Spring Wheat Belt was suited to the growing of wheat, and only to the most rapidly maturing variety. The area was in fact more widely and more completely suited to barley than to wheat, and it was only by breeding special varieties of wheat, tailored as it were to the climate, that the Canadian Spring Wheat Belt could become the Spring Wheat Belt and assume its present extent and character. The crop best suited to the conditions of rainfall and length of growing season, barley, did not dominate the farming or the region itself, but was outdone by one that had to suffer considerable modifications to enable it to do so. It is interesting to note, however, that in the changed market conditions of more recent years barley has made considerable headway, especially in the Red River valley of Manitoba. (Amongst ancillary advantages for this is the fact that its earlier harvesting dates allow a more thorough war on the weeds that wheat monoculture had encouraged.)

The truth is that, even accustomed as we now are to supplying our wants by buying and selling, we geographers are still prone to overlook the fact that it is consumer demand, direct or derived, as expressed in the state and trend of markets, against which the claims of a product to utilize a particular set of physical conditions must be viewed. The crop that best fits the physical conditions will be the preferred crop if, and only if, its advantage in physical yield over its competitors is reflected in an advantage in financial yield. That may well be normally the case; it is not necessarily so. The rise of corn to its dominant position in the later nineteenth century is to be set in the context of the rapidly rising demand for meat and perhaps especially for animal fats in the days before vegetable oils had made any significant advance as substitutes for butter and cooking fats. Famous as was, and is, the Corn Belt for the fattening of beef cattle, it is the lard hog that has been its peculiar contribution and the lard hog that most efficiently used the supreme fattening capacity of the maize in a rapid turn-over of stock. Directly contributory, too, was the development of lake shipping and the vast proliferation of railways about the middle of the nineteenth century, widening the home market and opening up international markets before the Cotton Belt or the great pastoral countries of the Southern Hemisphere were able to compete. In summary it was the sustained demand from accessible markets for corn-fed livestock products, constituting a derived or indirect demand for corn itself, that kept the price of corn per bushel broadly similar to that of wheat, while the yield per acre of corn in the Corn Belt was normally twice that of wheat, or more, and this relationship of wheat to corn epitomizes the net effect of the manifold outside influences to which the Belt and its agriculture were deliberately adjusted. Analysis of these and other aspects of the nearer and the wider economic environment forms no part of Baker's work or purpose. Baker's descriptive treatment of the Corn Belt as a going concern stands unrivalled, even by other parts of his own work, but should, it would seem, better be regarded as a contribution to regional than to economic geography.

This brings me to the final point arising out of Baker's work. Baker himself suggested that his boundaries might not themselves be permanent, and I have myself elsewhere discussed the geographical margin as one aspect of the lack of fixity of boundaries.[5] In the Corn Belt we have a more complex example, arising not only out of shifts in demand occasioned by events elsewhere, but also by alterations in supply conditions within the belt itself. In the first place the breeding of more rapidly maturing varieties of corn has had the effect of enabling the northwest boundaries of the belt to be pushed outwards in Minnesota and South Dakota. That is a simple extension of area, an outward movement of the margin, and does not of itself necessarily involve any change in the criterion or any recalculation of the numerical value assigned to the criterion.

Apart, however, from such biological changes, simple intensification in the demand for maize might well result in an increase in the amount of production of maize wherever it is grown in the United States, and along with that general increase might go either an increase or a decrease in the disparity between the Corn Belt and the rest of the producing area in the amount of production per square mile. The critical amount might then alter up to, say, 4000 bushels, or down to, say, 2500 bushels, with or without any significant change in the position of the boundaries themselves; and similar reasoning can be applied to a prolonged decrease in demand.

Such a simple sequence would of itself involve no change in the character of the belt, a point I shall return to later, and only relatively slight changes in its extent. In fact the actual trend of events has been complicated by other considerations. Here, as elsewhere, there has been a continuous intensification of urbanism, and the constantly increasing urban populations, largely but not wholly on the periphery of the belt, have required increasing supplies of dairy produce and market garden produce, most of which has to be produced locally. So the belt has been progressively bitten into by expanding areas devoted to the production of other things than corn, with a corresponding decline of corn-growing. Small as these areas are in total extent and in their proportion to the belt as a whole, they do something to alter the beautiful simplicity of outline of the belt and to remind us that corn-growing in the Corn Belt, no less than elsewhere is still dependent on the ability of the corn to hold its own in market value against the competition of other possible products.

More widespread and more continuous, however, is another change which has come about wholly since Baker was doing his work in the early 1920s. The rise of the vegetable oils as sources of margarine and cooking fats and of mineral oils as substitutes for animal fats in most of their other uses has greatly decreased the demand for lard and therefore for the lard hog. In compensation, however, it was discovered that the general physical and climatic conditions that are differentially good for corn are also differentially good for that recent vegetable oil seed immigrant into the United States, the soya bean. The great spread of soya bean growing shows the belt adjusting itself to a decrease in demand for its particular kind of animal fat and a growing demand for vegetable fats. In so doing it is altering its internal character[6] independently of and additionally to any fluctuations of the margins induced by new varieties of corn or by trends in price of corn or in cost of its production.

You may well by this time have begun wearily to wonder why I have devoted so much of my time and argument to a piece of work that is now more than thirty years old, and perhaps to feel that flogging this dead, or at any rate retired, horse is sheer waste of your time. There is indeed more to it than just corn-growing, and I deliberately chose the Corn Belt as a peg to hang a hat on because it illustrates so admirably the general points I want to leave with you about the nature of agricultural geography in a commercial world. In the first place commercialized agriculture does in fact express itself regionally in our present-day world and the definition and the delimitation of agricultural regions demand rigorous concepts and methods, demands which because the logical problem involved is not always understood are not always satisfied even now.

As a corollary of that it would seem to follow that satisfactory delimitation of agricultural regions, even if accompanied by a good descriptive treatment of the current system of agriculture, is strictly an exercise in regional geography rather than in economic geography. It does indeed contain much of the material for a study in economic geography, and may well be an essential step on the road to an adequate study in economic geography, but, without an analysis of the economic conditions, local and general, against which the specialization developed and to which it is adapted, it lacks the essentials of a study in the systematics of economic geography. Account must be taken of demand, which originates essentially outside the region and expresses itself in a general world price with appropriate local modifications. It is the ratio of local costs to this available price that indicates the desirability of the particular specialization. In more technical and general form this means that correlations are established at the margins, but that, even if completely valid, they solve no problems. They are in fact no more than a revealing and a defining of the problems, and themselves become the subjects of the investigation. Their value for this purpose arises in no small part from the fact that it is at the margins, the limiting instances of the forces involved, that they are established.

The other broad characteristic of the agricultural region and its specialized products or methods is its tendency, once established, to maintain itself. The very existence of such a specialized area implies the accumulation of much specialized fixed capital—in our Corn Belt, for instance, corn silos, corn pickers, pig sheds, cattle yards and so on—and of knowledge and skills peculiar to the particular form of production practised. It implies, too, a whole host of commercial and financial institutions ancillary to the special production, their efficiency, like that of the farmers themselves, deriving from long and intimate experience of handling the special product. It implies, finally, developed channels of communication, contacts, reputation. Not one of these categories of equipment will be sacrificed willingly and the attendant losses accepted. The specialized area, like the specialized worker, will fight to the last ditch before accepting a change in specialization, and stability of character, except perhaps at the margins, is a natural, almost inevitable, result. Demand, it is true, keeps on altering, but changes in demand are normally gradual and time is available for the specialist area and its personnel to adjust themselves little by little to the changes. So, though the regions are certainly stable, they are just as certainly not static, still less stagnant. Sooner or later persistent pressure of a permanently changed demand would ensure that a specialized area either changed its productive character or was abandoned. The present pattern of agricultural regions reflects events of the recent past in the growth and spread of white populations and in their application of scientific research, technological achievement and commercial organization to the business of farming. In all of these change is constant, and the Corn Belt, related to a particular phase, now passing away, of the opening up of North America, and to a particular stage, now being left behind, of Western economic evolution, may well be a portent of the replacement in some more or less distant future of the existing world pattern of agricultural regions by new regions and a different pattern.

REFERENCES

[1] D. Whittlesey, 'Major Agricultural Regions of the Earth,' *Annals of the Association of American Geographers,* vol. xxvi, 1936, pp. 199-240.

[2] Baker does use the term 'dominant' in the note to Fig. 12 in his first essay 'Agricultural Regions of North America. Part I. The basis of classification', *Economic Geography,* vol. ii, 1926, p. 472.

[3] *Ibid.,* p. 460: 'Especially have changes in land surface or soils been used in assigning an exact boundary to an agricultural region. The southern boundary of the Corn Belt, across Ohio and most of Indiana, for instance, is drawn along the southern margin of the Wisconsin glaciation, . . .'

[4] Cf. W. Warntz, 'An Historical Consideration of the Terms 'Corn' and 'Corn Belt' in the United States,' *Agricultural History,* vol. 31, 1957.

[5] R. O. Buchanan, 'Some Features of World Wheat Production,' *Scottish Geographical Magazine,* vol. 52, 1936, pp. 313-324; and 'Approach to Economic Geography,' *Indian Geographical Journal,* Silver Jubilee Volume, 1951

[6] L. Haystead and G. C. Fite in their *Agricultural Regions of the United States,* recently published (Oklahoma, 1955), re-christen it 'The Corn and Soy Bean Belt'.

V

The Empire & World Trade *

The question may well be asked why in such a book as this separate treatment is accorded to the British Empire. In normal times trade between any one part of the Empire and any other is financed and controlled in exactly the same way as trade with any foreign country, and is subject to precisely the same kinds of limitations. In the strict economic sense there is indeed no British Empire at all. Equally, however, there is no British Empire in any strict legal or political sense, and yet in two consecutive world wars the overseas areas embraced by the term have given a demonstration of political and military solidarity not surpassed by any unitary nation. Similarly, despite its international character, trade between the United Kingdom and its overseas 'dependencies', which had long been a major element in the economic health of the mother country, became in the pre-war years of the nineteen-thirties the undisputed dominant element, largely responsible for saving the export industries of this country from complete collapse. The character, magnitude and direction of the trade of the Empire is, therefore, worth some study, no less for its implications for the future than for its importance in the past.

Clear ideas on Empire trade imply clear ideas on the Empire itself, but, understandably enough in the circumstances, such ideas are rather conspicuously lacking in the intellectual equipment of the average man. This Empire of ours is a loose agglomeration of more than sixty political

*A contribution to Mark Abrams (ed.), *Britain and her Export Trade*, Pilot Press, London, 1947.

entities, scattered in large areas and small on all the continents, over all the seas, and in almost all latitudes, aggregating
an area of approximately thirteen million square miles (equal
to a third of the habitable land of the globe), and supporting
some 540 millions of people (about a quarter of the total
population of the world). Size, discontinuity and variety are
the keynotes, with the emphasis perhaps on the bewildering
diversity of climates, products, races of man, and stages of
political and economic development. So some preliminary
simplification of the complexity is desirable, to the end of
bringing the major features into better focus.

A first distinction, of cardinal importance in trade matters,
is between those countries that are completely self-governing
and those that are not.[1] These latter may be further divided
into India and the Colonial Empire. Table IV indicates the
orders of magnitude of area and population of these great
divisions.

TABLE IV.–BRITISH EMPIRE: AREA AND POPULATION

	Area	Population*, 1938	
	000 Sq. Miles	000,000	Per Sq. Mile
United Kingdom	94·3	47·48	503·6
Eire	27·1	3·0	111·1
Canada	3729·7	11·2	3·0
Australia	2974·6	6·93	2·3
Union of South Africa ...	473·1	10·0†	21·1
Southern Rhodesia	150·3	1·4†	9·3
New Zealand	103·6	1·6	15·4
Newfoundland	42·7	0·3	7·0
India	1575·2	380·5	241·6
Colonial Empire	2252·0	62·0	27·5

*Estimated.
†Including non-white.

Outside the British Isles the self-governing Dominions are
lands of nineteenth-century colonisation by European, chiefly British, emigrants. With the notable exception of the
South African countries their populations are entirely white,
and together with the British Isles they account for almost
the whole of the white population of the Empire. The period
of their effective colonisation was that in which the progressive industrialisation of Britain had given rise to the concept

(almost, indeed, an article of faith) that the rôle of the colonies was to provide foodstuffs and raw materials for the mother country, and dependable markets for her exports of manufactured commodities. Up to a point events fulfilled that expectation. In the colonies highly selected populations turned to the exploitation of virgin resources with energy, initiative and a marked freedom from the hampering effects of custom and tradition, to such effect that by the early years of the twentieth century primary production, as, for example, of timber or wheat in Canada, wool or wheat in Australia, lamb or butter in New Zealand, or gold in South Africa, had been 'industrialised' to a degree previously parallelled only in the great manufacturing industries of the Old World. And it is still true that the high standard of living of the relatively small populations of these young communities, no less than their contribution to the economic life of the world, depends to a very large extent on their exports of the products of agriculture, forestry, fishing or mining, either raw or little processed.

That, however, is only part of the story. The acquisition of progressively widening powers of self-government gave the opportunity, in some cases almost from the very beginning of colonisation, to formulate policies for future national development, and to take any measures considered appropriate to translate policy into practice. With the exceptions of Newfoundland and Southern Rhodesia, the Dominions have all followed the model of the United States rather than that of the United Kingdom. The ideal, expressed or implied, is the 'balanced economy', and the promotion of that ideal in lands, where for the most part the advantages so conspicuously present for primary production were at best much less in evidence for manufacturing industries, has been expressed in the setting up of industries behind protective walls of varying degrees of rigidity. For our present purpose the wisdom or justice of such protectionist régimes is quite irrelevant. The essential point is that a young industry in a young dominion could be attacked by British no less than by German, American or Japanese competitors, and quite deliberately the defensive tactics of protectionism were employed against competition from all external sources, foreign

and Empire alike. In practice (and that long before the
Ottawa Agreements) individual Dominions often accorded
some measure of preference to goods of British origin, but
the degree of such preference was very carefully limited; and
it is highly significant that when the Ottawa Agreements were
negotiated the United Kingdom was required to recognize
explicitly the right, even the duty, of the Dominions to
develop their own secondary industries. By the beginning of
World War II Canada had gone far along the road to
industrialisation, Australia and the Union of South Africa
were following some way behind, and even Eire and New
Zealand, with their relative lack of resources for the maintenance of large-scale industry, were fostering a certain range of
industrial enterprises.

Both the Colonial Empire and India afford striking con-
trasts with the Dominions. The Colonial Empire includes over
fifty administrative units, some of them large (many in
Africa), most of them small or very small (chiefly islands),
with a total area less than one third that of the Dominions,
but a population more than twice as great. These lands,
however, lie almost wholly within the intertropical belt, the
density of population varies from the 1,600 per square mile
of Bermuda down to the 0.5 per square mile of Falkland
Islands, and white population is almost restricted to officials,
traders, missionaries, mining engineers and so on, who, once
their term of duty is over, retire to their own homeland to
spend their declining years.[2] Broadly, the standard of economic achievement of the native populations is low. Even
under European administration the patterns of life and
standards of living in vast areas of the Colonial Empire are
built upon a somewhat primitive agriculture, producing food
crops for direct consumption and contributing little to
international trade. Important exceptions are not without
considerable significance. Examples are the two great entrepot centres, Singapore and Hong Kong, which have capital-
ised the outstanding advantages of their geographical position; the areas where European-controlled plantation agriculture has been established, as in Malaya and Ceylon; and still
more limited areas where native agriculture has succeeded
under British guidance in producing important export crops,

such as the cacao of the Gold Coast or the cotton of Uganda; some islands, usually small, where high specialisation on a single export crop has developed, as, for instance, Mauritius with its sugar or the Falkland Islands with their wool; and finally those areas where mineral wealth is being exploited by European enterprise, such as Northern Rhodesia (copper), Gold Coast (gold and manganese), Nigeria and Malaya (tin), Trinidad (oil) and so on. The fact remains, however, that even where great commercial enterprises have been established the amount by which the aggregate native purchasing power has been increased and standard of demand raised remains extremely small judged by any European standard.

So far there has been no basis in prospective manufacturing developments for the growth of protectionist sentiment and practice in the Colonial Empire, but customs duties have been the normal method of raising revenue, and with few exceptions preferences were not accorded to United Kingdom or Empire suppliers of dutiable goods until after the Ottawa Conference. Even then practically the whole of British inter-tropical Africa, including the Gold Coast, Nigeria, Uganda, Kenya, Tanganyika, and part of Northern Rhodesia, was covered by treaties or agreements which prevented the introduction of imperial preferences.

The Indian Empire occupies a unique position. Its continuous land mass of over one and a half million square miles (not including Burma) carries a population of not far short of 400 millions, and thus accounts for almost three-quarters of the total population of the whole of the British Empire. Traditionally India's teeming millions have been engaged in a subsistence agriculture that provided the vast majority of them with a living little above starvation level. The introduction of such plantation crops as tea and coffee, the enormous development of perennial irrigation in the drier areas, the building of great railway systems and the improvement of medical and sanitary services have done much to alter conditions of life, especially in the last two generations or so. Agricultural production has increased, its reliability has been improved and the risks of famine have been reduced, while large quantities of agricultural produce have been made available for export. Industrialisation has begun, and India's cotton and jute crops provide raw materials for industries that are already of world significance. The coal and iron resources are limited and severely localised, but occur sufficiently close together to form a technically convenient basis for a developing iron and steel industry. Up to the present the increased productivity has gone to the support of an amazing increase of population, while the standards of living of the masses seem to have improved little, if at all. Today more than three-quarters of the total population is still rural, depending directly upon the fruits of a soil taxed almost to its uttermost, and industrialisation has very far to go before it does more than scratch the surface of the problem of so raising general standards of living as to convert the potentialities of the Indian market into values that would be commensurate with its physical size.

India, like the Colonial Empire, has not yet achieved responsible self-government, but the Government of India has long pursued a fiscal policy designed for the benefit of India itself, and not for that of the United Kingdom. Prior to 1932 some preference was given on cotton piece goods and on certain classes of protected iron and steel goods, but otherwise British goods in the Indian market had to meet open competition. Here, as elsewhere, the Ottawa Conference, born of the terrible depression of 1930 and 1931, resulted in a considerable extension of the range of British goods on which preference was granted, and these preferences were further extended to certain of the Dominions.

Against this very general background it should now be possible to appreciate some of the characteristics and trends of Empire trade, and we shall begin by considering its amount. Table V gives a bird's-eye view of the aggregate values involved in two sample years, the year 1929 being selected as in general the peak year before the onset of the great slump of the 'thirties, and 1938 as the latest year unaffected by the war. By 1938 a considerable measure of recovery had been made from the trough of the depression in 1931-2, but price levels and aggregate values were still generally lower than those of 1929.

From our present point of view the differences between 1929 and 1938 are irrelevant. The essential fact in both years is the very large values involved. They amount indeed to not less than one-third of the value of the whole of the trade of the world. Even more striking is the individual supremacy of the United Kingdom, whose 47 millions of people conducted a trade that only in the nineteen-thirties fell below the aggregate of all the rest of the Empire put together. Even in 1938 it still amounted to 70 per cent. of that aggregate. This was the position built up on early and intensive industrialisation, the development of shipping and financial services with world-wide ramifications, and the long-continued export of surplus capital. Britain had become the world's great creditor nation, her shipping and financial services and her overseas investments brought in an annual income of some £400,000,000 a year over and above the payment for her current exports, and these interests were in the strictest sense international, foreign as well as imperial. Clearly this state of affairs set narrow limits to the power of the country to implement a policy of Empire Free Trade or even of thorough-going Imperial Preference. Conversion of 'The World's Best Customer' into merely the Empire's best customer carried all too plainly the prospect of an inevitable and drastic decline in the prosperity of its industrialised and urban population.

TABLE V.—SUMMARY OF TOTAL TRADE OF THE EMPIRE, 1929 & 1938.

	1929 £000			1938 £000		
	Exports	Imports	Total	Exports	Imports	Total
United King.	839,051	1,220,765	2,059,816	516,789	919,509	1,436,298
Dominions ..	594,283	598,219	1,192,502	523,925	570,381	1,094,306
India	239,069	180,570	419,639	122,093	114,248	236,341
Colonial Emp.	278,572	302,438	581,010	361,161	342,164	703,775

N.B.—The figures for the Dominions are obtained by adding together the figures for the separate Dominions. They do not, therefore, refer to net trade of the Dominions with non-Dominion areas, and so are not strictly comparable with the figures for the U.K. and India. The same limitation applies to the figures for the Colonial Empire.

What has not been so widely understood is that the Dominions too, are mighty trading nations. Expansion of their trade in the twentieth century has been proportionately more rapid than that of the United Kingdom, and by the outbreak of World War II their aggregate trade amounted to about three-quarters of hers, though their populations were still only half of hers. Canada alone had by 1937 attained fourth place for exports, eighth for imports and sixth for total trade among the nations of the world. Both the absolute figures and the relative rate of growth would seem to imply a high degree of specialisation of production on commodities for export, and the devotion of a large part of the national capital, labour and natural resources to that end. In fact wide differences of economy from one Dominion to another have emerged. At one end of the scale New Zealand, capitalising its ample rainfall, brilliant sunshine and mild winters, has specialised on permanent-grass farming which supports animals that provide 94 per cent. of the total exports of the country. At the other end of the scale Canada derives only a minor part of her exports from the far-famed prairie wheat lands. Increasingly she has exploited the forest, mineral and water power wealth of the Canadian Shield, as well as the Great Lakes connections with American coal and iron ore, to equip herself to export her raw materials in more or less completely manufactured form. By 1938 two-thirds by value of Canadian exports were of fully manufactured goods, while fully manufactured and partly manufactured together accounted for three-quarters of the total. Australia and the Union of South Africa are intermediate between these two extremes. From each the exports are overwhelmingly of little-processed primary products, pastoral and agricultural (especially wool and wheat) from Australia, minerals (outstandingly gold) from South Africa. In all these three Dominions the recent pressure of urgent war requirements has considerably extended the range of manufacturing activities— and not all of these war-founded industries will vanish now that the immediate urgency is over.

This general picture of the importance of the trade of the self-governing countries of the Empire is sharpened if the trade is expressed in values per head of population. Table VI gives such values for 1929 and 1938, and it should be noted that the broad effect, though not the precise figures, would have been the same at any time this century. These per head values are remarkable. They demonstrate beyond all possibility of doubt that for the Dominions, no less than for the

United Kingdom, overseas trade is not merely a means of adding a slight fringe of luxury or semi-luxury goods to the every day necessaries produced at home. Their exports are sold in the world market to obtain a significant fraction of just those necessaries, and imports form a by no means negligible part of the daily consumption of every citizen. The extent of this dependence on sea-borne trade is not exceeded anywhere else in the world, though Japan (before the war), Norway, Denmark and Holland approximated to it.

TABLE VI.–TRADE PER HEAD OF POPULATION, 1929 & 1938.

	1929			1938		
	£	s.	d.	£	s.	d.
United Kingdom	43	7	8	30	5	0
Canada	56	15	8	34	12	2
Australia	40	15	2	32	5	1
Union of South Africa* ...	22	19	2	20	4	5
New Zealand	70	7	1	77	5	7
India	1	19	5		19	7
Colonial Empire	8	12	10	11	7	4

*For total population. Reckoned for European population alone the values become:

> 1929: £102 11s. 4d.
> 1938: £96 18s. 11d.

Tables V and VI display a very different state of affairs in the Dependencies. The aggregate trade of India and the Colonial Empire is of the same order of magnitude as that of the Dominions, but the trade per head of population is relatively low, in India very strikingly so. It is to be remembered that the value given for the trade per head of the Colonial Empire is an average computed for a very heterogeneous collection of colonies, and here we may return to a point which has already received passing mention, namely that trade activity in the Colonial Empire is very unequally distributed among the constituent parts. Some few and limited areas live just as much on their external trade as do the United Kingdom or the Dominions. The great entrepot ports in South-East Asia (Hong Kong, Singapore and Penang) are excellent examples. Each of them maintains a constant and heavy flow of commodities that figure both as imports and as exports. From Singapore and Penang domestic (i.e.,

Straits Settlements) exports are very minor, and Hong Kong, with a trade per head of £117. 5s. 6d. in 1938, has effectively no domestic exports at all. Even more striking are the Falkland Islands, where a tiny, isolated community, specialising exclusively on the rearing of sheep, supported a trade in 1938 of £459. 8s. 3d. per head. Bermuda, with visible domestic exports of little more than £1 per head, contrived to make its tourist trade pay for imports of over £70 per head. Trinidad owes its per caput £30 to the exploitation of its oil resources. Practically all the rest of the colonies had an external trade per head of less than £20 per year, in some twenty of them it was less than £10 per year, and in more than half of those twenty it was less than £5. In assessing the value of these facts it is well to remember that the low-trade areas make up by far the bulk of the area and the population of the Colonial Empire, and that Malaya and Hong Kong by themselves account for almost two-thirds of its total trade.

The obvious deduction, good for both India and the Colonies, is the enormous scope for increase of trade that is implied in these low per caput figures. Even a slight rise in the standard of living multiplied by the hundreds of millions of the populations concerned, would add many millions of pounds sterling to the aggregate annual import requirements. Expansion of trade and improvement of living standards have elsewhere been most effectively promoted by the development of manufacturing industries, as in Great Britain, or of highly specialized agriculture, as in New Zealand. In the Colonial Empire there seems small prospect of any significant development of manufacturing industries, except perhaps in Singapore and Hong Kong, where its stimulus is in fact least required. It is rather in the commercialising of agriculture that the solution will be found, but very great care will be necessary in putting such a policy into effect. The history of hastily and unwisely exploited areas in the United States, Africa and elsewhere is too painfully clear to leave any doubt about the dangers involved. The millions of acres of once productive land that have had their soil completely stripped from them by man-induced erosion are effective testimony to the fact that the short-term risks of commercial crisis are paltry compared with the long-term risk of the destruction of

productivity. There is, however, much knowledge available of
the nature of soil-erosion, of its cure and its prevention, and,
given a reasonable modicum of wisdom in the British administrators of the Colonial Empire, much further development
can be undertaken safely. In India, on the other hand, where
agricultural progress has already contributed much, and will
no doubt contribute still more, quicker results seem likely to
follow from continuing the expansion of manufacturing industry. In neither case are rapid and spectacular results likely,
but an upward trend of productivity, persistent if not abrupt,
and a continued increase in the absorbing power of these
potentially immense markets may reasonably be expected.

The directions taken by the external trade of the constituent parts of the Empire owe much to the ideas and to the
conditions prevalent in nineteenth-century Britain. The
Colonial System, under which the kind, amount and direction of the trade of a colony were prescribed by the mother
country, was already discredited and largely abandoned.
Coercion of the Colonies had become a deadly sin, and even
benevolent guidance was suspect. Further, in an era of
currencies convertible into or linked to gold, stable exchanges
and multilateral trading provided an easy, almost automatic,
means of balancing international indebtedness. Every colony,
therefore, was free to sell where it could and buy where it
pleased, and with some of them trade with the United
Kingdom counted for relatively little from the beginning.
Newfoundland found its main markets for its fish in the
Catholic countries of Europe and South America. Hong Kong
and the ports of the Straits Settlements built up an enormous
trade with the adjacent Asiatic mainland and islands, to such
effect that over 80 per cent. and 70 per cent. of their
respective totals is with foreign countries. Zanzibar, when it
became a British Protectorate, continued and still continues
to exploit the Indian Ocean connections it had formed in the
days of Arab dominance. More usually the trade of a new
colony was dominantly with the United Kingdom. Sentiment, no doubt, played a part—British settlers in the temperate zone colonies and officials and traders elsewhere were
naturally biased in favour of their own mother country—but
the basic fact was that Great Britain was the only country

capable of absorbing all their surplus primary production and of supplying all their deficiency in manufactured commodities. The Free Trade policy that had won its victory there by the middle of the nineteenth century was a recognition of that fact, and it assured the overseas dependencies of unrestricted access to Britain's expanding market, even if in strict trade matters it prevented their being differentially favoured.

As events proved, that was a passing phase. Production of the great primary staples of the temperate zone colonies began to outstrip the capacity of the British market, where the expansion of industrialisation and the increase of population were both slowing down. Other countries, notably the United States, Germany, Italy, Belgium and Japan, were reducing their industrial leeway and becoming internationally significant both as markets and as suppliers. By the beginning of the twentieth century the new pattern of Empire trade was taking shape. The United Kingdom remained in most instances the chief single market and supplier, but her share of the total Empire trade, and particularly of the total Empire market, was declining. In the Dominions and Dependencies as a whole geographical relationships were more and more expressing themselves in regional trading. This is best seen in the West Atlantic, where Newfoundland, Bermuda, the Bahamas and, to a less extent, the rest of the West Indian colonies, had been pulled in to the North American orbit. Canada has a dual character. On the one hand she has become a 'commercial colony' of the United States, from whom she draws more than three-fifths of her imports, and to whom she sends over a third of her exports; on the other hand, she is in her own right a major market and supplier for the British islands of the West Atlantic. Australia and New Zealand were similarly developing their trade with Eastern Asia and North America, and to a smaller extent with each other. Apart from trade with the United Kingdom, inter-Empire trade has so far remained relatively small. The Dominions require little from each other and their absorbing capacity for the products of the Colonial Empire is not yet great in aggregate. It does, however, account for the bulk of 'Rest of the Empire' trade of India and the Colonial Empire. Tables VII, VIII, IX and X

TABLE VII (a).—U.K. Exports to Various Areas, 1929 and 1938.

Year	Dominions		India		Col. Empire		For. Countries		Total £000
	£000	% of Total	£000	% of Total	£000	% of Total	£000	% of Total	
1929	204,643	24·4	77,310	9·2	65,560	7·8	491,538	58·6	839,051
1938	256,998	49·7	34,868	6·7	69,098	13·4	155,825	30·2	516,739

TABLE VII (b).—U.K. Imports from Various Areas, 1929 and 1938

Year	Dominions		India		Col. Empire		For. Countries		Total £000
	£000	% of Total	£000	% of Total	£000	% of Total	£000	% of Total	
1929	222,283	18·2	50,490	4·1	86,069	7·1	861,923	70·6	1,220,765
1938	277,639	30·2	41,633	4·5	73,319	8·0	526,918	57·3	919,509

TABLE VIII (a).—Dominions: Aggregate Exports to Various Areas, 1929 and 1938.

Year	To U.K.		Rest of Empire		Foreign Countries		Total £000
	£000	% of Total	£000	% of Total	£000	% of Total	
1929	262,547	44·2	61,998	10·4	269,738	45·4	594,283
1938	277,639	53·0	47,221	9·0	199,065	38·0	523,925

TABLE VIII (b).—Dominions: Aggregate Imports from Various Areas, 1929 and 1938

Year	From U.K.		Rest of Empire		Foreign Countries		Total £000
	£000	% of Total	£000	%of Total	£000	% of Total	
1929	204,643	34·2	46,189	7·7	347,387	58·1	598,219
1938	256,998	45·1	69,051	12·1	244,332	42·8	570,381

TABLE IX (a).—India: Exports to Various Areas, 1929 and 1938

Year	To U.K.		Rest of Empire		Foreign Counties		Total £000
	£000	% of Total	£000	% of Total	£000	% of Total	
1929	50,490	21·7	32,760	14·1	149,849	64·2	233,099
1938	41,633	34·1	22,395	18·3	58,065	47·6	122,093

TABLE IX (b).— India: Imports from Various Areas, 1929 and 1938.

Year	From U.K.		Rest of Empire		Foreign Countries		Total £000
	£000	% of Total	£000	% of Total	£000	% of Total	
1929	77,310	42.8	17,088	9.5	86,172	47.7	180,570
1938	34,868	30.5	31,553	27.6	47,827	41.9	114,248

TABLE X (a).—Colonial Empire: Exports to Various Areas, 1929 and 1937.

Year	To U.K.		Rest of Empire		Foreign Countries		Total £000
	£000	% of Total	£000	% of Total	£000	% of Total	
1929	56,590	22·5	39,993	15·9	154,509	61·6	251,092
1937	70,162	26·3	43,353	16·2	153,721	57·5	267,236

TABLE X (b).—Colonial Empire: Imports from Various Areas, 1929 and 1937.

Year	To U.K.		Rest of Empire		Foreign Countries		Total £000
	£000	% of Total	£000	% of Total	£000	% of Total	
1929	64,411	24·5	58,547	22·3	139,751	53·2	262,709
1937	74,052	28·3	44,838	17·1	142,942	54·6	261,832

give a summary view of the general position in recent years, using 1929 as a not too untypical pre-depression year.

The most recent phase dates from 1930, when the failure to rebuild the pre-1914 economic system culminated in the Great Depression, with its calamitous break in prices. Inevitably it was international rather than domestic trade that was hardest hit, and the United Kingdom and the Dominions, just because their standards of living depended so directly on international trade, were particularly vulnerable. Further, the price collapse was most marked in primary, especially agricultural, products, and these formed the main export items of most of the overseas Empire. Finally, market after market was being closed as multilateral international trade degenerated into bilateral international barter. The situation was desperate, and desperate remedies were required.

This was the background of the Empire Conference held at Ottawa in 1932 to find a basis of mutual aid in the economic blizzard. It has already been indicated that existing interests and commitments limited the extent to which concessions could be granted to one another and barriers be erected against the foreigner. Nevertheless, sufficient community of view was achieved to permit the negotiation over the next two years of a remarkably complete series of agreements, which instituted by means of tariff rebates on Empire produce and/or quota limitations on foreign produce a very considerable measure of Imperial Preference. The aim was the maximum possible development of Empire markets for Empire produce, and in so far as that meant diverting trade which before the depression had 'naturally' flowed in other channels may be regarded ideally as the acceptance of a second best. It is, however, difficult to see what better measures could have been devised in the circumstances.

The comparative figures for 1929 and 1938 in Tables VII-X need to be used with caution, but they do give some indication of the results of this experiment in formal Empire co-operation. It will be seen that in general the aggregate value of Empire trade was smaller in 1938 than in 1929 (for the United Kingdom and India very much smaller), though the Colonial Empire is exceptional in showing some increase. Of this aggregate the percentage accounted for by Empire markets and Empire suppliers had increased, in most cases very materially, though again the Colonial Empire shows in its imports figures a solitary and very slight exception. In many cases, indeed, despite the lower values of total trade, not only the percentages but also the absolute values of the inter-Empire trade were significantly greater in 1938 than in 1929. Not all of this relative and absolute upward swing of inter-Empire trade can be attributed to the Ottawa Agreements. In some respects and to some degree it represented an accentuation of trends already in existence rather than the introduction of new trends. In any case the virtual closure of the major foreign markets to much of the Empire commerce during the nineteen-thirties would have compelled more and more restriction of Empire producers to Empire markets. It is difficult to avoid the conclusion, however, that the specific arrangements of the Ottawa Agreements did succeed in aiding the development of substitute markets, in arresting the decline of total trade and in saving to a considerable degree the current standards of living of Empire peoples.

It does not follow that the sea-anchor that saved the ship in the storm would be equally useful as a power-unit for the vessel when the storm had blown over. The basic facts are that production capacity of the Empire as a whole is in many important commodities far beyond Empire consuming power, while in others there is a permanent deficiency. This is perfectly obvious and widely understood with regard to some of the great primary products, such as rubber among the surpluses and tin among the deficiencies. What has been more commonly missed is that widespread development of industrialisation has involved enormous interchange among manufacturing countries of manufactured and partly manufactured goods. In the United Kingdom, for example, before the recent war the imports of articles wholly or mainly manufactured were almost equal in value to those of raw materials and articles mainly unmanufactured. The plain fact is that no country can specialise in everything, that 'manufacturing industry' covers an almost infinite variety of types and grades of industry, and that a country in the peculiar position of Great Britain can get the best return for its expenditure of labour and capital by progressive specialisation on the production of goods requiring a high degree of finishing rather than a large amount of raw material. That the trend in Great Britain is in fact in that direction is indicated by the rise to domestic and export dominance of the new light industries and the decline of the old staples of cotton and heavy engineering products.

Both at the raw material, the semi-manufactured and the fully manufactured stages, therefore, the optimum development of the Empire as a whole and of its constituent parts requires a trading area much wider than itself, wide enough indeed to include the whole world. Bretton Woods, emphasised by the implications in the American loan, indicates the acceptance of multilateral world trade as the immediate objective of high policy. The implementing of that policy will require adequate monetary arrangements, backed by coherent, non-restrictive, national trade policies, none of which will be easy of achievement, but which, if and when achieved, can ensure to the United Kingdom and its Empire partners and dependencies an economic prosperity not less than the best it has achieved in the past.

REFERENCES

[1] Newfoundland, which has temporarily abandoned Dominion status, and Southern Rhodesia and Ceylon, which have not quite achieved it, are borderline cases. In this essay Ceylon will not be included with the Dominions but Newfoundland and Southern Rhodesia will.

[2] Obvious exceptions are Kenya and Nyasaland, which have small settled white populations.

THE
ECONOMIC GEOGRAPHY
OF NEW ZEALAND

VI

Geographic Influences on the Dairying Industry of New Zealand *

This paper, itself part of a wider study, is an endeavour to examine the dairying industry of New Zealand as an adaptation of economic effort to geographic environment. It assumes a back-ground of world economic organisation of which the following characteristics are true:

(1) The localisation of industry, which in turn implies a high degree of specialisation of function within the industry. In origin such localisations always owe something to geographic advantages, whether of site or situation, of climate, of relief and soils, of mineral resources or of water supply, though later the economic momentum, acquired by an established industry by virtue of mere size, developed and appropriate financial organisation, large supply of highly skilled labour, and an established reputation, may carry it on despite the apparent absence of any particular local geographic advantage.

(2) The determination of world price by demand and supply, each of which is, itself, affected by various influences. The world price so determined sets an upper limit to the total production expenses, including profits and transport charges, that may be incurred by any producing region. These total costs are an aggregate of different elements—labour costs, capital costs, transport charges, costs of raw materials, profits, and so on—and the proportions of these different elements will vary from one region to another: economic advantages may be balanced by geographic disadvantage and vice versa.

*Contributed to *Geography*, 15, 1930

New Zealand suffers, in comparison with her chief rival, Denmark, from certain economic disadvantages, among which may be mentioned the smallness of its population (1,443,323 at 31/12/28). This has two corollaries: first, a

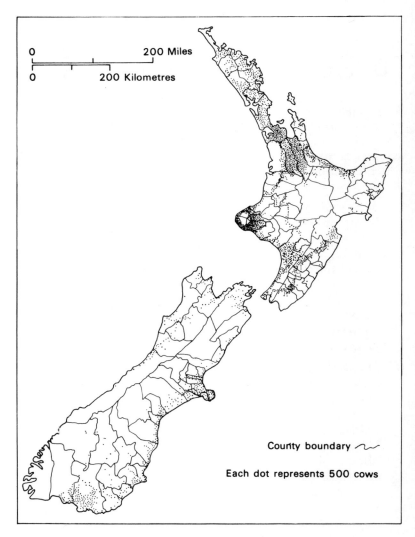

Figure 3. New Zealand: distribution of dairy cows

labour supply that is small in proportion to the natural resources, which in turn involves high wage rates;[1] secondly, a small home market. These characteristics both arise from the remoteness of the country from Western Europe, and its consequent late discovery and tardy colonisation, but this remoteness has also two direct effects: it causes relatively infrequent and irregular delivery of supplies to the British market and thereby has, on the whole, a depressing effect on the wholesale market prices for New Zealand produce, and secondly it is responsible for relatively high transport costs, not merely because of the extra distance the produce must be carried but also because of the necessity for keeping it cooled. Finally, as is always the case in new countries where demand is great and supply is small, the price that must be paid for the use of capital is high.

The practical problem for New Zealand, therefore, is how to counteract the effects of these elements in total costs of production so that it may be able to compete in the world market. Broadly, the solution is found in the localisation of the industry in those parts of the country geographically most favourable to it, and in the evolution on the one hand of a farming technique, and on the other of an industrial and commercial organisation appropriate to the local and general geographic and economic conditions. The enquiry into the nature of the geographic circumstances and the way in which they influence the industry is most conveniently approached by way of a study of the actual distribution of dairy farming in the country. The unit dot map (500 cattle to the dot) shows the location of dairy cattle as accurately as the available statistics allow.

The first fact that emerges is the overwhelming importance of the North Island, as compared with the South Island, with a dairy cattle population of 1,067,866 as against 264,784 (31/3/27), or roughly four to one. In the South Island, only one region, the Southland Plains, plays a major part in exporting, and therefore the remainder of this paper will have specific reference to the North Island. In the North Island, then, there are two regions of maximum concentration. South Auckland and Taranaki. The former comprises the counties of Hauraki Plains, Piako, Waikato and Waipa, and from this hub radiate three arms of secondary, but still considerable, importance; the North Auckland Peninsula, one narrow ribbon along the Bay of Plenty as far as Opotiki, and another following the main Trunk Railway southwards to link up with the Taranaki nucleus. The latter, which consists essentially of a somewhat narrow girdle around Mount Egmont, is connected by a thin coastal band to the secondary area of the Manawatu and Wellington West Coast Plains. East of the mountain backbone a further ribbon runs southward from Napier through south west Hawke's Bay and the Wairarapa Valley to Cook Strait.

The two maps in Figure 4, shewing different methods of indicating dairy cattle distribution, being proportional maps, require to be used with some care. High density per 100 acres of improved land may be an indication of the small proportion of improved land rather than of the importance of dairying. Similarly, a high proportion of dairy to total cattle may be a reflex of the unimportance of cattle rearing

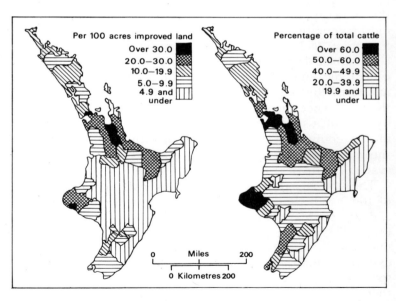

Figure 4. The North Island: dairy cows per 100 acres and as percentage of total cattle

compared with other forms of agricultural activity, sheep
rearing, for example. Nevertheless the remarkable correspondence of the three maps in Figures 3 and 4 brings out not
merely the absolute importance of dairying in the particular

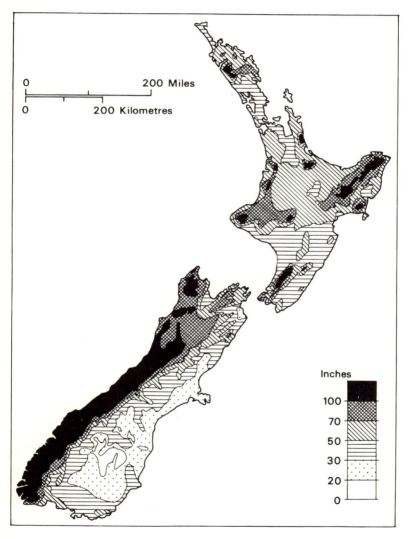

Figure 5. New Zealand: average annual rainfall

areas enumerated above, but also its relative importance, the fact of severe specialisation in the main areas.

One obvious factor in this distribution is situation; all the areas, except the minor Hawke's Bay-Wairarapa strip, lie west of the mountain backbone, and this points to climate as the general control. The rainfall map (Figure 5) shews the areal distribution of the rainfall. The North Island, situated in Mediterranean and immediately extra-Mediterranean latitudes, receives its precipitation mainly from westerly cyclones generated by tongues of low pressure from the great Antarctic Lows. There is naturally a winter maximum, but the significant fact is that not even in the far north in typical Mediterranean latitudes is there the characteristic Mediterranean summer drought; convectional rains facilitated by the proximity of the two coasts, occasional ex-tropical cyclones, and easterly winds representing incipient and irregular Trade Winds, provide considerable summer precipitation. *Effective* precipitation, it is true, is less than the figures would suggest (Auckland City has 2.6 inches in January, its driest month) owing to the evaporation induced by the high proportion of hours of bright sunshine. Within the dairying regions the average annual precipitation is less than 40 inches only on the west coast plains of the Wellington Province, and exceeds 70 inches practically nowhere.

Temperatures also differ in significant respects from typical Mediterranean: Auckland, New Plymouth and Tauranga, which may be taken as representative, have the following mean figures:

TABLE XI

	Jan.	Feb.	Mar.	Apl.	May	June	July	Aug.	Sept.	Oct.	Nov.	Dec.	Year
Auckland °F	66·5	67·0	64·9	61·2	56·8	53·5	51·7	52·2	54·6	57·2	60·3	63·9	59·1
Inches	2·67	3·05	3·02	3·43	4·63	4·92	4·95	4·22	3·64	3·69	3·32	2·90	44.44
New Plymouth °F	61·4	64·6	62·9	59·3	55·3	52·0	50·5	50·8	53·4	55·7	58·3	61·7	57·2
Inches	4·42	4·00	3·62	4·51	6·23	6·14	6·29	5·33	5·22	5·61	4·65	4·33	60·35
Tauranga °F	64·3	64·6	62·2	57·9	53·7	50·1	49.0	49·6	52·6	56·3	58·0	61·5	56·7
Inches	4·34	3·58	4·16	5·08	5·16	5·42	4·86	4·08	4·41	5·25	3·29	3·47	53·1

They illustrate the general characteristics of relatively high winter, and low summer, temperatures. At sea level, frosts, though unknown only in the far north of the Auckland Peninsula, are rare and never severe, while heat waves in the summer are quite unknown.

It is these temperature and rainfall conditions, combined with the high sunshine records, that encouraged the growth of the dense New Zealand 'bush' or forest. The character of the bush was somewhat mixed, but the predominant element in the Auckland Peninsula was the giant kauri, on the lowlands of Taranaki, the kahikatea or New Zealand white pine. The fact that the white pine, useless for building purposes owing to its susceptibility to attack by wood borers, was odourless, tasteless, easily worked, and therefore ideally suited to the manufacture of butter boxes, no doubt contributed towards the replacement of the forest by dairy farms. The main factor, however, was the suitability of this climate to the growth of all English grasses, grasses which in the main were surface sown, without ploughing, in the ashes left by the burning of the useless remnants of the bush after the saw mill had taken its toll. High rainfall, much sunshine and favourable temperatures promote the growth of green juicy grass all the year round, subject only to a slight risk of checks to growth through frost in the winter and insufficient moisture in the summer.

This year-long growth of grass in turn has determined not merely the general location of the industry, but also the farming methods employed. Dairy farming in New Zealand may be characterised as pastoral dairying, in contrast to the Danish system which is essentially arable, intensive grass growing, as contrasted with intensive crop raising. Grass growth alone can provide sufficient fodder, on a small area, to support a herd as large as can be conveniently managed. Consequently, holdings are small, the typical size being from 50 to 150 acres, though even smaller are common. Under the most advanced practice these small farms are sub-divided into a number of fields, which are grazed on a rotational plan—next to the laborious Danish system of tethering animals, the most systematic and economic method of grazing known. At present, despite the increasing intensification in the post war

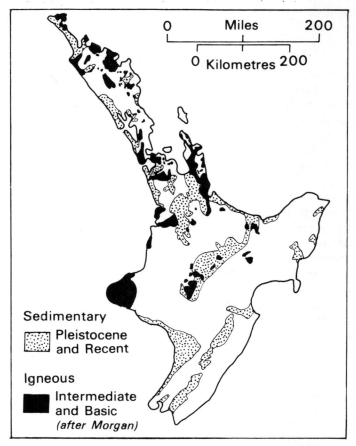

Figure 6. The North Island: distribution of basic volcanic rocks and Pleistocene and Recent sedimentaries

years, supplementary feeding plays a minor role, and even for this, grass is still the most important element. Systematic top dressing,[2] mainly with phosphatic fertilisers, is now very widespread, the extra yield being preserved in the form of hay or ensilage, particularly ensilage, against the possibility of shortage of succulent fodder in the late summer months, January to March. Where soils are suitable, lucerne is rapidly coming to the front, while maize and root crops, such as carrots, form less important elements.

A further effect of the climate is that the cattle live out of doors all the year round, not even the dainty Jersey requiring to be housed, though sometimes canvas covers are worn by the animals. Apart from the indirect effect of promoting the good health of the herd, an item by no means negligible, this open air life does away with the necessity for investing large quantities of capital in the provision of extensive stables and barns, and for employing labour in feeding the animals and keeping them and their stalls clean.

The whole farm economy then, thanks to the climate, is a labour-saving economy. The provision of food and the care of the animals requires probably less expenditure of human effort than in any other dairying region in the world, with the result that the labour costs per unit of output are low, despite high wage rates. But labour saving does not stop short with the organisation of the general farm economy—it is carried into the particular operations of the daily routine. The outstanding example is the invention and adoption of the milking machine. While the hand milking of a herd of eighty cows would require the services of six expert milkers for at least two strenuous hours, with machines, a man and two boys are sufficient. The spread of the milking machine was slow till after the Great War; petrol-driven engines did not supply power smoothly enough for complete satisfaction, and petrol in a small country far from the sources of supply, was a very expensive fuel. The comprehensive development of hydro-electric power, rendered possible by the youthful topography and the heavy, evenly distributed precipitation, has overcome both of those difficulties, and led to an increase in the number of machines in use from 7,577 in 1919 to 18,049 in 1928.[3]

So far we have been concerned with climatic effects, but inside the belt of most favourable climate great variations of cattle density occur. The relief map indicates one correlation: the industry is almost confined to elevations below the 200 metre contour, due partly to the fact that the lowlands are coastal, so that accessibility for settlement is at a maximum, while transport outwards is minimised, and partly to greater frost incidence on the higher lands in the interior. But the lowlands themselves are not uniform. Rugged, broken country covers a larger area than flat land, and, what is even more important, soil varies greatly. Naturally enough, density of concentration and intensity of specialisation are a function of soil fertility. The extract from the geological map shows the distribution of basic volcanic rocks, mainly basalt, and Pleistocene and recent sedimentaries, mainly alluvium, the correspondence of which with the cattle distribution maps is striking. The basaltic soils, so-called 'volcanic soils,' vary in colour from a red brown to deep black, are always inclined to lightness, and therefore greedy of moisture, and always very rich. The main area is Taranaki, but scattered patches occur further north. The alluvial soils are less uniform, but in general they also are very fertile, though occasionally, as in the case of the Hauraki and Piako Plains, extensive drainage may be necessary. The alluvial deposits form the only considerable areas of flat land, and the very flatness is in itself one of the reasons for the predominance of the middle Waikato, and of the Hauraki-Piako Flood Plain.

A map of the dairy factories of the island shows a much larger number in Taranaki than in South Auckland, an indication not of the greater dairy produce output of Taranaki, but of the smaller size of its factories. In 1928, twenty factories, nineteen of them in Auckland, had an annual output of more than 1,000 tons of butter each, and five, all of which were in Auckland, exceeded 2,000 tons each. The key lies in the much greater relative importance of butter in Auckland than elsewhere; In 1928, 64.2 per cent. of the New Zealand export of butter came from Auckland.[4] This is partly a climatic effect, the mildness of the winters favouring Jersey and Jersey cross cattle, which are noted for the high butter fat content of their milk rather than for the quantity of milk yielded. Auckland Province, as a whole, however, was traditionally the province of bad roads, more especially in the stoneless silts of the flood plains, and the logical adaptation was the development, on the one hand, of home separation of the cream so as to minimise the quantity of material to be transported, and on the other, of a centralised system of cream collection by motor waggon, thus giving the factories the possibility of a wide area of supply.

The displacement of the farm by the factory[5] in the

manufacture of butter and cheese, like the development of farming methods, was an economic adaptation to the shortage of labour. The organisation of the factories,[6] overwhelmingly co-operative, is similarly an adaptation to the shortage of capital. Both of these economic characteristics, as indicated earlier, have their roots in the geographical circumstances of the country, but it may be suggested here that the necessity to supply an export market (a market which, for New Zealand produce, is effectively confined to a limited number of great firms in Tooley Street, London), favoured the development of co-operation both in manufacturing and in selling. Not even Denmark has succeeded in applying co-operation to the supplying of her own home market with dairy produce.

Thus far, the problem of keeping costs within prices has been examined wholly from the point of view of costs, but obviously world prices are just as important. In the play of demand and supply, high quality of product, by virtue of its relative scarcity, ensures relatively high prices. Further, high quality of produce can be achieved without adding to the cost of production in the same proportion as prices may be raised. It costs no more to feed a good than a bad cow, and little more to manufacture with stringent regard to quality than without, and New Zealand, recognising this, has concentrated on the production of first quality butter and cheese. For this effort the local climatic conditions provide a very favourable basis; the health and cleanliness of the herds, promoted by the outdoor life in a climate which, while warmer and much sunnier than that of the British Isles, finds its nearest analogy there, together with the natural food of fresh, rich grass all the year, conditioned by the same climatic factors, not merely keep down working expenses, but give each animal a good chance of realising its potentialities in both quantity and quality of milk yield. That, however, is nature's limit. It is man's responsibility to see that the highest possible quality of manufactured product is obtained from the raw material.

The bulk of the credit must be given to the State acting through the Dairy Division of its Department of Agriculture. Suppliers' cream is graded on arrival at the butter factories, and the bonus given on first grade cream is an incentive to the farmers to see that their cream is first grade. Stringent regulations prescribing standards of health in milking herds, standards of cleanliness in every process from the milking of the cows to the packing of the finished article, and standards of quality for that finished article, are enforced by a staff of inspectors and graders, while field officers also give instruction and advice to farmers, and secure their co-operation in the carrying out of group field experiments. Close touch is kept by the Department with the distributing agencies in Britain, and every effort made both in the field and in the Department's research laboratories to remove the cause of any complaint that may be received. The grading at the ports is particularly rigorous, and no produce that fails to reach the national standard can be exported from the country. From the geographic point of view it should be noticed that the maintenance of a *uniform* standard, so essential to the commercial success of the industry, is facilitated, if not rendered possible, by the small size of the country, which permits the interchange of graders among the different ports, the frequent meeting of graders at conferences, and regular combined work in judging dairy exhibits at agricultural shows. In contrast one can understand the difficulty faced by the Australian dairying industry, scattered through six States from Queensland to Western Australia, in attempting to produce Australian butter as distinct from numerous Australian butters. This is one of the reasons why, on the weekly average, prices in London for the period 1921-1927, both inclusive, Australian choicest salted butter brought 7s. 3½d. per cwt. less than New Zealand.[7] It does not, however, afford any explanation of the fact that the average of New Zealand butter top prices for the same period was 13s. 11½d. per cwt.[8] less than corresponding prices for Danish butter. The difference is not wholly due to quality differences; Denmark has a very considerable alternative market in Germany,[9] which she can and does use to prevent a glut in her chief market, Britain, a course which is not open to New Zealand or Australia. To some extent also it is a question of custom, the established preference for one type of flavour rather than another. But when all that has been said, it remains true that the long period of cold storage does detract something from the first fresh bloom of the butter—a further consequence of remote situation.

New Zealand now ranks second only to Denmark as a dairy produce exporter,[10] very rapid growth of the industry,[11] particularly of butter production, having taken place in the post war years. The increase has been due partly to the development of new areas, by the normal progress of settlement, or by the draining of extensive swamp areas, as on the Hauraki Plains and at various places in North Auckland, but even more to the intensification of production on areas already in use. This has a double aspect; on the one hand, increasing the carrying capacity of the land per acre particularly by top-dressing, rotational grazing, and the growing of supplementary fodder; on the other, the raising of the yield per cow not only by increasing the amount of food available at critical seasons, but also by persistent attention to the tasks of improving the breed of the herds. In this connection the practice of herd testing provides the farmer with invaluable records of performance of the animals, and eases his task of progressive improvement of the herd very considerably.[12] The difference between the average carrying capacity of the land and of that farmed according to the best practice, and the difference between the national average yield per cow and that obtained from the best herds, give some measure of the possibilities of increase in the national output from the present dairying areas, by the further application of principles and methods already well established. In addition to that, however, much suitable land remains to be utilised. The most obvious region is the forested alluvial coast plain of Westland in the South Island, with its heavy rainfall, but also high sunshine records and good drainage, its equable temperatures, its low relief and good soils. The chief handicap of inaccessibility has already been met by the completion in 1923 of the Midland Railway through the Southern Alps. Similarly the progress of settlement along the main Trunk Railway on the western forested slopes of the Volcanic Plateau (the King Country), and the conditioning of the heavy clays of the Gum lands[13] in North Auckland will also add to the area under dairy farms. Finally,

one may expect in Canterbury and Otago a growing importance of dairying as one element in the mixed farming that the
character of the climate and soils has promoted there.

To sum up, the physical possibilities of dairying increases
are such that potentially New Zealand is a much greater
supplier of dairy produce to the world market than Denmark.
Whether those potentialities will be realised depends always
on whether, in the task of increasing yields from present
areas or in breaking in new lands, farming economy,[14]
manufacturing and transport organisation can be so adapted
to the geographic and economic circumstances that total
costs for the marginal product do not exceed world price for
that particular quality of product, and that, in turn, essentially depends on the trend of the world market price and on
the appreciation and intelligent utilisation of the various
elements in the local situation.

REFERENCES

[1] Agricultural wage rates range from 30s. to 50s. per week, with full
board and lodging.

[2] Statistics of New Zealand, 1927-28. "Agricultural and Pastoral Production":—

	Area Top-dressed. (Acres)	Amount of Fertiliser. (cwt.)
1926-27	1,521,259	4,383,002
1927-28	1,952,490	5,783,312

Increase per cent.:—
Area ... ... 28.4 per cent.
Amount ... ... 31.9 per cent.
Proportion of fertiliser specified as phosphatic:—
1926-27 ... ... 71.1 per cent.
1927-28 ... ... 72.9 per cent.

[3] New Zealand Official Year Book, 1929.

[4] Annual list of creameries, factories, etc.

[5] Factory butter exported 1928 ... ... 73,477 tons.
Farm butter made 1928 ... ... 2,697 tons.
Proportion of total farm butter to factory butter exported ... 3.7
per cent.

[6] In 1928 Co-operative factories manufactured 65,729 tons of butter
out of the 73,477 exported, 89.45 per cent.

[7] Weddell and Co. Thirty-third annual report for year ended 30th
June, 1927.

[8] 1½d. per lb.

[9] Danish Foreign Office Journal, April, 1929:—
Danish butter exports, 1928:
    To U.K.   ...   ...   101.1 million kilograms.
    To Germany   ...   40.0 million kilograms.

[10] Year Book of Internal. Inst. of Agric.:—
Dairy produce exports: Average 1923-26:—

	Butter		Cheese	
	1000 Quintals.	% of World	1000 Quintals.	% of World.
Denmark ...	1226	33.5	74.75	2.7
New Zealand	626.5	17.1	745.75	26.8
Holland ...	359.75	9.8	708	25.4
Australia ...	403.75	11		
Canada ...			593.25	21.3

[11] New Zealand Official Year Book, 1929.
New Zealand butter exports:—
    1919   ...   ...   16,830.3 tons.
    1927   ...   ...   72,776.95 tons.

[12] New Zealand Journal of Agriculture, 1929.
Herds under test:—
1927-1928—General average butter fat production per cow 224.68 lbs.
    Highest association or group average   ...   377.70 „
    Highest herd average   ...   .   484.88 „
    Highest cow average   ...   .   858.20 „
    Average per cow of all dairying cows   ...   200 „

[13] Gum lands, heavy clay lands that have been worked for fossil kauri gum.

[14] On the subject of grasslands and their management in New Zealand, see: Stapledon, R. G., 'A Tour in Australia and New Zealand. Grassland and other studies.'

VII

Sheep Rearing in New Zealand *

A useful introduction to a treatment of this topic is an indication of New Zealand's place in the sheep rearing industry of the world. The Table XII[1] shows the sheep population of the leading half-dozen countries in 1928. This table, however, neglecting as it does all reference to type of sheep and to kind and amount of sheep products, gives an inadequate idea of the importance of the country to the international trade in sheep products. Table XIII compares New Zealand with the other great wool exporting countries of the world, and shows that it ranks fourth, little exceeded by South Africa, which holds third place. Table XIV gives another aspect of the industry, and exhibits New Zealand as by far the greatest supplier of mutton and lamb to the world's market. Such an important contribution to the international trade in sheep products implies an important place for the industry in the agricultural and commercial economy of the country. Table XV gives one illustration of the dominance of pastoralism over agriculture in the narrow sense, but it should be noted that the table slightly over-emphasises the part played by grass in the cultivated area of the Dominion, for the portion of the area under the heading 'Remainder' is also cultivated and includes forest plantations, orchards, and vineyards to the extent of 326,000 acres. Table XVI separates some of the main products of the pastoral industries in the exports of the country, and besides emphasising the conclusion drawn from Table XV, gives a general indication of the relative importance of sheep-rearing

*Contributed to *Economic Geography,* 7, 1931.

TABLE XII

SHEEP POPULATION OF SIX LEADING COUNTRIES

U. S. S. R.	123,809,600
Australia	106,115,100
U. S. A.	47,171,000
Union of South Africa	42,500,276
Argentina (1922)	36,208,981
New Zealand	27,133,810

TABLE XIII

WOOL EXPORTS

(In Thousands of Quintals)

Countries	1909—1913 Greasy	Washed	1925—1928 Greasy	Washed
Australia	2,525	308	3,091	214
Argentina (1925—1927)	1,448	1	1,299	82
Union of South Africa	657	...	1,092	...
New Zealand	699	151	795	187
Uruguay	631	...	525	17

TABLE XIV

EXPORTS OF FROZEN MUTTON AND LAMB

(In Thousands of Quintals)

Countries	1909—1913	1925—1928
New Zealand	1,050	1,360
Argentina (1925—1927)	687	808
Australia	687	333
Uruguay	27	181

TABLE XV

DISTRIBUTION OF OCCUPIED AREA IN NEW ZEALAND

(In Thousand Acres)

Tussock and other native grasses	14,086
Sown permanent grass	16,864
Rotation pasture and fodder crops	1,187
Other field crops	697
Remainder	10,602
Total occupied area	43,436

TABLE XVI

SOME PASTORAL PRODUCTS EXPORTS OF NEW ZEALAND*

Total Exports	Total Pastoral Products	Wool	Frozen Meat	Tallow	Skins, etc.	Other Pastoral Products
100	91·8	29·1	18·9	1·5	6·7	3·3

*New Zealand Official Year Book, 1930.

among the pastoral industries. The percentages are calculated on the basis of average values for the quinquennium, 1924-1928, and, allowing for the fact that something is contributed by the cattle rearing industry to each of the last four columns in the table, it is safe to say that the sheep rearing industry alone is responsible for little short of 50 per cent by value of the total exports of the country. (Butter and cheese account for the overwhelming bulk of the remainder).

DISTRIBUTION

Figures 8 and 9, based on figures given in the 'Annual Return of Sheep Owners' and 'in Statistics of New Zealand: Agricultural and Pastoral Production, 1930,' indicate the present distribution and density of the sheep population. For the whole country the average density is almost exactly 700 sheep per 1,000 acres of *occupied* land, and 20 sheep per head of human population, on either count the heaviest density in the world. The maps show, however, that great variations in density occur from district to district. Contrary to popular belief, the North Island, which has held the leadership since 1907, has more than half the total (54 per cent), contains the areas of maximum density, and has a smaller area of very low density. In this island the southeast stands out: of the East Coast counties only two have fewer than 1,000 sheep per 1,000 occupied areas, while six have more than 1,500, and one has 2,500. A second group of eight counties, west of the mountain backbone, and running northeast from the South Taranaki Bight, exceeds in each case 1,000 sheep per 1,000 occupied acres. The rest of the island (which includes, however, the areas of maximum concentration of dairy cattle) has a relatively low density, and a long north-south strip running from Auckland City southward to include the centre and east of the Volcanic Plateau has a very low density. In the South Island it is again the east that is dominant, more particularly from the mouth of the Clarence River southward, and here the contrast between east and west is even more noticeable than in the North Island. The eastern side includes the famous Canterbury Plains, but nowhere on the Plains does maximum

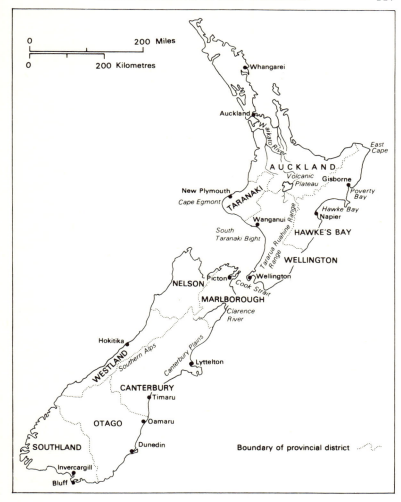

Figure 7. The provincial districts of New Zealand

density approach that of the southern portion of the Hawke's Bay district, or the west coast portion of the Wellington district in the North Island. It should be noted, however, that the unit dot map is here a better guide than the density map. The latter is based on county statistics, and as many of the

Canterbury counties include high country of the Southern Alps and foothills, county average densities are not usually a fair index of density on the plains.

FACTORS IN DISTRIBUTION

The predominance of the eastern portions of New Zealand invites a correlation with rainfall. Figure 5 shows the areal distribution of the annual rainfall, and Tables XVII and XVIII bring out some further features of the climate of the country. Those features may be summarised briefly as follows. There is an ample rainfall—only one relatively small area receives less than 20 inches annually, but considerable areas, usually elevated, receive a very heavy rainfall of over 100 inches. The seasonal distribution is very even, least so in the north, where in Mediterranean latitudes there is a marked winter maximum. Everywhere there is a high degree of rainfall reliability. Temperatures at low elevations are remarkably moderate, summer temperatures are low for the latitude, and annual range is very small. The allowance of sunshine is high, and (a feature not brought out in the tables, but associated with the dominance of cyclonic influences) perfectly still days are comparatively rare. In general, the east has lower rainfall and more sunshine than the west, though it will be noticed that in the North Island even the East Coast has a considerable area receiving more than 50 inches.

These climatic conditions are, of course, favourable to the rearing of open-air animals, but would not necessarily have given the original impetus to sheep farming, apart from other circumstances. From Britain, the source of its settlers, and the market for its products, the country is distant 12,000 miles, representing in the earlier days of colonisation a voyage time of from four to six months. The best commodity to produce was that which most effectively economised labour and utilised land, and at the same time was sufficiently durable and valuable to be able to stand long and expensive transport. Sheep and cattle fulfilled the first condition equally well: in the days before refrigeration sheep were much superior to cattle in meeting the second. (This fact is still important in the opening up of new areas to settlement: the sheep is the pioneering animal of New Zealand.) These theoretical considerations were reinforced by the example of Australia, which had had 40 years of successful wool export before the first attempt at organised colonisation in·New Zealand. The first sheep (merinos) were imported from Australia into the Wairarapa district of the North Island, but small progress was made until the grasslands of the South Island were exploited.

A comparison of the rainfall with the sheep distribution maps shows clearly that there is no absolute limit set by rainfall to sheep-rearing. Even Westland with a rainfall of over 100 inches a year has some sheep, and they are numerous and increasing throughout the West Coast of the North Island and in the North Auckland Peninsula, where almost the whole area has more than 50 inches, and much of it has more than 70 inches per annum. Crude rainfall figures indeed may be quite misleading as a guide to the effects of rain. Drainage, related both to the lithological character of the rocks and to the amount of slope, modifies the effect of any given quantity of rain on the soil and pasture, while sunshine and wind not merely do that, but modify as well the direct effect of the rainfall on the fleece of the animals. Further, different breeds of sheep react very differently to the same atmospheric and pasture conditions: the Lincoln and especially the Romney Marsh breeds flourish in wet conditions of rank pasture that would be fatal to the Merino. A heavy rainfall of itself, therefore, does not prohibit the rearing of sheep. Nevertheless it is clear that the industry on the whole is most important in the drier areas. The truth seems to be that the whole of occupied New Zealand is actually or potentially physically suitable to the rearing of either cattle or sheep, that there is a bias to cattle for dairying in the wetter areas, a bias to sheep in the drier areas, and a relatively wide transition area where the bias either way is not pronounced, and where it may even fluctuate between cattle and sheep according to movements of prices for their respective products. This means that over much of occupied New Zealand there is present or potential competition between sheep and cattle for the available grazing. The word 'competition,' however, expresses only part of the truth. In those areas that

TABLE XVII

AVERAGE MONTHLY TEMPERATURE AND PRECIPITATION AT SELECTED STATIONS

		Jan.	Feb.	Mar.	Apr.	May	June	July	Aug.	Sept.	Oct.	Nov.	Dec.	Year
Auckland	.. °F.	66·5	67·0	64·9	61·2	56·8	53·5	51·7	52·2	54·6	57·2	60·3	63·9	59·1
	Inches	2·67	3·05	3·02	3·43	4·63	4·92	4·95	4·22	3·64	3·69	3·32	2·90	44·44
New Plymouth	.. °F.	61·4	64·6	62·9	59·3	55·3	52·0	50·5	50·8	53·4	55·7	58·3	61·7	57·2
	Inches	4·42	4·00	3·62	4·51	6·23	6·14	6·29	5·33	5·22	5·61	4·65	4·33	60·35
Napier	.. °F.	66·1	65·5	63·0	58·7	53·8	50·1	48·9	49·9	53·6	57·5	60·7	64·1	57·7
	Inches	3·14	2·89	3·26	2·87	3·73	3·54	3·87	3·56	2·16	2·29	2·48	2·32	36·11
Wellington	.. °F.	62·5	62·5	60·5	57·0	52·7	49·4	47·7	48·6	51·6	54·4	56·9	60·4	55·4
	Inches	3·30	3·19	3·29	3·80	4·76	4·87	5·55	4·43	4·19	4·19	3·44	3·30	48·11
Hokitika	.. °F.	60·3	60·6	58·5	54·7	49·9	46·4	44·8	46·3	50·2	52·7	54·9	58·4	53·1
	Inches	9·92	7·37	9·75	9·39	9·82	9·55	8·99	9·28	9·32	11·81	10·78	10·62	116·60
Dunedin	.. °F.	58·0	57·7	55·4	51·7	47·1	43·8	42·4	44·0	47·9	51·0	53·3	56·3	50·7
	Inches	3·34	2·75	2·96	2·78	3·26	3·15	2·99	3·14	2·75	3·13	3·28	3·53	37·06
Invercargill	.. °F.	57·2	56·8	54·7	50·8	45·8	42·7	41·4	43·8	48·1	51·3	52·8	55·2	50·0
	Inches	3·97	2·97	3·85	4·34	4·49	3·59	3·24	3·38	3·18	4·44	4·39	4·20	46·04

TABLE XVIII

AVERAGE PERCENTAGE DEVIATIONS FROM AVERAGE PRECIPITATION AT SELECTED STATIONS

	Jan.	Feb.	Mar.	Apr.	May	June	July	Aug.	Sept.	Oct.	Nov.	Dec.	Year
Auckland ..	53·4	64·7	51·5	56·1	33·3	31·4	34·5	36·5	35·9	39·6	53·7	39·1	11·5
New Plymouth	46·1	40·8	60·2	42·3	39·3	48·7	27·2	27·6	30·9	27·3	39·8	43·4	12·3
Napier ..	54·8	50·2	70·9	45·3	66·8	63·0	45·0	43·0	43·5	81·2	48·8	45·7	23·4
Wellington ..	46·8	55·0	49·4	47·9	39·5	37·1	33·1	34·2	36·6	41·9	40·9	33·7	14·7
Hokitika ..	43·3	37·9	33·8	37·3	24·9	33·9	34·6	39·9	29·7	27·4	30·7	29·6	8·7
Dunedin ..	38·1	49·1	53·7	42·2	39·0	49·5	57·1	52·5	49·7	54·0	44·0	38·2	15·3
Invercargill ..	30·5	66·7	48·3	21·2	29·3	36·5	27·5	32·8	38·1	27·9	23·5	23·3	9·0

are marginal to both types of livestock, the most economic utilisation of the pasture normally demands the rearing of both: the cattle graze the ranker pasture and keep it in more suitable condition for the sheep. The minimum ratio of cattle to sheep necessary to keep the pasture in the best condition for the sheep varies considerably, but in any case it is only beyond that minimum that cattle compete with sheep.

A further inspection of the maps shows that both in the North Island and in the South Island the 50-inch isohyet fits fairly closely round the areas of greatest sheep density. In the North Island the general east-west 50-inch isohyet from Hawke's Bay to Cape Egmont closely delimits the northern extension of the southern area of heavy density. The density map, which spreads the total sheep of any county evenly over the whole county, would indicate this as one belt, but the unit dot map shows it divided longitudinally by a strip where sheep are absent or few, a strip that corresponds to the position of the mountain backbone of the Island, the Tararua and the Ruakine Ranges. These ranges, owing to their greater elevation, are areas also of heavier rainfall, especially the Tararuas, where, along a narrow summit strip, 100 inches is exceeded. It is, however, not the rainfall directly that is responsible for the decrease to zero of the sheep density along this strip. Rather it is the combination of the heavy rainfall with the extremely rugged, broken character of the ranges, in part heavily forested, that makes the establishment of permanent grass almost impossible owing to the rapidity of soil erosion. Outside the main southern area two further areas call for special notice. The northern part of the East Coast, from Hawke's Bay to East Cape lies, except for a small area round Gisborne, beyond the 50-inch isohyet, yet it has a sheep density comparable to the heaviest in New Zealand. Nor in the area as a whole are cattle important, the one exception to this being in the area round Gisborne already mentioned for its lower rainfall. This apparent paradox is explained by the fact that the low rainfall area round Gisborne is the rich river alluvium of the Poverty Bay flats, where even the lower rainfall is sufficient to produce grass growth adequate to grass-farm dairying. Most of the remainder of this region is a dissected plateau, where tertiary

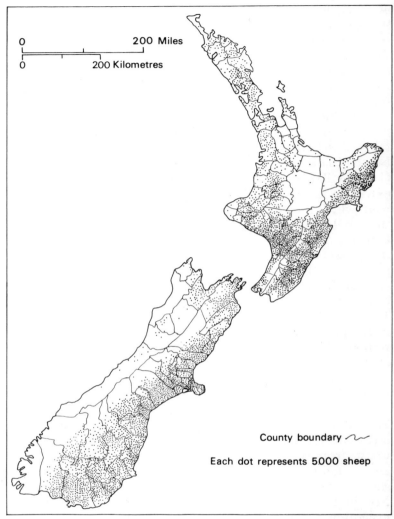

0   200 Miles

0   200 Kilometres

County boundary

Each dot represents 5000 sheep

Figure 8. The distribution of sheep depends upon the relief, the climate, and the soil. The areas of greatest concentration naturally indicate the most favourable conditions.

limestones are prevalent, the country is very hilly, and the hours of bright sunshine are high, thus greatly decreasing the effectiveness of the rainfall. The second area to be noticed is the central portion of South Auckland, comprising much of the basins of the Thames, Piako, and middle Waikato Rivers. Here with rainfall *less* than 50 inches dairy cattle are overwhelmingly more important than sheep, while immediately to the west and southwest, with rainfall *more* than 50 inches sheep become more important than cattle. The rich, level, alluvial flats of the rivers, low lying and originally somewhat swampy, are now drained, but still have a considerably moister soil than the rainfall figures would suggest, while the relative importance of sheep to the west is largely due to undeveloped transport.

In the South Island, too, the 50-inch isohyet indicates pretty accurately the western limit of sheep rearing from the Clarence River to the south, but here also we must beware against taking a correlation for proof of causal connection. The eastern side of the South Island mountain backbone is at similar elevations less rugged and less forested than that of the North Island. Elevation *qua* elevation, however, is a much more important factor in the South Island, since the Southern Alps rise several thousand feet above the snowline. Elevation achieves its effect through temperature: on the one hand fodder decreases and finally vanishes; on the other the winter precipitation takes the form of snow and is accompanied by very severe frosts, so that losses of stock by death may be very heavy. It is scarcely too much to say that the temperature limit conditioned by elevation is the only absolute limit to the industry in the country. The precise position of the upper limit varies somewhat with latitude, and considerably with season. The range between the summer limit and the winter limit is greatest in Canterbury, approximately from 3,000 feet in the winter to 6,000 feet in the summer. The existence of seasonal limits implies the practice of transhumance, and a modified form of transhumance, in fact exists. 'Summer country' and 'winter country' are included in the confines of the same hill-country run (ranch), and the sheep are 'mustered' up and down according to the season.

LOCAL CHARACTERISTICS

The foregoing argument may be summarised by saying that

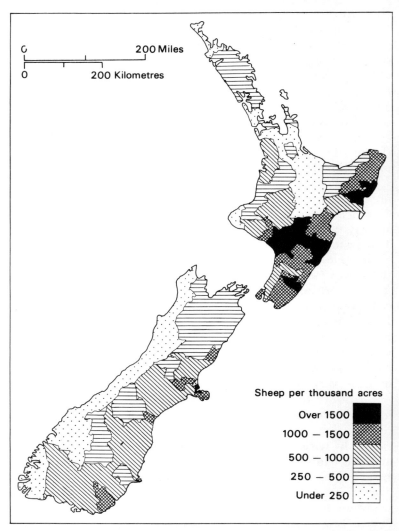

Figure 9. The density of the sheep population indicates the carrying capacity of each area, as well as the relative advantages and disadvantages in the environment.

sheep became popular in New Zealand because of the compelling effect in the earlier stages of colonisation of local and general economic conditions and the existence in the country of areas that were, or could be made, suitable to the rearing of one or other of the many breeds of sheep. Variations of sheep population density, due to variations in local geographic conditions, have been pointed out: it remains to indicate variations in farming method based on those conditions. A broad primary distinction must first be made between the North Island and the South Island. In the latter, east of the crest of the mountain backbone, there is relatively little forest except along the south and southeast coast and on some of the mountains. The great bulk of the area, including most of Canterbury and of North and Central Otago was natural grassland, the country of the native tussock. This grassland, originally held mainly in great runs, provided almost ideal conditions for the merino, but gradually with increase in population and growth of settlement the low country was split into smaller holdings and came under the plough, 'English' grasses of higher utility (cocksfoot, timothy, rye grasses, and clovers) replacing the tussock. At higher elevations and in the more rugged areas, this has not been feasible: the tussock remains, though its carrying capacity has been frequently much reduced through overstocking, over-burning, and rabbits. The adult tussock is tough, wiry, unpalatable, and little nutritious. The young growth induced by occasional burning provides good fodder, but over-burning saps the vitality of the plant and promotes soil erosion. Here, too, remains the large run, varying in size from about 20,000 to over 100,000 acres, but typically about 40,000, carrying about 8,000 sheep. Finally, this is the last stronghold of the merino, the animal best adapted to the conditions. Nervous by nature, with more than a hint of the wildness of their distant ancestors, merinos pine and wilt in small paddocks, magnificent climbers, they will graze to the very crests of the steepest hills, thus utilising the fodder resources to the utmost and at the same time suffering the minimum mortality through burial in snowdrifts in the gullies; finally they are dowered with great capacity to survive hardship, and instances are known where merinos, snowed up without food for ten days, have emerged apparently little the worse for their exhausting experience. Attempts to replace the merino in the high country by half-breds (*i.e.* half merino) have not been very successful, and after a period of decline, the merinos are once more increasing.

On the low country the winters are mild enough to ensure little risk of mortality through exposure in the flocks, yet just severe enough to render necessary the provision of supplementary winter fodder (especially root crops) if the full summer capacity of the land is to be utilised. Here, too, over considerable areas, notably the Canterbury Plains and North Otago, the summers are sufficiently dry, warm, and sunny to favour the growing of wheat and oats. Holdings naturally became small, typically 200 to 400 acres, and there arose a system of diversified farming of a very flexible type. This flexibility is partly climatic in origin since any of the usual crops can be grown equally successfully either as a winter crop or as a spring crop; partly social and economic, owing to the freedom of the farmer from the cramping effects of a fixed traditional rotation, and to his constant striving to evolve a system that economised labour. Amid the almost infinite variety of detail, sheep always form a very important element, but sheep marked by great changes from the original merino. The introduction of freezing in 1882 rendered possible the supply of meat to the English market, and the exploitation of that possibility rendered necessary a change in breeding policy. Not that the pure merino was a failure as a meat producer: on the contrary merino mutton, even from an old sheep, has excellent flavour and a high degree of tenderness. But the merino is very difficult to fatten, and the appearance of merino joints is not such as to attract purchasers among the undiscerning public. English breeds were already replacing the merino in the wetter areas of the South Island (South Otago and Southland, for example) before the introduction of refrigeration, but refrigeration widened the area and increased the speed of merino replacement. The main flocks gradually came to consist of half-breds, and these, crossed again with one or other of the English breeds (increasingly Southdowns), provided the lambs that supplied the English tables. The importance of the merino strain in contributing to the quality of the meat is not generally realised, but it is safe to say that it was no small part of the reason for the fact that Canterbury gave its name ('prime Canterbury') to the highest grade of exported mutton and lamb, and that, though the province is no longer the greatest quantity producer, it still holds pride of place for quality.

In the North Island conditions were different. At similar elevations the rainfall is normally higher than on the eastern side of the South Island, but east of the mountain backbone, below elevations of about 2,000 feet, usually not sufficient to support forest growth. The open grasslands of the South Island, however, were not repeated in the North, and the original vegetation was either bracken fern or the dense scrub of the manuka, both alike thoroughly unsuitable for sheep rearing. The establishment of the industry here had to await the evolution of a technique of economical conversion of this country into grassland. Burning of the fern or scrub was followed by the sowing of grass-seed in the ashes, followed in turn, when both grass and fresh fern growth had appeared, by the introduction of sheep in numbers sufficient to tramp out and eat down the fern. This implied overstocking the land and underfeeding the sheep, but was essential to obtaining control over the fern and scrub. Even then the burning, sowing, and 'fern-crushing' might have to be repeated more than once before the grass could obtain possession. On some of the steeper slopes and poorer soils success was never achieved, but over most of the East Coast regions fine swards of 'English' grasses were sooner or later established. In these conditions the merino never throve, and almost from the beginning reliance was placed on English breeds, of which the Romney and its various crosses are now everywhere predominant. Here, as in the South Island, the large runs were gradually sub-divided, but the milder winters and higher rainfall gave a higher carrying capacity on grass growth alone and rendered the growing of supplementary fodder less urgent. The average size of holding in the lower country, consequently, is larger than in the mixed farms of the South Island. Crops are not absent, but they are grown specifically for fodder, and are, in the American phrase, 'marketed on the hoof,' or 'in the wool.' The net result is that here, especially on the rich plains of Southern Hawke's Bay, is the most intensive sheep-rearing area in the world. Elsewhere in the North Island it was forest that the grass replaced, and despite numerous sheep, the bias is usually to dairying.

GENERAL FEATURES

Reference has already been made to the changes introduced by freezing. At first the production of meat was carried on merely as a form of insurance against adverse movements of wool prices, but gradually the peculiar advantages of New Zealand for this aspect of sheep rearing came to be realised and exploited. The mildness of the winter temperatures on the one hand permits a certain amount of winter grass, even in the far south, and on the other enables fodder crops such as oats and rape, sown in the autumn or early winter, to provide quick fattening green fodder in the spring. In this critical period, August to January, granted an abundance of lush green fodder, grass or other, rapid fattening of lambs is possible, and it is precisely this that constitutes the differential advantage of New Zealand over the other great sheep-rearing countries of the Southern Hemisphere, more particularly Australia and South Africa: an advantage related directly to the relative abundance and reliability of the rainfall during these months. It may be noted at this time that lambing commences in July (mid-winter) in the north of Auckland and is over by the beginning of October in Southland. Supplementing of the grass by other green fodder crops for fattening is not universal, and in general is more in evidence in the South Island than the North. Under these conditions lambs may reach prime condition for killing in as short a period as ten to twelve weeks from birth, so that it is not surprising to find that New Zealand specialises on lamb, not on mutton. But the provision of fodder is by no means the whole story. Breeding changes have been referred to: it should be added that breeding has been directed not merely to the production of meat, but to the production of lambs that will take the maximum advantage of the spring fodder, lambs, that is, that will fatten rapidly, attaining prime condition before the frame of the animal has become too large; that will carry a minimum amount of offal and show a minimum amount of waste when dressed; and that will, finally, if they escape the butcher, provide a marketable fleece. Complete success in breeding with two purposes in view is always difficult, and it would seem that while New Zealand prime lamb will challenge comparison with the world's best, the quality of New Zealand wool has suffered somewhat.

A second general feature that should be stressed is the economic organisation of the industry as a response to economic rather than narrowly geographic conditions. These economic conditions may be summarised as high wages rates, high interest rates, high transport charges to a market 12,000 miles distant, and high prices of land. High-priced land may seem strange in such a new and distant country, and may, therefore, merit some explanation. New Zealand has never, as did the United States with their home-steading system, provided settlers with free land. When organised colonisation commenced in New Zealand in 1840, official circles had adopted more or less completely the views of Edward Gibbon Wakefield, an essential element of which was that land should be sold 'at a sufficient price.' There was, too, the example of Australia, where free gifts of land had led to the aggregation of enormous estates, held by common opinion to be a social evil. From the beginning, therefore, the New Zealand Government alienated land only by sale. Most of the desirable land has for long been in private hands, and twenty years of agricultural prosperity before the recent war, due quite as much to a steady upward trend of world primary produce prices as to local geographic conditions, had the effect of forcing land prices at least up to the utmost that the land was worth regarded as an instrument of production. Professor Condliffe, indeed, has argued very convincingly in his 'New Zealand in the Making: A Survey of Social and Economic Development,' that during those years prices of land at any moment were higher than could be justified by the productivity of the land, and contained a speculative element due to anticipation of continued rise in primary produce prices. The war with its unprecedented prices for wool and meat, butter and cheese, increased real values of land, and increased land speculation still more, so that land prices rose extremely rapidly. After the war prices of primary produce, except for a short slump in 1921-1922, fell less than those of most other commodities, and delayed the deflation of land prices from the unhealthy levels reached at the end of the war.

The New Zealand sheep farmer, then, has always been faced with three heavy cost elements (wage rates, interest rates, and transport charges), and over long periods has also had to contend with high land prices. Feeding costs have been kept low, as indicated above, by favouring climatic conditions, but conscious planning was still essential if total costs, including normal profits, were to be kept within the limits set by the prices obtainable in an open market against world competition. The characteristic organisation was worked out in the days of the large runs, before refrigeration, and owed much to the experience of the Australian 'squatters' or wool-kings. The permanent labour force consisted of a few specialist shepherds, well mounted, and with strong teams of highly trained dogs. At the present day, for example, a Canterbury hill-country run of 40,000 acres, carrying 8,000 or 9,000 sheep, would employ three permanent shepherds. Heavy seasonal demands for extra labour were met by the employment of temporary, but still specialist, workmen. At shearing time, for example, the shepherds were reinforced by a team of 'musterers' to assist in assembling the flock at the wool shed, where the shearing was done. The wool shed itself was designed for the rapid handling of large numbers of sheep, and the work was minutely organised to promote efficiency and speed. Shearer, sweeper, classer, and presser were a few of the specialist employees to be found in every shed. Results may be judged from the fact that 100 sheep a day per shearer for a working day of rather less than ten hours was accepted as a standard rate, over 200 per day was not an uncommon performance, and several instances of over 300 a day are on record. In England where no such organisation exists, 80 sheep per man per day is regarded as a high figure. Evolved on the large runs, the system remains practically unaltered where the large runs remain, but has been adapted by informal co-operation to the needs of the smaller farmers with almost equal effectiveness. Shearing machines, driven at first by petrol engines, now almost universally by hydro-electric power, eased somewhat the physical strain of the work, and enabled the sheep to be more closely shorn, but do not seem to have added greatly to shearing speeds.

The informal co-operation of the farmers to the end of achieving greater efficiency and lower costs in the major operations of shearing and dipping has not been followed to any significant extent by organised formal co-operation in preparing the fat sheep and lambs for market—a strange anomaly in such a co-operatively minded nation as the New Zealanders. The freezing works are mainly a product of ordinary capitalism, but in organisation resemble the farms and the co-operative dairy factories in having as their aim the minimising of labour requirements by specialisation of men and machinery. Unlike the dairy factories, however, which are among the largest to be found in the world, the freezing works have attained only moderate size. Growth of the industry has taken the form of increase in the number of works rather than of constantly increasing size of the works already in existence, until the country now has a total of 34, with an aggregate capacity for daily killing of 3,220 cattle and 128,000 sheep and for storage of 160,000 tons of meat. (Compare Argentina with only 17 frigorifices.) It would seem probable, therefore, that even if the internal organisation be perfectly appropriate to the size of the works, the maximum possible economies of large scale operation are not being achieved; but whether that is so or not the number of works is to be related directly to the long drawn-out shape of the country, to the existence of numerous harbours, and to the prevalence of relief conditions difficult enough to hinder the development of cheap and rapid land transport. It is at least arguable that any loss of works' economies has been offset by the minimising of land transport charges and the avoiding of the loss of condition always suffered by animals that are subjected to long inland transport. It is certain, too, that the establishment of freezing works at various points along the coast and in touch with the railways has been a not unimportant factor in preserving the activity of the smaller ports and saving the country from excessive centralisation of its shipping in the larger ports. Such minor ports that might be mentioned are, in the North Island, Wanganui, Napier, Gisborne, New Plymouth, and Whangarei; and, in the South Island, Picton, Timaru, Oamaru, and Bluff, all of which have a considerable direct export of frozen lamb and mutton.

TABLE XIX

SHEEP POPULATION OF NEW ZEALAND IN SELECTED YEARS*

Year		Year	
1900	 19,348,506	1924	 23,775,776
1913	 24,191,810	1925	 24,545,955
1919	 25,828,554	1926	 24,904,993
1920	 23,919,970	1927	 25,649,016
1921	 23,285,031	1928	 27,133,810
1922	 22,222,259	1929	 29,051,382
1923	 23,081,439	1930	 30,841,287

*New Zealand Offical Year Book, 1930

THE FUTURE

The slaughter of about ten million sheep and lambs a year involves a very heavy drain on the flocks; yet they increase in numbers—a testimony to their fecundity and healthiness, in turn, to some degree at any rate, reflecting the suitability of the environment. Table XIX shows the numbers in selected years. An increase during the war years, due to soaring prices for wool involving some decrease in killing, a decrease accentuated by the difficulty of finding shipping space, was followed by a rapid decline, till 1922 showed the smallest number of sheep of any year since 1907. And this decline was being paralleled elsewhere. Australia, United States, Argentina, South Africa, New Zealand, British Isles, Spain, and Uruguay, the great caterers for the world market in sheep products, had in round numbers in 1913, 310 million sheep, but in 1922 only 260 million. Human population in the meantime had increased. Accordingly, despite the accumulation in Australia, South Africa, and New Zealand of war-time wool stocks, the slump in 1921-1922 was relatively short lived for wool and meat, and stimulated by a continuing high level of prices the sheep-rearing countries set themselves to make good the world deficit. This had been practically accomplished by 1926, by which year the flocks of the above-mentioned countries had mounted to about 320 millions. By 1928 they were not far short of 330 millions. There can be little doubt that regarded in the light of post-war general price levels, the gap had been already overfilled by 1928, and prices had begun to decline somewhat seriously before the present world depression commenced. In New Zealand the increase in numbers was largely carried out by improvement in technique, the widespread adoption of top-dressing of pastures with artificial fertilisers, combined with closer attention to rotational grazing. On permanent pasture top-dressing increases the amount of growth; on temporary pasture it not only increases the amount of growth every year but also lengthens the productive life of the pasture. Top-dressing, therefore, means an increase in yield per unit of labour involved, and, other things being equal, enables the industry to withstand successfully some price shrinkage. But wool prices are now below pre-war level, mutton and lamb prices have also fallen, though not so much, and total income from the flocks is at present quite inadequate. It would seem that when the world has emerged from the present depression, the price position is likely to be more favourable to the dairying than to the sheep-rearing industry. It is consequently to be expected that the next few years will witness no appreciable growth in the Dominion's flocks (there may even be some recession), any increased carrying capacity that may be achieved being utilised rather to increase the dairying herds.

REFERENCE

[1] This table and also Tables XIII, XIV, and XV are all taken from the International Year Books of Agricultural Statistics, 1928-1929.

VIII

Hydro-Electric Power Development in New Zealand *

The development of hydro-electric power has made considerable progress in New Zealand, especially since the war, during which time the installed horse-power increased from 49,000 in 1919 to 149,000 in 1927. Within the last few months the first stages of two new stations have been put into operation, adding a further 90,000 horse-power. In comparison with the power production of Canada, for example (5.3 million horse-power in 1928), this seems trifling, yet it represents a production of 0.17 horse-power per head of population, which is exceeded by only four countries: Norway, Sweden, Canada and Switzerland. It is, too, a very small fraction of the potential power of New Zealand. Two comprehensive inquiries have been made as to New Zealand's resources in this respect, the first, in 1904, by Mr. P. S. Hay, Government engineer-in-chief, who in his report estimated the total, neglecting sources of under 1000 horse-power, at 3,700,000 horse-power, of which the South Island share was 3,200,000. The second report, by Mr. Evan Parry, chief electrical engineer, appeared in 1918, and according to his estimate, still accepted as authoritative, the total was assessed at 4,870,000 horse-power, of which the South Island accounted for 4,100,000. That represents a potential power of 3 horse-power per head of present population, an allowance greatly in excess of the utmost that is likely to be utilized for a very considerable time to come. The *Electrical World* of New York, January 1923,[1] estimates water-power wealth by expressing it in terms of potential horse-power per square mile of area, and on this basis ranks New Zealand with 47.8 horse-power per square mile second only to Switzerland with 87.9 horse-power per square mile, and followed by Norway with 44.2, Italy with 31.6, and Sweden with 26.0.

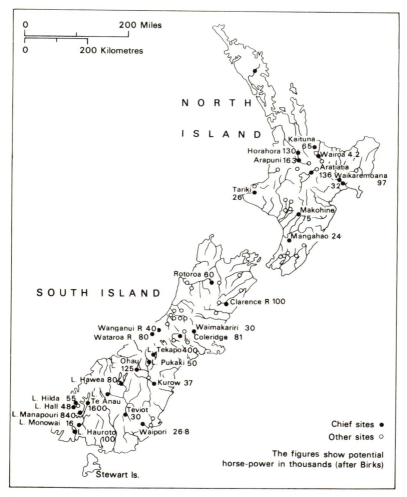

Figure 10. Sketch-map showing Potential Power Sites in New Zealand. The chief sites only are named, with figures for potential horse-power

Physical Background

This generous reserve of water-power is obviously a result of the topography and precipitation of the country. In both islands the main topographic feature is a mountain backbone running in a general north-east/south-west direction. In the South Island the backbone is high, especially in the Southern Alps, where the average elevation, about 8000 feet, exceeds the height of the snow-line by a full thousand feet. The range is unbroken except for a few high passes, and in the south rises directly out of the sea. In the northern portion of this island wide branching spurs of the main range, together with a parallel eastern system, occupy practically the full width of the island. Less striking than the Southern Alps and their continuations is the Otago Plateau, an upraised and very deeply dissected peneplain, giving the appearance of a series of north-south ranges, separated by comparatively narrow valleys, and gradually dropping in elevation from about 8000 feet in the north-west to about 2500 feet in the south-east.

The North Island backbone, running from Wellington to East Cape, is less high than that of the South Island, less continuous, and with less of its island to the east of it. Immediately west of it, and occupying the centre of the island is the Volcanic Plateau, a great triangular mass, characterized topographically by considerable areas of rather level country crowned here and there by ranges and peaks that rise above the general level of 2500 feet. Smaller elements are the isolated cone of Egmont in the west and the low ridges that lie parallel to the east coast from Cook Strait to Hawke Bay.

In brief, a large proportion of the country is mountainous, and much of the mountain area is high. Only Ruapehu (9175 feet) and Egmont (8260 feet) rise above the snow-line in the North Island, but in the South Island 25 per cent. of the area is above 3000 feet and 1 per cent. is above the snow-line. The low plains are all coastal and of limited extent. River gradients consequently are steep, rapids and waterfalls numerous.

For an appreciation of amount and regularity of water supply the most useful materials are measurements of amounts and variations of river flow and of variations in lake-levels. Such data certainly exist for some of the lakes and rivers, but they have not been published. It remains therefore to consider the precipitation.[2] The rainfall map indicates the distribution of the average annual rainfall in area, and illustrates at the same time the topographic control of the distribution. It will be noticed that precipitation is heavy: only 13 per cent. approximately of the total area has less than 30 inches per annum, while 17 per cent. has more than 70 inches, and half of that has more than 100 inches. The South Island, with its higher and more continuous mountain ranges, shows a greater contrast between east coast and west coast, and contains the areas both of greatest and of least precipitation of the Dominion. In the North Island the striking feature is the large proportion (87 per cent. approximately of the area of the island) receiving between 40 and 70 inches. (Figure 5)

Seasonal distribution is on the whole even (Table XX). This is particularly true in the South Island. In the North Island there is characteristically, though not universally, a winter maximum, but even in the far north there is no appearance of the summer drought typical of these latitudes in other parts of the world. At Auckland City, 36° 5′ S., January, the driest month, has an average rainfall of 2.66 inches, and December, with 2.84 inches, is the only other month that drops below 3 inches.

Possibly even more important than seasonal distribution of the rainfall is its reliability, and of this a useful method of assessment is given by an examination of deviations of actual from average monthly rainfalls.[3] For the eight stations examined the absolute values of the deviations, irrespective of whether they were positive or negative, have been averaged in the ordinary way, and the result for each month expressed as a percentage of the average precipitation for the month in question (Table XXI).

These results may be summarized as follows: Average monthly deviation percentages range from 21.2 for April at Invercargill to 81.2 for October at Napier. Of the 96 monthly records represented, 25 show percentage deviations of more than 50 per cent., 44 of less than 40 per cent. Five stations have at least six months in the year with deviations of less than 40 per cent.

TABLE XX

TABLE OF AVERAGE MONTHLY TEMPERATURE AND PRECIPITATION AT SELECTED STATIONS.

		Jan.	Feb.	Mar.	Apr.	May	June	July	Aug.	Sept.	Oct.	Nov.	Dec.	Year
Auckland ..	°F.	66·5	67·0	64·9	61·2	56·8	53·5	51·7	52·2	54·6	57·2	60·3	63·9	59·1
	Inches	2·67	3·05	3·02	3·43	4·63	4·92	4·95	4·22	3·64	3·69	3·32	2·90	44·44
New Plymouth	°F.	61·4	64·6	62·9	59·3	55·3	52·0	50·5	50·8	53·4	55·7	58·3	61·7	57·2
	Inches	4·42	4·00	3·62	4·51	6·23	6·14	6·29	5·33	5·22	5·61	4·65	4·33	60·35
Napier	°F.	66·1	65·5	63·0	58·7	53·8	50·1	48·9	49·9	53·6	57·5	60·7	64·1	57·7
	Inches	3·14	2·89	3·26	2·87	3·73	3·54	3·87	3·56	2·16	2·29	2·48	2·32	36·11
Wellington	°F.	62·5	62·5	60·5	57·0	52·7	49·4	47·7	48·6	51·6	54·4	56·9	60·4	55·4
	Inches	3·30	3·19	3·29	3·80	4·76	4·87	5·55	4·43	3·99	4·19	3·44	3·30	48·11
Hokitika ..	°F.	60·3	60·6	58·5	54·7	49·9	46·4	44·8	46·3	50·0	52·7	54·9	58·4	53·1
	Inches	9·92	7·37	9·75	9·39	9·82	9·55	8·99	9·28	9·32	11·81	10·78	10·62	116·60
Dunedin ..	°F.	58·0	57·7	55·4	51·7	47·1	43·8	42·4	44·0	47·9	51·0	53·3	56·3	50·7
	Inches	3·34	2·75	2·96	2·78	3·26	3·15	2·99	3·14	2·75	3·13	3·28	3·53	37·06
Invercargill	°F.	57·2	56·8	54·7	50·8	45·8	42·7	41·4	43·8	48·1	51·3	52·8	55·2	50·0
	Inches	3·97	2·97	3·85	4·34	4·49	3·59	3·24	3·38	3·18	4·44	4·39	4·20	46·04

TABLE XXI

TABLE OF AVERAGE PERCENTAGE DEVIATIONS FROM AVERAGE PRECIPITATION AT SELECTED STATIONS

	Jan.	Feb.	Mar.	Apr.	May	June	July	Aug.	Sept.	Oct.	Nov.	Dec.	Year
Auckland	53·4	64·7	51·5	56·1	33·3	31·4	34·5	36·5	35·9	39·6	53·7	39·1	11·5
New Plymouth ..	46·1	40·8	60·2	42·3	39·3	48·7	27·2	27·6	30·9	27·3	39·8	43·4	12·3
Napier	54·8	50·2	70·9	45·3	66·8	63·0	45·0	43·0	43·5	81·2	48·8	45·7	23·4
Wellington	46·8	55·0	49·4	47·9	39·5	37·1	33·1	34·2	36·6	41·9	40·9	33·7	14·7
Christchurch	45·4	60·9	55·9	50·3	57·9	43·3	51·9	50·0	58·9	50·3	24·5	54·3	14·2
Hokitika	43·3	37·9	33·8	37·3	24·9	33·9	34·6	39·9	29·7	27·4	30·7	29·6	8·7
Dunedin	38·1	49·1	53·7	42·2	39·0	49·5	57·1	52·5	49·7	54·0	44·0	38·2	15·3
Invercargill	30·5	66·7	48·3	21·2	29·3	36·5	27·5	32·8	38·1	27·9	23·5	23·3	9·0
Valencia (Ireland) ..	28·7	37·8	40·3	37·7	35·9	35·9	37·1	31·4	38·2	29·9	33·6	27·9	10·9

These figures may be claimed to indicate a high degree of regularity of rainfall, and to give a strong presumption of regularity of river flow. They are somewhat strengthened by two other circumstances. In the first place, the records disclose on the whole a remarkably even balance between the number of positive and the number of negative deviations. The negative instances are slightly more frequent, ranging from 50.8 per cent. of the total at Dunedin up to 69.6 per cent. at Napier. Under such circumstances extraordinary deviations in either direction are unlikely. The second point is that out of all the months examined for these eight stations, totalling 2568, only three were found in which no rain at all had fallen, one at Auckland, one at Napier, and one at Wellington.

These precipitation conditions go far to account for New Zealand's fortunate position in water-power resources, but other factors have a share in determining the degree of regularity of river flow. The table of climatic statistics given opposite shows that temperatures are moderate, and implies that little reduction of river volume takes place by freezing in the winter or excessive evaporation in the summer. Some winter reduction of volume does, however, occur in those rivers which rise in the glaciers fed by the snowfields of the Southern Alps, though on balance it can scarcely be doubted that such rivers have a more regular régime than those which depend wholly on rain. Lakes, the best natural regulators of river flow, are numerous, and many of them are of considerable size. In this respect, too, the South Island is more richly endowed than the North Island. Finally much of the headwater areas up to elevations of about 5000 feet is forested, and even where the forest has been removed or never existed there is a continuous grass cover which checks run-off and helps to even out the effect of variations in precipitation on river flow. The importance of this filtering action of the vegetation has been demonstrated locally, notably in Hawke's Bay and Poverty Bay, where heavy floods in the low country have been caused by deforestation of steep headwater areas in a vain attempt to establish permanent pastures.

Historical

The early settlers of New Zealand built flour mills driven by water-wheels. With the development of railway transport most of these succumbed to the competition of steam mills situated in the larger centres, but a few still exist. The discovery of gold in 1852 inaugurated a period of water harnessing for 'sluicing,'[4] particularly along the Clutha River in Otago, and as early as 1887 a beginning was made on the production of hydro-electric power, a small plant being installed at Reefton in that year.[5] During the next twenty years private companies and local authorities established a number of small stations, the most important of which were at the Waipori Falls in Otago (Dunedin City Corporation) and at Horahora on the Waikato River (Waihi Gold-mining Company).

Meantime the national government had become alive to the part that hydro-electric power might play in the development of the country, and had passed a series of measures which progressively defined the attitude of the state to the water-power resources.[6] By 1903 water-power was recognized as a national possession, and its ownership vested in the state, which was given the sole right to develop hydro--electricity *for sale*, with, however, the power to delegate the right. It was not until 1910 that the government proceeded to avail itself of its right. In that year a site was selected at Lake Coleridge in Canterbury for the first government station. Work was commenced the following year, and the station was opened in 1915. The war had delayed progress there and postponed government action elsewhere, but in 1918 came Evan Parry's report, which not only surveyed the water-power resources of the country but also considered the amount and distribution of probable demand, and put forward a scheme for national development. Effect was given to this report by legislation in 1919 and 1920.

Briefly put, the aim is the production by the government of the necessary power at a few large inter-connected stations,[7] and the retail distribution of current by specially constituted local authorities (Electric Power Boards). Local stations already in existence are incorporated in the scheme,

where necessary as auxiliary producers, otherwise as trans-
forming stations. At present there are in existence forty-two
power districts, administered by elected power boards, some
few of which produce their own power, but most of which
purchase current in bulk from government stations.

Carrying through a scheme of this scope obviously involves
considerable expenditure of public funds. The policy is to
make it 'productive expenditure' by charging wholesale and
retail prices that will cover interest and sinking fund on the
capital outlay. In fact, experience has shown that for the first
year or two prices low enough to attract consumers will not
cover these charges, but that thereafter, with growing consumption, both profits and reduced prices are generally
possible. The explanation lies in the fact that overhead costs
are much greater than operating costs, that the bulk of the
overhead costs are incurred in the original installation of the
generating plant and the reticulation of the consuming areas,
and that they increase only slightly with extensions of the
undertaking. Prices naturally vary from one part of New
Zealand to another, according to the amount of current sold
and the capital expenditure that has been necessary to enable
that current to be provided, but taking a general average of
prices for current over all power districts and for all purposes,
a reduction was effected from 1.82 pence per unit in 1920 to
1.58 pence in 1927. It is anticipated that, as consumers
increase, further reduction, probably to a general average of
less than one penny per unit, will be possible.

Power Developments[8]

We may now examine in greater detail the scheme
adopted by the government to prevent the technical inef-
ficiency and economic waste that would result from over-
lapping and competing enterprises.

The map (Figure 11) shows the proposed electrification of
the North Island, based on the three key stations of Mangahao, Waikaremoana and Arapuni (eventual horse-power
24,000, 140,000 and 160,000 respectively). It illustrates,
too, the linking up with the main system of the various
smaller stations already operating. Of these the most important is on the Waikato River at Horahora (17,000 horse-

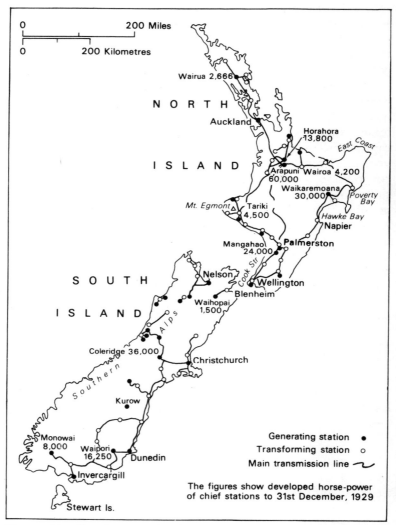

Figure 11. Sketch-map showing Government Hydro-electric Power Scheme (after Birks) and Developed Power of chief stations to 31 December 1929

-power), installed by the Waihi Gold-mining Company, but now owned and operated by the government,[9] and supplying besides the industrial demand of the Waihi mines the urban and rural demand of the rich dairying plains of the Waikato, Piako and Thames rivers. Others are Wairua Falls on the Wairoa River, North Auckland (3250 h.p.), Tauranga (5600 h.p.) and Tariki and New Plymouth in Taranaki (4400 and 5000 h.p. respectively).

Of the main stations, Mangahao is situated on the Wellington West Coast Plains at the foot of the steep western slope of the Tararua Ranges, 15 miles south of Palmerston North. It draws its water from the Mangahao River, which formerly flowed north between two of the ranges of the Tararuas into the Manawatu River, but is now diverted by 2¼ miles of tunnels through the mountains into three-quarters of a mile of pipeline to arrive at the power house with a head of 850 feet. Already up to its full capacity of 24,000 horse-power, Mangahao is supplying current to an area that reaches to Napier in the east, to Wanganui in the west, and to Wellington in the south.

Waikaremoana, east of the main divide and about halfway between East Cape and Southern Hawke's Bay, has an area of 21 square miles and an elevation of 2000 feet above sea-level. Its catchment area, though not large, has an average annual rainfall of more than 70 inches. The peculiarity of the lake is that it has no natural surface outlet, the surplus water escaping by underground channels and reappearing some distance away to form one of the headstreams of the Wairoa River. Harnessing the lake to its ultimate capacity of 140,000 horse-power will involve the stoppage of these channels and the provision of a surface outlet. The first unit, providing 30,000 horse-power, was put into operation in October 1929, and now supplies besides its own immediate thinly populated area the easternmost portion of the Southern Hawke's Bay area previously supplied by Mangahao. Further development will permit still greater assistance to Mangahao as increasing population makes further demands on that already fully taxed station.

The Arapuni Rapids station, which also came into operation in 1929 with 60,000 horse-power, is already the largest in New Zealand, but this is merely the first stage of a planned 160,000 horse-power development. It is situated on the Waikato River a few miles above Horahora, and was selected in preference to any of the other rapids farther up the Waikato River partly for economic reasons and partly for technical reasons associated with the site. At Arapuni the river flowed through a narrow gorge, rather over three--quarters of a mile long and with almost vertical sides. A 150-feet dam at the upper end diverts the river into an old deserted course, from which at the lower end it is led down to the power house at the bottom of the gorge. The head so obtained is 175 feet. Arapuni's market is threefold: first, Auckland City and its environs; secondly, the Waikato-Piako-Hauraki Plains, already growing beyond the capacity of Horahora; and thirdly, the ribbon of settlement along the main trunk railway, and thence through the as yet scantily settled country west of the railway to link up with the local stations operating in Taranaki.

The South Island system, though lacking the beautiful symmetry that the triangular shape of the Volcanic Plateau has given to that of the North Island, is essentially similar in its comprehensiveness and economy. The largest station is at Lake Coleridge, one of the numerous South Island glacial lakes. Development has involved damming the natural outlet (which was at the western end), diverting the Harper River into the lake, and tapping the eastern end by a tunnel whose intake is 12 feet below average lake-level. The power house is situated a mile and a quarter away, and the water reaches it with a head of 480 feet. The main consumption is by Christchurch, 63 miles distant, but reticulation covers the whole of the East Coast Plains from Kaiapoi in the north to Oamaru, beyond the Canterbury boundary, in the south. The rapidity of the increase in demand for electricity may be gauged from the fact that since it was opened in 1915 its capacity has been twice enlarged, till it now stands as 36,000 horse-power, that it is being further enlarged to 46,000 horse-power, and that a new station is being established on the Waitaki River, near Kurow, to take over part of the district at present supplied by Coleridge. Details as to the area to be served by the Kurow station are not available, but presumably on the east coast it will supply from Timaru in the north to Palmerston in the south.

The Waipori Falls station, on the Waipori River, 30 miles

from Dunedin, is owned and operated by the Dunedin City Corporation. The main river and some of its tributaries are dammed at the head of a deep narrow gorge, and the water is led by tunnel and pipeline to the power house at the other end. The volume of water is smaller than at most of the stations, but the head of 700 feet that is attained helps to compensate for that. The present capacity of 15,000 horse -power is being enlarged to 25,000 horse-power, to cater for increasing rural demand from as far south as the lower Clutha.

The last link in the present South Island chain is the Southland Electric Power Board's plant on the Waiau River, 66 miles from Invercargill. The water is obtained from Lake Monowai by open canal and pipeline, and arrives at the power house with a head of 180 feet. Since it was opened in 1925 its capacity has been enlarged from 5000 to 8000 horse-power, and is capable of further enlargement to 16,000 horse-power as required.

The small scattered stations in the thinly populated north and west of the island may ultimately be connected with the main part of the scheme in the east and south, but that is a distant prospect.

Economic Aspects

This section is concerned mainly with the extent and character of the market for power, and with such new outlets for power as the presence of cheap power may induce. It should be noted that distribution and density of population are not necessarily safe guides to the amount of probable demand. Canada, for example, in her wood pulp and paper industries consumes large amounts of power in areas that have no dense concentration of population. Consideration must therefore be given to the character of the demand, and this depends on the nature of the occupations as well as on the distribution of the population.

Population in New Zealand is almost confined to the coastal lowlands, where climate, soil and the isolation of the country have combined to make one or other of the branches of the pastoral industry the chief national occupation.[10] Broadly, the drier east coast lowlands whose grasslands are associated mainly with sheep rearing may be distinguished from the wetter west coast lowlands (including the Auckland Peninsula), where the original vegetation was forest, and which are now the dominant cattle-rearing areas. Here warm winters and sufficiently moist summers give with fertile soils an all-year growth of grass that will permit very close rural settlement based on dairy farming, and already the North Island west coast plains show a rural population density somewhat greater than other parts of New Zealand.

A further fact of importance is the wide scattering of the chief points of concentration of population. Greater Auckland (202,400), Greater Wellington (126,750), Greater Christchurch (122,000), and Greater Dunedin (83,250) (N.Z. Statistics, *op. cit.*), with an aggregate of 37 per cent. of the total population, are situated at wide intervals over a distance from Auckland to Dunedin of 850 miles as the crow flies. In only three other urban areas (Wanganui, Palmerston North and Invercargill) is 20,000 exceeded. The basis of these concentrations is essentially commercial: the severe rural specialization, exemplified particularly by the dairy industry of the North Island, and by the fact that 95 per cent. by value of New Zealand's exports are pastoral products, involves very active commerce, both domestic and foreign. Evidence of this may be found in the average value of the foreign trade of the Dominion per head of population for the period 1923-27, which was £70,[11] by far the highest of any temperate-zone country in the world.

Manufacturing is of quite minor importance even if one includes such elementary operations as the making of butter and cheese and the freezing of meat. These, though they bulk large in the economy of the country, are capable of utilizing only small amounts of power. The smallness of the market and of the labour supply (population, 1 April 1928: 1,453,517)[12] has prevented large-scale organization and the consequent economies that would permit successful competition with the great industrial countries. This disadvantage is increased by the lack of available coal and iron. Lignite and brown coals are widespread and can cater more or less adequately for domestic needs, but high-grade bituminous coals occur in only two small areas on the west coast of the

South Island. There transport difficulties are considerable: not until long after Coleridge was in operation was there railway connection with the east coast of the South Island, while shipping suffered from the stormy nature of the west coast and the presence of bars across the mouths of the Buller and the Grey rivers. Iron presents another difficulty. No commercially feasible method of smelting the rich iron-sands of the Taranaki beaches has yet been devised, and the smelting of the high-grade iron ore near Onahaka in Nelson Province is carried on under the same disadvantage of small-scale organisation that hampers the manufacturing industries.

Industrial demand, then, in the sense in which it would be understood in the United States, Canada or Sweden, does not at present exist. The cities provide the major part of the demand for power—utilized for tramway systems, for numerous small industrial enterprises (flour mills, boot factories, freezing works, rope works, furniture factories, confectionery works, and so on), and especially for public lighting and domestic purposes. Rural demand, however, forms in New Zealand probably a larger proportion of total demand than in any other country, and of this rural demand the most important element is the purely domestic. It should be mentioned that no statistics exist which enable rural demand to be separated accurately from urban, but the following table gives an indication of the great importance of domestic consumption:

TABLE XXII

HORSE-POWER OF WATERPOWER IN USE IN NEW ZEALAND AT
31 MARCH 1928 (FROM N.Z.O.Y.B. 1929)

Total	Mining	Elec. Sup.	Flax Mill	Saw Mills	Flour Mills	Dairying	Constr.	Freez. Works	Paper Mills	Miscellan
149,485·75	1603	141,949	279	297·5	287	1242·5	37	1295	450	2045·75

Apart from domestic consumption the purely rural demand is for such purposes as the driving of water-pumps, milking, separating and shearing machinery, and the heating of water for the cleaning of dairy plant. For these purposes electric power has considerable advantages. It is easy to apply, and it can be used in small quantities and for short periods without waste. Further, the power is applied smoothly—an important point where animals are concerned, and one which gives electricity a definite advantage in use over its competitor, the petrol engine. It should be mentioned, too, that from the time it was first available electricity was cheaper than petrol, which, imported in tins from California and Sumatra with high freight and insurance charges, was an expensive source of power.

Population distribution, then, is in New Zealand a sufficiently accurate guide to probable distribution of demand for electric power, and so the immediate necessity in creating a national supply was the installation of adequate stations as close as possible to the population centres of gravity of the lowland areas. In the South Island the selection of Lake Monowai in preference to Lake Manapouri or Lake Te Anau, the neglect of Lakes Hawea and Wanaka, and the acceptance of the Kurow site on the Waitaki River to the exclusion of Lakes Tekapo, Pukaki and Ohau in its upper basin are all perfectly sound on this view. Similarly the greater proximity of Arapuni to the Auckland and Taranaki populations and to the main trunk railway line decisively reinforces the claims of this site as against those of the upper rapids of the Waikato River.

As has been shown, the direct effect of the geography of the Dominion has been to fix the sites of the water-powers, and the indirect effect has been to place between the power sources and the small city centres a relatively large rural population engaged in the main in such forms of exploitation of the land as offer a good market for electric power. It is natural, therefore, that primary attention in distribution should have been directed to the country districts. In no case since the inauguration of the national scheme has power been transmitted directly to the nearest city before the intervening rural areas were reticulated. Kissel, writing at the beginning of 1928, was of the opinion that though New Zealand stood only sixth in order of average consumption per head, it had 'the most fully developed and perfectly organized rural reticulation in the world' (Kissel, *op. cit.*). It is the rural areas that are most responsible for the rapid increase in consumption in the post-war years, an increase according to the same writer, during the period from 1920 to 1927, of consumers from 10.8 to 20.1 per cent. of the population, and of consumption per head per annum from 148 to 310 units.

It remains to glance at some of the effects of cheap electric power on economic conditions. Naturally, effects on rural industry, especially dairying, are most evident. Particularly in Auckland and Taranaki, the small specialized dairy farm carrying a large herd is characteristic, and here, though the absence of winter hand-feeding of housed animals reduces feeding and labour costs, total costs in a country of high wage rates are apt to be very high if much labour has to be employed for milking. With machines a man assisted by two boys can do the milking that would require about six experienced hand milkers. The rapid spread of the milking machine since electricity became available[13] has either reduced the labour demand of the farmer, or made more labour available for increasing the yield of the farm per cow and per acre by increasing cultivation of supplementary fodder—a valuable contribution to the efficiency of the national agriculture. In so far as any of the labour force is rendered surplus to demand, it may help to swell the 'drift to the cities.' Contrary to the opinion of most publicists, this is not, at any rate in countries of predominantly primary production, a feature to be deplored: essentially it is an indication of increasing efficiency of rural production, and therefore of real material progress. But if it is in any measure due to the superior amenities of city life, hydro-electric power by banishing much of the drudgery formerly associated with farm life, especially for the women, should prove a powerful ally of the motor-car, the telephone and the wireless set in tending to check it. In any case, the improvement in living conditions and the reduction in the amount of exhausting physical labour are a sociological effect of prime importance.

It seems unlikely that hydro-electric power will enable New Zealand to become an industrial country. Against the possession of cheap power and of raw materials for certain industries must be set the major problems of an adequate supply of cheap iron and the organization of any industry on a scale large enough to secure all possible manufacturing economies. It would seem impossible under conditions of modern competition from countries already industrialized to repeat in the woollen industry the record established in the cotton industry by Lancashire, which from the beginning depended upon foreign markets rather than upon the home market. For a front rank wood pulp and paper industry there is insufficient raw material, and the only industry that seems to hold out much hope of developing to a size of world importance is the manufacture of artificial nitrate, which the experience of Norway seems to prove has least need of a large and expanding home market. That industry however, while it may use great quantities of power, will absorb altogether inconsiderable amounts of labour.

We may conclude that cheap power solves only one of the problems incidental to making New Zealand a manufacturing country, and by itself cannot affect the transformation. Its chief function in the immediate future would seem to be the increasing of the national efficiency in the various stages of the production of wool, meat and dairy products, and, in the more distant future, with increase of population, in improving transport by the electrification of both the suburban and the trunk railways. If, without altering the fundamental economic organization of the country, it can increase the output per head, and *pari passu* decrease the social cost in terms of labour and hardship, it will have achieved no small result.

REFERENCES

[1] Quoted by 'New Zealand Official Year Book,' 1925.

[2] Climatic statistics from the 'New Zealand Official Year Book' and from 'New Zealand Statistics,' Meteorology Section.

[3] The stations quoted in this paper are all coastal, but though available records are short there is no reason to doubt that the case for regularity of precipitation in the mountainous areas is even stronger than is here argued.

[4] 'Sluicing' was the name given to the process of using powerful jets of water to wash down banks of gold-bearing river gravels preparatory to recovering the gold.

[5] Kissel: 'Electricity in New Zealand' in the *New Zealand Journal of Science and Technology*, February 1928.

[6] 1896 Electric Motive Power Act.
1903 Water Power Act.
1908 Public Works Act, incorporating and modifying the 1903 Water Power Act.
1910 Aid to Water Power Works Act.

[7] In 1929 the four chief stations in the North Island and the four chief stations in the South Island accounted for 187,000 horse-power out of a total of 239,000

[8] See Birks, 'Hydro-electric Power Development in New Zealand'. Wellington, Govt. Printer, 1925.

[9] This station was bought by the government in 1919.

[10] New Zealand Statistics: Population and Buildings. Estimated populations, 1927.

[11] New Zealand Official Year Book.

[12] *Ibid.*

[13] Milking Machines in use (N.Z.O.Y.B. 1929): 1919, 7,577; 1928, 18,049

GEOGRAPHY
AND THE COMMUNITY

IX

Some Aspects of Settlement in the Overseas Dominions*

'Settlement' is a term which, like many others adopted by the geographer from lay usage, has several distinct, though related, meanings and uses. Currently the geographer's use of the term is tending to restrict itself to the material evidences, particularly the buildings, and perhaps even more particularly the dwellings, of the people who live and work in an area. This is a perfectly defensible usage, appropriate especially in the 'older' lands, and much interesting and valuable recent work, including the whole range of urban geography, bears witness to the fruitfulness of the field. In the 'newer' lands, however, until with the passage of time the settlements in this sense acquire some stability of site and form it is the human processes producing these concrete results that rivet the attention, and in these areas the emphasis in lay usage tends to be on the process rather than on the village or town. This is the aspect on which Isaiah Bowman seized in his own 'Pioneer Fringe' and in the series of studies of pioneer settlement that he stimulated, and it is with settlement in this sense that this paper is concerned.

The basic idea of settlement of this kind is the taking possession of unused or little used land by incomers whose aim and expectation is to utilise the resources of the land, to make homes for themselves and their children, and ultimately to develop as full a range of community amenities as their times, their culture and their numbers can provide. Permanent settlement implies permanent resources and conserva-

*Presidential Address to Section E of the British Association for the Advancement of Science at the Belfast Meeting, 1952. (*The Advancement of Science*, 34, 1952)

tional use of those resources, and is pre-eminently based on a stable agriculture. This is not to deny the importance of forest and mineral resources. Forests can, if wisely used, support permanent settlement, though the settlement will be thin and the population small in relation to the area used. But commonly their history in new areas has been different: where they grew in good soil, they were removed to provide land for farming; elsewhere their wealth was ravaged and they were commonly abandoned. Minerals are notoriously a wasting asset, and settlement dependent wholly on minerals is inevitably temporary. Such a relatively stable mineral as coal, even in its more massive occurrences, can produce in time such problems as that of south-west Durham, where a not insignificant population has been bereft of its mainstay. In the Union of South Africa cheap labour, cheap power, technological progress, the rise in gold prices, and, finally, the discovery of the new gold fields of the Orange Free State have pushed the economic exhaustion of the gold resources much further into the future. It remains nevertheless one of the two major problems of the Union. Partly then for these reasons, but partly also because the problems of settlement in the overseas dominions of the British Commonwealth have in fact been overwhelmingly the problems of establishing farming settlement, this paper will concern itself essentially with land settlement, the progress of the occupation and working of new agricultural land in these several countries. This is a problem of many facets, economic, political, legal, administrative, all of them set in the areal framework of the region concerned and against the historical background of the people concerned. To put the matter in a different way, the process of settlement in the pioneering areas and the pioneering stages reflected the attitudes and capacities of the pioneers themselves and of their distant governments and markets as well as the character of the lands they were attempting to subdue, and that process has left its objective imprint on the geography of the settled areas, and indeed, if we may borrow the thesis of Francis Jackson Turner from the United States in many less tangible ways in the outlook, the history and the character of the peoples of these dominions.

In so far as land settlement is our topic, a short examination of Turner's views may not be inappropriate. Turner, an American historian, sprang into fame in 1893 with his essay entitled 'The Significance of the Frontier in American History.' A short extract will make vivid his concept of the moving frontier:

> 'Stand at the Cumberland Gap and watch the procession of civilisation, marching single file—the buffalo following the trail to the salt springs, the fur trader and hunter, the cattle rancher, the pioneer farmer—and the frontier has passed by. Stand at the South Pass in the Rockies a century later and see the same procession with wider intervals between. The unequal rate of advance compels us to distinguish the frontier into the trader's frontier, the rancher's frontier or the miner's frontier, and the farmer's frontier.'

It has been well said that Turner supplied for the first time a master key to American history. He saw American development as a series of successive stages towards full utilisation of the natural resources of the land of the United States, accompanied by progressive growth of economic and social organisation. In tune with that, and despite the title of his essay, it is the frontiersman rather than the frontier that focuses his attention. It was the frontiersman in Turner's view who contributed so strikingly to the distinctive character of American democracy, to the consolidation of national sentiment as against sectionalism and to the nature of the development of American religious and intellectual life. But the frontiersman is the product of the frontier, and while in human affairs the trader and the miner may (or may not!) impinge on society in much the same way as the pioneer rancher or cultivator, in so far as a true frontier implies continuity, the trader's frontier and the miner's frontier are not frontiers at all, but merely outposts. The rancher's frontier and the farmer's frontier are the true frontiers, and in the United States, as in the Dominions, they were not merely continuous but they marched with one another.

So far as I know, no geographer and only one historian[1] has attempted to test Turner's concept against conditions in

any of the British Dominions and no comparative treatment
of the Dominions themselves has been undertaken. Yet each
of them has shown something of the same kind of progress as
the United States through a moving frontier to a virtually
static area of occupation and a high degree of stabilisation of
use of the resources of the land; and some appreciation of the
differences in frontier conditions from one to another will
provide useful aid towards the understanding of some of the
present differences in their cultural geography. This, however, is much too vast a subject for detailed consideration in
the short space of one hour, and my purpose at the moment
is merely to take one or two of the more obvious points of
difference and touch on some of their causes and some of
their effects.

Probably the first thing that strikes any student of the
colonisation of the Dominions is the length of the period
over which it was spread. Champlain founded the first
permanent French settlement in Canada in 1608 and van
Riebeck established the Dutch East India Company's settlement at the Cape in 1652. At the other end of the scale New
Zealand was not declared a British possession until 1840 and
the same year saw the arrival at Wellington of the first
organised band of settlers. Settlement of the Canadian prairies in any real sense did not begin until the last quarter of
the nineteenth century and has been largely the work of the
twentieth. There is a spread of two and a half centuries,
remarkable not so much for the fact that it is two and a half
centuries as for the changes it witnessed. During that time
Holland and France both sank from their proud position as
world leaders, and their loss to Britain of the Cape and
French Canada was an early symptom of their inability to
maintain the role of active colonising powers. The United
States had grown from a series of separate and often
quarrelsome colonies, almost confined to the Atlantic coast,
and numbering only a few million people, to a mighty unified
nation already setting new standards for the world in economic and social organisation. Britain had lost her American
colonies and received in exchange a lesson in colonial administration that she was never to forget, even though she was to
have for a century afterwards occasional and partial lapses.

Almost immediately afterwards she had had to endure the long strain of the twenty years of the French Revolutionary and Napoleonic Wars. Most significant of all, however, she had initiated the Industrial Revolution and ushered in a new age. From that Revolution she was in the later nineteenth century to reap a very rich harvest, but the immediate picture for three decades after Waterloo was one of greater misery for more people than had ever been known before or has been since. The enclosures, the ruin of the domestic industries by the factories, the absence of control of either working conditions in the factories or housing standards for the factory workers, a savage penal code, the twin influences of laisser-faire and the repressive political atmosphere that was an understandable reaction from the French Revolution, the difficulties, at that time without any precedent, of the change over from war to peace—all these combined with a greatly increased rate of population growth and a drastic redistribution of population to produce among the masses of the people a state of economic and social misery and seething political discontent.

This close-up, with its emphasis on the foreground of the conditions of life of great masses of British people, is very relevant to one aspect of overseas migration, but it dims a background of even greater importance. In the long run the significant elements of the Industrial Revolution were the increased productivity of labour armed with power-driven machinery and the specialisation of labour necessitated by the specialisation of machinery. In combination they provided both the incentive to and the means for the extension of active trading into more and more widely flung areas and into an ever widening circle of commodities. This was the background of the new era colonisation of the nineteenth century. No longer was the settler prepared to go forth into the wilderness to cultivate his own food, make his own clothes and implements and lead a selfsubsistent life, limited in material consumption and in intellectual outlook by the character of his own small plot set in its own small neighbourhood. True, such an extreme subsistence character of overseas settlements had never in fact fully existed. Even the New Englanders had early commenced trading, especially in fish, and trading in the product of a highly specialised agriculture had been the essential condition of the foundation and the maintenance of the plantations, but the very limited coastal areas over which these settlements could be successful is the proof of the general point. From about the end of the eighteenth century, then, new colonisation was likely to succeed only if it could produce efficiently commodities that were in demand in the industrial areas and if those commodities were physically and financially able to stand the long transport from the point of production to the point of consumption. With the proceeds of such exports the settlement could import both consumption goods and the capital equipment necessary to promote further development of economic production and social amenities. The logic of that position is easy enough to see from the vantage point of the mid-twentieth century. It was not so easy to see, at any rate in the United Kingdom, up to the middle of the nineteenth century, and the actual process of settlement, particularly in Australia and New Zealand was from one point of view a struggle by the settlers to get command of the right kind of land in the right kind of amount and the right kind of location. Clearly the conception of 'right,' whether in kind, in amount or in location, would change as technological advances enabled new commodities to comply with the conditions or previously sub-marginal lands to become economic producers, but at each stage there were non-geographical obstacles to be surmounted before new settlement could adjust itself satisfactorily to the changed conditions. In the Southern Hemisphere colonies these obstacles bore in general a certain family resemblance to one another, though South Africa had certain ones peculiar to itself, and in all the colonies the exact nature and degree of common influence varied considerably.

At the Cape the tightly monopolistic Dutch East India Company, intent only on its trade with the Indies, established its settlement as a means to providing fuel, fresh water, meat, vegetables and flour to its own ships on their way to and from the east. Its initial policy of having all the production of these goods done by its own paid servants was soon given up, but its determination to be the sole trader was not, and officials and settlers alike were forbidden to undertake private trading. What the Company had in mind was a small, compact settlement, in which working farmers would produce food on holdings of about 120 acres (60 morgen) and sell it to the Company. It was clear that extension of settlement would progressively decrease the control the Company was able to exercise and increase the expenses of administration and defence, while, further, if production were correspondingly increased, there would be little prospect of disposing of it: ships, even on this high road to the Indies, and even with the multiplying of French and British vessels, were normally too few to support much trade. Control from Europe, though hardly such close and strict control, and the attempt to restrict settlement within narrowly drawn boundaries are features that appear again in the nineteenth century in Australia and New Zealand. In all three countries a leading element, if not indeed the chief element, in the history of settlement was to be the deliberate efforts by the people on the spot to free themselves from both kinds of restrictions.

It would seem that despite various commissions sent out from Holland and numerous reports submitted by governors, the Council of Seventeen never formed an adequate appreciation of the local circumstances at the Cape. Limited areas of reasonably good soil and rainfall, the long summer drought, the necessity for irrigation almost within sight of Capetown gave conditions for farming alien to the Dutch, the German, and even some of the French settlers. By a long process of trial and error farmers had to win through to a command of Mediterranean concepts and techniques. Only in vine-growing and the making of wine and brandy did a measure of success come at all quickly, and that owed everything to the expertise of some of the French and German settlers. At the same time relations had to be stabilised with the previous inhabitants. The Bushmen hunters were themselves hunted and driven out. With the Hottentots, however, owners of cattle and sheep, relations were on the whole friendly, trading in animals became established despite official ban, and the Hottentots, progressively detribalised, set the tradition of a menial class. This tradition, accentuated by the importing of slaves and the complete cessation of immigration from 1707 till the arrival of the British 1820 settlers, was to have a profound influence on the history of South Africa. In the initial stages the hunting of Bushmen and trading with the Hottentots, the inheritance provisions of Roman-Dutch law and the cramping effects of the economic and political system combined to tempt the bolder spirits out beyond the borders of settlement. Here is the origin of the Boers and their trekking habits, a feature of development completely at variance with the established policy and the current desires of the Company. Yet it had to be given some recognition, since it could not be stopped, and, grudgingly, provision was made for land to be held on loan from the Company in blocks as large as 3000 morgen (6000 acres). The rent could in fact be seldom collected and as time went by these holdings virtually acquired the status of freehold. Not uncommonly a man might have more than one, and practise a kind of transhumance from one to another. This was especially so on the western Karoos, with their chronic deficiency of both winter rain and summer rain. These Boers were essentially cattle farmers, eking out their livelihood by hunting and a minimum of tillage. Their cattle they bred, and augmented by trading with the Hottentots and, later, by raiding the Bantu. Their lack of interest in wool, so marked that various consignments of merinos to the colony were allowed to become diluted and finally lost in uncontrolled breeding with the native hairy sheep, is perfectly understandable in the conditions of the late seventeenth and early eighteenth centuries—there was as yet no factory industry to create a demand for wool that could not be satisfied locally in north-west Europe, and no sign that the Company would be any less arbitrary in buying wool than in buying wheat or wine.

Here, then, was a real frontier and a moving frontier, with northwards and eastwards its own forward screen of elephant hunters and Bushmen hunters. The frontiersman himself, born out of dislike of and resistance to distant authority, achieved almost complete independence with his cattle, his hunting and his distance from the closely settled country of the Cape and the seat of authority at Cape Town, but he achieved it at the cost of an almost self-subsistent life that brought its own penalties, in isolation, impatience of any form of external restraint or even guidance, narrowness of interest and outlook, an extreme fundamentalism in religion and a developed tradition of yielding to the lure of far horizons.

A glance at the relief and rainfall maps of South Africa will disclose a good deal about the physical nature of the frontier area up to about the middle of the eighteenth century and suggest its contrast with Australia beyond the Great Dividing Range and, still more, with the United States beyond the Appalachians. The analogy would have been closer if Australian settlement had commenced at Adelaide and worked eastward, though the advantage would still lie with Australia. Briefly it was a country capable of carrying only a thin population and a scattering of animals, and it needed no very high rate of increase of people or animals to point the desirability of hiving off fresh pioneers who would continue the advance into fresh territory. When the better rainfall areas of the Eastern Cape Province were reached about the middle of the eighteenth century and the Boer advance guards were probing across the Great Fish and then the Kei rivers, contact was joined with the advanced wave of the Bantu, another expansionist people, cattle rearers and part-time cultivators, with a much more highly developed social, political and military organisation than the Hottentots and a recent history of successful territorial advance.

So here was joined a conflict greater in magnitude and fraught with much more serious implications for the future than the previous contacts of the Boers with the Bushmen and the Hottentots. It was conflict in the most literal sense of the term, punctuated by a series of nine Kaffir wars, and the frontier in the narrower sense became and long remained an armed frontier in which the gaining of new land depended on successful fighting. The question was complicated, but not essentially altered, by the assumption of control by England in 1806, and by the consequential injection of the English settlers of 1820 into the advanced border of the frontier zone in the Eastern Cape. In passing we may note that the plan of small tillage farms for these settlers was reminiscent of the original Company's settlement at the Cape, and fore-shadowed the later settlements at Adelaide, Dunedin and

Christchurch—all of them destined to lose their planned character almost from the moment the settlers landed. The basic difficulty, however, lay in the expansion impetus on both sides of the line of contact and in the irreconcilable, and generally misunderstood, concepts of land ownership. Elsewhere only New Zealand, and there only the north and west of the North Island, repeated this phenomenon in any significant way. New Zealand had its Maori wars, won them in the end, largely in the same sort of way in which the Kaffir wars were won, by the irregular forces of the men on the spot, who could and did develop their own local military tactics to meet their own local situation. In each case victory made more land available for white settlement and left a heritage of resentment and distrust on the part of the defeated. But there the parallel ends: New Zealand was fortunate in the smallness of the numbers of the Maori, in their high potential capacity for assimilating European civilisation and reaching European standards, and in acquiring a degree of understanding of and sympathy for the native people, which, partial and inadequate as it was, was yet a unique feature of nineteenth-century white-native contacts.

The Great Trek of 1836 and 1837, preceded by several reconnaissance expeditions, was the culmination of the already long history of Boer dissatisfaction with distant control and their ever-present urge to the acquisition of more and yet more land. The basic attraction was the vast extent of better land reliably reported on the summer rain plateaux of what are now the Orange Free State, the Transvaal and Natal. There were indeed new elements in that the control was now foreign, that the British Colonial Office had banned free grants of Crown land in 1832, that the abolition of slavery in 1834 had been accompanied by quite inadequate compensation, and that the freedom for the Boer to deal with the Bantu as he wished was being severely curbed. These gave a political complexion previously absent and promoted an ambition to found new and independent states, expressed in the organised movement of large bodies of people under chosen leaders to the distant destinations of the High Veld and Natal. There is nothing parallel to this in the other Dominions, and nothing in their history to match the train of events set in motion by the fact of the Trek and the attitudes of mind that supported it. The immediate effect in the Eastern Cape frontier zone was a drastic reduction of both people and occupied land. Walker has estimated that 'by September (1837) some 20,000 souls, "the flower of the frontiersmen" as D'Urban called them, had crossed the Orange River.' Their going made room for sheep on their deserted lands, and it was in the few years following the Great Trek that the great wool-growing enterprise of South Africa began to develop. The times were now propitious, Australia was showing the way, and within twenty years the value of wool exports was to outstrip that of all others combined.

Let us now turn to a more direct look at Australia. Sydney was founded simply as a penal camp, and doubtless its isolation, much more pronounced than that of the Cape, was regarded as an advantage rather than otherwise. Phillip had at first only convicts and soldiers, while the first grants of land were made to officers and the first actual settlers were freed men. Here, as in the Cape, the government was the only buyer of grain, and prices to the farmers were arbitrarily fixed by the government. The obvious requirements were free settlers and capital, and official land policy varied according to the views of the governor and his success or otherwise in getting the approval of the Colonial Office. Free grants of land— sometimes large, as witness the famous Macarthur estate at Camden or the 8,000 acres of the Blaxlands—outright sales, conditional sales with rebates according to the number of convicts maintained or free labourers brought from England, and leases were all tried. As late as 1821, nearly half a century after Phillip's landing, the total population was still below 40,000, and less than one acre per head was in cultivation. Clearly progress had been slow, and such as there was had been accomplished with much friction. There were two outstanding difficulties: the poverty of the soil overlying the Hawkesbury sandstone, that stretched away to the north and south of Sydney and westwards to the crest of the Blue Mountain plateau; secondly, the acute shortage of labour and its frequently unsatisfactory character. Virtually unpaid labour by convicts promised small prospects of advancement for immigrant free labourers, and the mere fact of labour shortage was a discouragement to the entry of capital. Contributory, however, and not insignificant, was the inadequacy of survey, which failed to keep up with alienation of land and often made it impossible to prove title to land when it had been issued and to obtain legal protection against squatters.

It was in the eighteen-thirties that the two movements that were so vitally to affect settlement in Australia, and later in New Zealand, came into full strength and into full conflict. The first was the triumph in England of the ideas of Edward Gibbon Wakefield, their conquest of the Colonial Office and their expression in the formation of companies to organise actual settlements. In Australia South Australia (1836) was the only such colony. In New Zealand Wellington, Nelson, Otago and Canterbury were all founded by such companies, and the latter two benefited considerably from their planning, though there as elsewhere the system was to break down. Wakefield saw colonial settlement as a problem of how to get people and capital on to the land in the right proportions. Australia had the land, England had the capital and the surplus labour. The obvious policy was to sell the land at a 'sufficient price,' use the land fund thus created to finance immigration into the colony, and in due time, but not so soon that they left the existing farms without labour, the labourers would be in a position to buy their own land and employ labour in their turn. Implied in all this are the concepts of compact settlements, small to medium holdings and mixed agriculture on the British model. A prime difficulty not appreciated by the Wakefieldian apostles was how to fix on the 'sufficient price.' If it was to be fixed in relation to the needs of the colony, it might be out of tune with the value of the land and so discourage investment by those who had the capital. If it were fixed to represent a fair value of the land, it would have to vary according to the attractiveness of the land, and in any case might be quite inadequate to promote the development of the colony as visualised by the theorists. Its main weakness, however, was that it completely overlooked the competing attractions of land for squatting beyond the official borders of the colony, and this was the rock on which the Wakefield scheme ultimately broke. In the eighteen-thirties squatting in New South Wales was not new. It had begun with small men, ex-convicts or free men, squatting on crown land or even on alienated but not demarcated holdings on the coastal side of the Great Divide. The squatters rapidly acquired a most unenviable reputation, and the term 'squatter', there as in England, became a term of opprobrium. By the 'thirties, however, the picture was very different. Blaxland, Lawson and Wentworth in 1813 had discovered a practicable, though not easy, route across the Blue Mountains to a 'fine grazing country facing the west.' Others had gone north to the Hunter River and beyond, others again to the south, all to be followed by a stream of successors. The official colony in its expanded form, as proclaimed in 1829, was confined to the Nineteen Counties, and comprised the coastal belt from the Manning to Moruya together with the nearer edge of the western slopes, but already, despite official insistence, this defined an obsolete position.

If it was true (and it was) that the Nineteen Counties were themselves a real frontier area in a strictly pioneering stage, it was no less true that the scantily timbered grasslands beyond the divide promised freedom from cramping governmental restrictions and offered the prospect of great rewards to the successful. Here the sheep, the stabilised but still improving Australian merino, was the pioneering animal, Australian wool was beginning to squeeze the Saxon and Silesian fine wools from the expanding West Riding market, and the 'wool rush' was in full swing. In Roberts's words, '... every able-bodied man thirsted for the bush and pined to ride in the dust behind masses of smelling sheep and live on an unchanging diet of mutton chops, unleavened damper and "post-and-rail" tea.'[2] As with the Cape Boers of nearly a century and a half before, this expansion was against government policy, wedded as it was to concentration of settlement and sale of land, but Governor Bourke, in 1835, recognising that it could not be stopped, eased the situation by issuing annual licences conferring the right to graze stock over as much land as the squatter could manage. Unlike the Boer expansion, however, it was a commercial movement in a commercial age, it had little difficulty with natives, though much with nature, and it advanced with spectacular rapidity so that by 1860 there was a continuous pastoral frontier area from Bass Strait to the Gulf of Carpentaria. Squatter now meant a stockman of substance, the backbone of the country, and the squatters had gathered to themselves the political as well as the economic power of the country.

In New Zealand the process of settlement commenced later and the pattern of development showed marked differences in the two islands. It was the North Island that in 1840 received the first band of colonists organised according to Wakefield's ideas. The forest and swamp of most of the island gave no encouragement to the broad-fronted advance of a pastoral frontier, but demanded rather a slow and painful small-scale war of attrition on those formidable natural obstacles, and success, if and when it came, meant the establishment of small-scale farms in a slow advance of close settlement. There were serious deficiencies in the organisation of the Wellington and Taranaki settlements; and the later Maori Wars, originating mainly out of conflicting conceptions of land ownership, further delayed progress. The South Island on the other hand provided a remarkable parallel to New South Wales. Nelson (1840, an offshoot from Wellington), Dunedin (1848) and Christchurch (1850) were all designed to demonstrate the superiority of the Wakefield system, and all alike, almost from the day of their founding, found their prosperity in the rise of squatting. The grasslands of the eastern side of the South Island, from the Wairau to the Waiau, with only a handful of Maori at a few scattered points, provided similar opportunities to those of New South Wales, though different difficulties. The tussock grass was far from ideal grazing, but it sufficed for the merino. The country it covered was largely mountainous and the slopes were steep. The rivers, fed from the eternal snow were torrential and when in spate with the spring snow melt were fearful obstacles. Winter cold and snow and flooded rivers rather than sun-scorched, drought-smitten plains were the hazards faced by the New Zealand squatter. His first sheep and his methods of handling them came largely from Australia, though he himself was mainly not Australian.

By 1860, then, this grassland frontier had been occupied, essentially by a scatter of great sheep runs on no more secure a tenure than short-period licences to graze. Here and in Australia the squatters could not rest content with that hazardous status, and set themselves to the task of getting complete control of the land they depastured. Only in Queensland, and there not until 1916, did any of the governments take the extreme step of abolishing alienation of land, though in the end all of them reached the point of giving long leases of land in the less attractive areas, the arid plains of the far interior in Australia and the difficult 'high country' of Canterbury and north-west Otago. Elsewhere all governments reserved the right to sell land for closer settlement as population increased and demands for land grew. To evade this danger the squatters adopted many ingenious devices, including the buying of strategically placed pieces of land such as river banks or the land around water holes, possession of which rendered the land behind useless to anyone else. Their measure of success was sufficient to ensure their conversion of most of the desirable land into private estates, consecrated to the golden fleece, but capable so long as it was so consecrated of carrying only an almost negligible population. The squatters in fact had escaped too successfully from the dangers of their insecurity of tenure, and had converted security into a status of privilege that sat ill with the youth of the colonies and the aggressive democracy of the rapidly growing landless populations.

This rapid growth of population was very recent, even in Australia. Not until the eighteen-thirties was there any very significant inflow of free settlers and the disappearance of the distaste and even contempt that the penal settlements of Sydney and Van Diemen's Land had inspired. Capitalistic scepticism of the commercial prospects of these antipodean experiments had been slow to go, and their banishment had not been helped by the early tribulations of the great land companies, the Australian Agricultural Company and the Van Diemen's Land Company, that were given their charters in the middle eighteen-twenties. New Zealand settlement did not begin until the Australian tide had begun to flow, and it started free from the handicap of the early Australian

reputation. The discovery of gold, however, in the 'fifties in
New South Wales and Victoria, in the 'sixties in Otago
stimulated an unprecedented inrush of gold-seekers, few of
whom made fortunes from gold, but very many of whom
remained to contribute a vigorous, independent and unortho-
dox element to the existing pastoral society. The significance
of this at the time lay in the fact that the colonies had
recently acquired responsible government, the solving of land
problems was now a matter for the local colonial governments and the power of the ballot box could be used to
break the 'land monopoly' that stood between the landless
men and the good land fit for close settlement in countries
that were destined to support millions of people in comfort.
The introduction of refrigeration, in 1882, which opened up
vistas of success for small men supplying the European
larders with perishable foodstuffs from small farms intel-
ligently and carefully managed, provided a strong reinforce-
ment to the increasing pressure for closer settlement.

The problem was not solved at once. In each of the
colonies a long series of measures bore witness to the success
of the squatters in defending their interests, but also to the
gradual advance towards what had become the community
ideal of the family farm capable of providing an acceptable
standard of living for a hardworking owner. In detail the
measures varied from colony to colony and from time to
time, but they bore a strong family likeness to one another.
Provision was made against the further alienation of Crown
land in large blocks to individuals; for repurchase and
subdivision of suitable land already alienated; for survey of
farms of size appropriate to the reasonable support of a
family, the size naturally varying according to soil quality, to
rainfall, to relief and elevation, to accessibility; for assistance
to the small settler by government loans at low rates of
interest, by an early form of hire purchase known as deferred
purchase, or by lease with right of purchase. At the same
time conditions of personal occupation and of progressive
values of improvements were enforced to guard against the
danger of mere speculation in Crown land. The gradual
success of such measures ensured the conversion of the better
areas of the pastoral frontier zones into an agricultural

frontier of close settlement capable of supporting an expanding population. In Australia the over-riding general index to relative productivity was found in rainfall, and the gradual decrease of the rainfall inland has permitted a corresponding, though by no means an exactly corresponding, increase in size of holding from the small dairy farm of the New South Wales South coast, for example, through the progressively larger farms of the sheep-wheat belt and the small grazing run to the great run that remains and will remain undivided in the far interior. In the South Island of New Zealand it was not rainfall but relief and elevation that distinguished the more productive from the less productive land, and broadly the smooth lowlands are wholly occupied by farms, typically within the range of 200 to 500 acres, the lower and easier hill country has small runs of several thousand acres, while the great runs necessarily remain in the high country.

In summary Australia and New Zealand had their period of effective settlement at a time when Europe provided an intense demand for commodities, beginning with wool, that they were well fitted to produce. Ample land, scarcity of labour and complete reliance on a distant overseas market encouraged a severity of specialisation that early became a national habit and still distinguishes the farming countryside from that of South Africa with its entirely different tradition. We cannot doubt that if the nineteenth-century colonisation of Australia and New Zealand had been by Chinese instead of by British people, or if the British colonisation had been seventeenth instead of nineteenth century the rural landscapes of these two dominions would have been very different from what they are.

There is little room left for discussion of Canada, and I must content myself with a brief reference to the Prairie Provinces. The Canadian prairies differed from the Southern Hemisphere colonisation areas in almost every respect. Physically they were a great continuous area of smooth surface, admirable soils, grass vegetation, and a climate characterised by the length and severity of the winter. They were in the far interior of a great continent, separated from long settled eastern Canada by the hundreds of miles of rough Canadian Shield and from the Pacific coast by the great cordilleran belt, but marched on the south by the expanding settlement of the United States. Yet they had long been used in the fur trade by the Hudson's Bay Company, which enjoyed special rights over the whole area, and indeed until the coming of the railways no other possible product could have been profitably transported to a market. Furs were in some sense the Prairie equivalent of wool in Australia, but sheep were not a reasonable venture in the Prairie climate. The difficulties were well illustrated by the ill-fated Selkirk ventures at settling the Red River valley, even apart from the hostility of the North-West Company. Preliminary measures to settlement in any effective way, then, included resumption of the land by the Canadian government from the Hudson's Bay Company and the building of railways. So it was not until the last two decades of the nineteenth century that the process of settling these grasslands acquired any significant momentum, and even then its precise course and nature depended on three other elements, all of them borrowed from the experience of Canada's great southern neighbour. One of these was the breeding of wheat types to suit the difficult climatic conditions, and but for the success achieved in breeding rapidly maturing wheats almost the whole of the Prairies would have remained beyond the limit of wheat growing. The second was the Homestead Acts, which extended into the Canadian prairies the quarter section of 160 acres and the regular rectangular pattern of fences and roads already standardised on the prairies of the United States. It may indeed be queried whether the adoption of 160 acres as the standard size of farm was altogether wise in view of the shorter growing season and the more restricted range of possible products than in the more southerly United States, and the pretty continuous increase in the average size of holding over the years tends to support that doubt. Nevertheless it was 160 acres that was decided upon, and it proved large enough for the immediate application in one-crop wheat-growing of the contemporary large scale methods of American farmers. Many of the farmer settlers were themselves immigrants from American farms, still following the frontier that had retreated beyond the bounds of their own country, and they were able to demonstrate in practice the economies in prairie settlement of the great machines and the massive teams of horses. On her prairies, then, Canada solved at one operation the legal, administrative and production problems that had cost South Africa some two centuries, Australia over a century and New Zealand over half a century to solve. That does not mean that the pattern of either settlement itself or the production on which it lives is fixed for ever. It does mean that change can be gradual and evolutionary, produced by individual adjustments as opportunity offers or necessity decrees, and not requiring a social revolution powered by a national dissatisfaction and operated by a political party victorious at the polls.

The aim of this paper has been to suggest how differences in the course, pattern and results of settlement in the overseas dominions have been influenced not merely by the inherent nature of the areas in which settlement took place, but very vitally by the human circumstances of the particular time at which the settlement took place. It is a very large canvas, the brush strokes have been very wide, and even so have left most of the canvas untouched. Much valuable contributory work has been done by historians, especially economic historians, but the corresponding definitive work by geographers still offers considerable opportunities.

REFERENCES

[1] Alexander in his *Moving Frontiers* briefly applies Turner's ideas to aspects of Australian development.

[2] Roberts, S. H. *The Squatting Age in Australia*, p. 11.

X

Air Transport
Some Preliminary Considerations*

A study of the geography of air transport, like that of any other form of transport, is a study of the fitting of the medium into the pattern of world economy. It is concerned with air routes, air bases, nature and amount of air traffic, and their reflex effects on trends in production and population patterns. This essay deals directly with none of these elements. It is rather an attempt to distinguish something of the economic character and problems of the aircraft and the ground installations that are the working tools of commercial air transport, in the hope that it may serve as useful groundwork for the study of the actual and potential geography of air communications.

It was not till 1903 that the first heavier-than-air machine, that of Wilbur and Orville Wright, made a successful flight, and the aeroplane was still in the hit or miss stage when war broke out in 1914. From 1914 to 1918 developments were almost wholly conditioned by military requirements, civil air transport did not begin until 1919, and the Second World War saw again a practically complete concentration of design, production and operation on military types. Now military requirements (particularly in the stress of total war) differ from civil requirements in that within the limits of technical possibility they must be satisfied regardless of costs. The military machine, therefore, however good it is for the purpose for which it was designed is normally a wildly extravagant machine to use for civil purposes,[1] and there are

*Contribution to *London Essays in Geography* (Rodwell Jones Memorial Volume), London School of Economics and Longman's Green and Co., 1951.

limits to the losses that even a nationalized air transport organization can face. But, if the military machine is not directly appropriate to civil air transport, the advances made during the war in the design of air-frames and of power units and in the evolution of ground control devices for military air operations can be adapted for civil purposes, and a period of rapid development in design and operation of civil aircraft and in the general organization of air transport services is a natural corollary of the end of World War II.

Among the characteristics of the aircraft, those most commonly mentioned are speed, small size, independence of surface obstacles and costliness. Only the first three of these are 'prime' characteristics. The fourth, costliness, is derivative from other features, and as much of the rest of this essay will be concerned with cost elements no more need be said on the point here. The small size of the vehicle is of course obvious. The air giants of the present have about equalled the tonnage of the mediaeval ship, and even that statement does not adequately indicate the disparity in size between the air vehicle and the ocean vehicle of today. More significant than over-all size is the pay-load capacity. In the aircraft that capacity is to be measured in weight, rather than in volume, and the proportion it bears to all-up weight of the loaded vehicle is much smaller than for any surface transport vehicle.

Speed of vehicle, in miles per hour while flying, is already high, both absolutely and relatively, and will continue to increase. It is a function partly of the aero-dynamic qualities of the airframe and partly of the power provided. 'Aerodynamic qualities' in this context includes the reduction of headward air resistance (drag) to the lowest possible point by the best possible streamlining of the air-frame as a whole and of all exposed parts, and by the refinement of smoothing of all outside surface. Both lines of attack have necessitated long-sustained, expensive research, and the attainment of the most exacting standards of workmanship. Power is still provided mainly by the orthodox internal combustion engine, and so remarkable have been the advances in design that 3,000 horse-power can be developed from a unit occupying only a few cubic feet. Nevertheless the ratio of engine weight to all-up weight is very high, and is a prime factor in reducing the ratio of pay-load weight to all-up weight as compared with surface vehicles. The other chief element in limiting pay-load weight is the amount of fuel that must be carried—and even the most economical aero-engine is greedy of fuel. A rough average fuel consumption rate may be taken to be rather less than half a pound weight of fuel per horse-power hour. An aircraft, therefore, powered with four 2,000 horse-power engines, uses about a ton and three-quarters of fuel per hour, or about fourteen tons on an eight-hour journey. It must of course carry enough additional fuel to afford a safe margin over and above estimated consumption. The longer the non-stop flight, the more drastically does fuel-load curtail pay-load, and the long distance and endurance records of the past have all been set up by craft that were in effect flying petrol tanks and nothing more. It is equally obvious that highgrade aviation spirit is a very expensive fuel. At half a crown a gallon the fuel cost of the fourteen tons mentioned above is £560. Compared with the orthodox type of aero-engine the newer 'jet' engine gives two significant economies: the weight/power ratio of the engine itself is decidedly less, and the disposable pay-load correspondingly greater, for the same all-up weight and power output; and, secondly, the paraffin fuel, though it is consumed at a comparable rate, is much cheaper than high-octane petrol. The commercial promise of these two sources of reduction of aircraft operating costs need not be laboured, but, important as they are, they are only part, ultimately perhaps only a minor part, of the contribution the 'jet' engine has to offer. Its most distinctive characteristic is that its efficiency increases as atmospheric density decreases. It gives its most efficient output of power at high altitudes, where the bugbear of drag is markedly reduced, where atmospheric turbulence and frequency and severity of icing conditions are noticeably less, but where the petrol aero-engine loses much of the efficiency it has at low levels.

    The significance of this power position lies in the fact that it must be costed against a relatively small weight of pay-load, with the result of high power cost per unit. Given full-loads, some progressive economy is gained with increasing size of aircraft: in general, disposable pay-load weight increases somewhat more rapidly than total weight of loaded aircraft. The advantage gained by the large aircraft in power cost per unit of pay-load may be offset, however, to a greater or smaller degree, at any rate for passenger airliners, by another significant element in direct operating costs. This is the cost of the operating crew. Like the power cost it is large as compared with surface transport, but unlike the power cost it tends to increase with increasing size of aircraft. A passenger train carrying 600 passengers requires no bigger crew than a passenger airliner carrying thirty passengers. In general, while power requirements per ton-mile in air transport may be very roughly averaged as about forty times the requirements in railway transport, crew requirements may be tentatively suggested to be about ten to fifteen times as much. These power and crew costs are the outstanding elements of the direct running costs incurred in the machine itself, most of the others partaking to a greater or smaller degree of the nature of overhead costs.

Among the overhead costs first mention should be made of the initial price of the aircraft. The amount of that price is related on the one hand to the nature of the aircraft itself and of its intricate equipment, and on the other to the conditions of its production. The new aircraft is a miracle of design and construction, but a miracle behind which lies an immense amount of research, experiment and development work, some of it directed specifically to the requirements of the new type, some of it not. The new type must bear its share of these basal overhead costs as well as its own specific costs if the aircraft manufacturing industry is to remain solvent. Nor has the manufacturer of civil aircraft anywhere in the world, except possibly in the United States, been able to avail himself fully of the economies of mass production methods. Apart from the difficulty of maintaining standards of workmanship required to approach closely to perfection, a difficulty that could probably be got over, the limited demand for any particular type has always kept production volume low. In addition obsolescence was extremely rapid before the recent war, and is very unlikely to be any less rapid during the next decade or so. In the nineteen-thirties a new type aircraft on first going into service already had its successor on the drawing-board, and its expectation of profitable working life was only about five years, which meant that the operator had to write off as depreciation some 20 per cent per annum of the intial cost of the machine. For a large airliner that could amount to more than £500 a week, whether the aircraft was employed or not.[2] If costs of this order of magnitude are to be covered by the operation of machines of which only 15 to 25 per cent of the all-up weight can be given to pay-load, then clearly air transport must be able to offer service for which the consuming public is prepared to pay a high price.

The specific service offered by the aircraft is usually said to be speed. More accurately it is saving of time, and this depends on other things as well as on the rate of movement of the aircraft in the air. It depends, for example, on the fact that the aircraft has a large measure of freedom from the effects of surface obstacles to straight line, or great circle, movement. It can save time by saving distance, and just how much distance can, in theory at any rate, be saved in an extreme case may be illustrated by route distances from London to Tokio. In rounded figures they are as follows: by sea via Suez and Singapore, 13,000 miles; via North Atlantic, Canada and North Pacific, 12,500 miles; by the trans-Siberian railway route, 8,600 miles; by great circle via the Arctic, 6,000 miles. It should be noted, however, that flying of regular services along great circle routes of this kind is still a matter for the somewhat distant future. The prime purpose of commercial air services is to move profitable pay-load, and for air services as for surface services those routes that provide the greatest supply of and demand for such pay-load movement will be the major world routes. It is not without relevance to add that such routes are precisely those on which the provision of airports, fuel, servicing facilities and so on are most easily and cheaply provided. It might be urged that since the aircraft is a small vehicle there should be no difficulty in filling it with through traffic,[3] so that the availability of point to point traffic would become a matter of indifference, and regular, if not frequent, express services could be flown over 'empty' routes. There is some force in this as an expression of faith, and the view may possibly be justified at some future time, but for the present and the more foreseeable future world-spanning great circle routes do not come into the picture—absence of bases and restricted economical range of aircraft alike forbid them.

Nor is the great circle route necessarily available even for the shorter distances. One of the major calamities of commercial aviation in pre-war Europe was the prevalence of government restriction of permissible routes over national teritory. The beginnings of this policy can be seen in the acceptance by the Paris Convention in 1919 of the complete and exclusive sovereignty of any power over the whole atmosphere above its national territory and territorial waters, with, as a corollary, the decision that any power might proclaim 'prohibited' areas and take any necessary steps to exclude foreign aircraft from such areas. It was left to Germany with its clandestine rearmament programme after 1933 to carry the idea to its logical conclusion, the prohibition of all foreign aircraft from using the German air except along a few specified narrow corridors of entry and of passage. Germany was by no means the only sinner, and the great majority of international routes in Europe was thus arbitrarily penalized. In the post-war world there is little indication that Russian treatment of foreign aircraft over U.S.S.R. territory will be any more generous than that of pre-war Germany. Complete freedom from inter-state restrictions of this kind over the continental territory of the U.S.A. was a major advantage enjoyed by American lines.[4]

A further point that is relevant to the amount of time-saving that air services can provide is the number and length of halts a vessel must make on its journey. This is a function of a number of variables, including, for example, the range and capacity of the aircraft type, the nature of the route and the organization and equipment of the airway and the airports. Much of the potential advantage of the early Imperial Airways route to India, and later to the Far East and to Australia, was still-born through the limitation of flying to daylight hours only. Real success on long trunk routes demands uninterrupted flight by night as well as by day. Up till 1939 commercial night flying was limited to routes provided with 'air lights', visual beacons whose distance from each other depended on visibility and varied from an average of about fifteen miles over Western Europe and Northeastern U.S.A. to about forty miles in the clearer atmosphere of the Middle East. By the end of the war radar installations had displaced visual beacons as the appropriate markers for the airways, but off the war routes little progress had been made, or has since been made, in providing the necessary equipment.

Apart from night flying the number of halts on a trunk route is largely a question of finding the optimum length of stage for the type of aircraft in use. This is a mean somewhere between the extremes of having a stage so long that fuel-load eats disastrously into the weight available for pay-load and a stage so short that even though a relatively large pay-load be carried all the way landing fees, servicing and total time taken become excessive. Technical developments imply in general a longer optimum stage for large aircraft and a progressive advance towards eliminating more and more intermediate halts by express services on the long trunk routes. It will be obvious that this will apply with particular force to aircraft designed to give their most economical performance at very high altitudes. For a really effective 'strato-line' it will cease to be a question of what is the longest stage that can be flown economically and become a question of what is the shortest stage that will justify the long climb upwards to the effective operating altitude.

At present, length of flying stage is not always a matter of choice. Up to 1939 it was still true that there was no world net of air routes comparable to the world net of sea routes. The Atlantic Ocean still formed a major gap, though two routes already crossed the Pacific Ocean. The problem of the 1,800 mile gap between West Africa and Brazil had been practically solved, and an experimental attack on the North Atlantic by flying-boat was in progress when war broke out. Here Greenland and and Iceland seem to provide stepping stones conveniently spaced to reduce to manageable proportions the distances of open ocean to be crossed, and this route approximates fairly closely to a great circle route between eastern North America and North-Western Europe, but possible airfield sites on these stepping stones have such a high proportion of bad flying weather that it was considered preferable to accept the penalty of longer total journey and longer ocean crossing for the sake of less difficult weather conditions at airports. Up to the end of the war, while the civil services were still run by flying-boat, two routes were used according to season. The summer route, London-Foynes-Gander-New York, had an ocean stage of 2,000 miles from Foynes to Gander in the total of 3,600 miles. The winter route, London-Foynes-Azores-Bermuda-New York, had its longest ocean stage, 2,100 miles between Azores and Bermuda, and a total length of 4,700 miles. With the land 'plane services inaugurated at the end of the war the Foynes-Gander route has become the all-season route. Even so the ocean crossing causes fuel-load to cut significantly into pay-load, and is probably twice as long a stage as operators would choose if their choice were free. The trans-Pacific routes from the United States to the Philippines and East Asia and to New Zealand are tenuous links making use of island stepping stones too widely spaced for maximum economy, and they diverge very widely from the great circles joining their terminals.

The day, then, of the non-stop express, or even 'limited,' service, flown in very long stages along strict great circle routes, is not yet. In the more foreseeable future the major contribution to be made lies in the provision of more and better services in and between the closer areas of dense population and heavy production. On the shorter routes these services can be flown point to point great circle, so far as governmental prohibitions permit. Ultimately the sphere of air transport is surely to provide a world network of routes with a range of specialized services, attuned to the varied requirements of different regions and different kinds of traffic, and analogous to the variety of service offered by ocean, by rail and by road transport each in its own domain. The general picture no doubt will include a backbone of express services of large, fast, high-flying aircraft, using first-class airports along intercontinental routes and supplemented by slow services and branch services catering for intermediate airports along the trunk routes and for airports not on them. But an essential prerequisite is that air services shall, in addition to speed, provide standards of safety and regularity of the same order as those already achieved by surface transport.

For safety the airliner is already a more efficient instrument than is commonly realized. Progressive improvement of the ability of the air-frame to withstand the severest stresses, the increase of the power and reliability of engines and the development of instrument flying have made the airworthy aircraft an effective answer to the meteorological hazards confronting it, and considerable progress has been made in dealing with such special problems as icing. The high degree of safety already achieved may be illustrated by the American civil aviation record for 1943 of 51,300,000 miles flown per accident,[5] a record very little inferior to that of American railways and superior to that of American roads. In general the meteorological hazards diminish with height above ground, but even in the stratosphere they do not disappear, and the atmospheric turbulence experienced there, though much less pronounced than in the troposphere, presents nevertheless a considerable problem at the very high speeds that are necessary to justify stratosphere flight.[6] The greatest risk of accident, however, occurs and will probably continue to occur during take-off and landing. Here fog is the chief enemy, more particularly in landing, and, despite the advances made with devices for blind landing, diversion of aircraft from fog-bound to fog-free airfields is still preferred.

Regularity has been achieved to a much less satisfactory degree than safety. Indeed the good safety record has been gained to a considerable extent by the sacrifice of regularity. Apart from daily aberrations such as keeping outgoing aircraft grounded or diverting incoming aircraft in bad flying weather, both winter services and night services have shown up to the present relatively poor results in number and dependability. In 1939, for example, European winter routes had barely 40 per cent of the mileage of summer routes, and were subject to much more frequent interruption. The performance on night routes was even less good. Much of the reason is to be found in the fact that dependability of flying services is as much a matter of ground facilities and organization as it is of aircraft and aircrew, and only in limited areas have the necessary ground developments kept pace with the evolution of the aircraft and its various instrumental aids to flying.

The hub of an airways system is the airport, the counterpart to the seaport, and, like the ocean port, increasing in magnitude and complexity with the increase in size and speed of the vehicles concerned. A modern first-class airport makes heavy demands on space, equipment and surface communications. It must provide taking-off, landing, parking, fuelling, repair and overhaul facilities for aircraft; lighthouses and beacons; flying control accommodation and equipment; an efficient meteorological service; radio and radar installations; customs office; post and telegraph office. It should also, and in the future will certainly have to, provide waiting rooms, shops, hotels, cinemas. Finally it must have fast services by surface transport, as frequent as air time-tables require, to the heart of the region served. Of these items— none of them distinguished by cheapness—the most expensive are those directly concerned with the landing ground itself.

The first point to notice is the area of land occupied. This is conditioned primarily by the number, length and arrangement of the runways, and the essential fact here is that modern large airliners, with heavy wing loading and high stalling speeds, touch down at not less than 80 miles an hour, many of them at more than 100 miles an hour, and some at more than 120 miles an hour. Runways, then, must be of great length and strength. Even main runways have not, indeed, yet reached the 5,000 yards' length foreseen in 1944 by the Air Ministry. [7] but rapid increase in length has marked the course of events in recent years. A width of 200 yards is already standard practice for runways in the larger airports. The orthodox lay-out of runways is basically $\times$ with the chief leg running in the direction of the prevailing wind, and this design lends itself to expansion and elaboration to handle increasing traffic at a busy terminal.[8] From the point of view of cost the significant feature of this land area is that it is situated within the range of suburban, if not indeed urban, land values. Cost of runways, which are built in solid concrete, preferably with a middle course of a material that will give a degree of resilience to the structure, and with a surface coating to damp down somewhat the initial landing shock, added to the site cost, goes far to explain the estimate, for example, of over £31,000,000 for the London Airport (Heathrow), a capital expenditure which at 3 per cent would require an annual revenue of £600,000 to cover airport overhead costs alone.

To the air transport operator the airfield costs are direct charges, since such share of them as he pays is chiefly in the form of landing fees. Clearly the real incidence of airport costs is related to the density of the traffic, and it would seem that unless traffic reaches the maximum capacity of the airport for a large part of every day landing fees adequate to cover airport costs would be crippling to the operators and would ensure the defeat of the purpose of the airport. Airport owners are commonly public authorities, either local or national, and able therefore at the expense of the rate-payer or the taxpayer to subsidize the airlines by charging landing fees at less than full cost rate. Whatever the view that may be held of the immediate or the ultimate desirability of such a practice, it must be recognized that part of the real cost of air transport is being paid by the community at large, and that until the practice ceases air transport remains in the nurseling stage, unable to stand on its own feet in level competition with other transport media.

On the subject of airport sites it might be mentioned in parenthesis that while they must be as close as possible to the centres of the great cities they serve, they are still somewhat distant as compared with the stations serving land transport, and the time taken in getting to and from the airports ('dead' time) may considerably affect the total time of journey. Just how significant the dead time is depends on the length of the flight and on the speed and frequency of ground services. In the extreme case, as, for example, between London and Birmingham before the war, it could neutralize the whole advantage of the greater travelling speed of the aircraft. More generally, it was the reason why, so long as aircraft speeds did not much exceed 100 miles per hour development of internal air services was slow in Great Britain, with its short distances and close networks of road and railway carrying fast and frequent services. The contrast is striking on the one hand with the trunk Imperial routes to West Africa, to South Africa, to the Far East and to Australia and New Zealand, and on the other hand with the internal air routes of the U.S.A., U.S.S.R., and Australia, with their continental magnitude and more open or even rudimentary networks of surface communications. Every increase of aircraft speeds and every addition to the frequency of air services reduces the effect of 'dead' time even in such countries as Great Britain or Belgium, and the advent of efficient helicopter service at the airports might well dispel the last vestige of such effect.

Other aspects of ground organization necessary to enable civil air transport to translate its potential contribution into actual performance include standardization of classification and control of airways, of traffic control procedure at and between airports, of radar equipment and service (including signals) not only at airports but at all necessary intermediate points, of meteorological information (actual and forecast), of rule of the road, of design of air navigation maps, and so on. These are obviously matters for international action, and international agreement in air matters is notoriously difficult to achieve. The inter-war organization of I.C.A.N. (International Commission of Air Navigation) achieved much, but there was much that it failed to achieve, and the very success of war-time technical developments has added new fields in which lack of uniformity in international practice will hamper the efficiency of air service operation. The Chicago Conference, 1944, gave small hope that post-war differences of national opinion would be noticeably less acute then pre-war.

These are technical and diplomatic matters, important not so much for their own sake as for the assistance they give, or do not give, to air service operators in finding a solution to their central commercial problem. This problem has already been indicated in part, but may be elaborated a little here. Since a very high proportion of total costs is represented by overhead costs, economy can be achieved only be spreading the costs over the maximum possible number of freight units. This implies a traffic flow sufficient to keep airports fully engaged, to eliminate empty cargo space from the individual aircraft, and to reduce idle time of aircraft to the essential minimum required for adequate maintenance. Such a traffic flow would have spectacular effects in the reduction of costs per ton mile, and would permit profitable working at low freight charges for suitable freight. But until some such flow is achieved low freight charges would merely increase losses and hasten bankruptcy. That is the dilemma which it was the purpose of government assistance to resolve, but government assistance before 1939, influenced by non-commercial considerations of national prestige and military security, for the most part degenerated into a bitter subsidies race in which the prime purpose of making civil air transport an independent, self-supporting element in the transport equipment of the world was completely lost.

REFERENCES

[1] This is not wholly of necessity a matter of direct running costs. The effect may be indirect. The Lancaster bomber, for instance, designed to carry a very concentrated load close to its axis of balance, would give a much poorer performance with the same weight of load distributed throughout the fuselage.

[2] This extreme rapidity of depreciation of the aircraft implies also rapid depreciation of manufacturer's specialized plant with further addition to overhead costs.

[3] Cf. E. P. Warner, Wilbur Wright Memorial Lecture to the R.A.S., 1943: 'In the United States before the war, of the passengers using domestic airlines:

(i) half travelled 250 miles or less
(ii) three-quarters travelled 400 miles or less
(iii) nine-tenths travelled 750 miles or less.

Even in air-minded U.S.A., through passenger traffic from terminal to terminal probably amounted to less than one-tenth of total passengers.'

[4] It is not wholly without significance that the flying-boat, when it used foreign seaports, inherited something of the age-old tolerance extended to foreign shipping in the commercial harbours of the world, and escaped some at any rate of the new suspicion that met the land 'plane.

[5] Civil Aeronautics Administration.

[6] Cf. Air Commodore L. G. S. Payne, in the *Daily Telegraph*, April 25, 1947

[7] Pamphlet, 'Technical Characteristics of Aerodromes,' 1944

[8] The more recent conception of a tangential lay-out of runways would appear to have the merits of reducing the risk of collisions on the ground and of economizing airport area. It is said, however, to have introduced difficulties of ground control of airborne traffic, and has not yet found general acceptance.

XI

The I.B.G.: Retrospect & Prospect*

I

The custom of having a presidential address at the Annual Meeting of the Institute is a comparatively new one, and I find myself regretting the care-free days when no such demand was made on the President of the Institute. The blame, it seems, must be laid on Mr. J. N. L. Baker, whose full-scale address, 'Geography and politics: The geographical doctrine of balance',[1] given in 1947, he explicitly refused to call a presidential address. Nevertheless, we find Professor A. Austin Miller in the following year, 1948, explaining that his address, 'The analysis and dissection of maps',[2] had been prepared at the request of the Council as a formal presidential address. His example has been faithfully followed, though whether renewed pressure by the Council has been required on each occasion I am in no position to say. Certainly my own Council gently but firmly insisted that this year's President should not take it upon himself to break the tradition, which, recent though it be, they regard as already binding. Committed, then, to the task, I found myself with relatively little choice of a topic upon which to address you. The outstanding feature of this particular meeting is that it is the twenty-first birthday of our Institute, and a twenty-first birthday is no unimportant occasion in the life of an individual or of an institution. It seemed fitting, therefore, that some attempt should be made to survey those twenty-

*Presidential Address to the Institute of British Geographers: printed in the *Transactions and Papers* of the Institute, 20, 1954

one years, to bring to the younger members some idea of the story of the early hopes and struggles of their organization, and to attempt some assessment of what has been accomplished and what are the tasks that lie ahead. What I have to say will be in no sense a detached, impersonal, critical history. Such a history may well be produced for the jubilee of the Institute or for its centenary, but for me such an attempt is impossible. The peculiarity of my position is that for the whole of those twenty-one years, with the solitary exception of the year 1952, I have been continuously in office—with the almost inevitable result that I have developed, if not a possessive parent complex, at any rate an intimacy of attachment that is quite inimical to an aloof, impartial examination of the record. If, however, what I say is essentially personal, I shall as far as possible avoid mere reminiscence, though I may on occasion be compelled by incompleteness of the records to rely on memory rather than on the primary document.

II

It is almost always difficult to put a finger precisely on the beginning of a movement or an organization, but for the I.B.G. I am going to risk the selection of a day in January 1931, when Dr. S. W. Wooldridge, Dr. H. A. Matthews[3] (then of Birkbeck College, later of Beford College, London) and I were lunching together. The talk turned to the research work that geographers were doing and the lack of opportunities for publishing the results. There was nothing very new about that. Probably most of the younger geographers of the country had at one time or another commented on the same thing: certainly each of us three had had similar conversations with other colleagues. The general situation was, indeed, curiously similar to that which has recently been exercising the minds of some of our Institute members. The years following the First World War had witnessed a great expansion of our subject in the schools and universities. In the universities, Liverpool and London had created the first full university chairs of geography in 1917. Other universities soon followed and still others created departments of geography. Staffing, it is true, was on a very meagre scale judged by present-day standards, but the increase in the total number of academic geographers during the 1920s was, nevertheless, quite remarkable. Most of the appointments, even to responsible posts, were of relatively young men, men with ideas and energy, men who were conscious of their opportunities and their responsibilities, even though they were heavily overburdened with teaching and administrative duties. Publication facilities, however, lagged behind the growing demand. The *Geographical Journal*, in spite of its twelve issues a year, was able to spare little space for academic geography, which lay outside the sphere of competence or interest of its large lay membership. Further, the Society had for years been financially pinched to pay for its new house and site, and its series of Supplementary Papers, which might have provided an outlet for much good academic work, had accordingly been discontinued. *Geography*, under the inspiring editorship of Professor H. J. Fleure, and reflecting the massive growth of the Geographical Association, had blossomed from a terminal into a quarterly periodical of enlarged size, and generous treatment was given to academic contributors; but the editor had already gone as far as he could without sacrificing the legitimate professional interests of the great body of teacher members, and no further concession seemed possible. The *Scottish Geographical Magazine* was understandably hardening its policy in favour of work on Scotland or work by geographers in Scotland. The publication pinch was, therefore, less acutely felt in the Scottish departments of geography, and for that reason there was perhaps less enthusiasm in Scotland for the new venture.

The triangular discussion over lunch, which I have already mentioned, differed from others of its kind only in the fact that a decision was taken to try to change the situation. The first step was to convene a meeting of all junior staff of the London schools of geography, and this meeting was held at King's College on February 8th, 1931. No minutes were kept, but I think I am correct in giving the attendance as eleven: Dr. Wooldridge, Mr. H. J. Wood, Mr. S. H. Beaver, and Mr. W. G. East (Joint King's College, London—London School of

Economics), Mr. Buchanan, Mr. R. E. Dickinson and Mr. G. Tatham (University College), Dr. Matthews and Mr. H. C. K. Henderson (Birkbeck College), Dr. D. K. Smee (Bedford College) and Miss B. M. Tunstall (the sole Geography lecturer at East London College, now Queen Mary College). That meeting endorsed the need for a new avenue of publication, decided that a professional organization of geographers, as comprehensive as possible,[4] gave the best hope of initiating and maintaining it, and even proceeded to sketch in some preliminary ideas of organization and management. A summary report of the discussion, prepared by Dr. Wooldridge, was sent to Professor C. B. Fawcett, with the request that he should discuss it with his London senior colleagues, and, if they supported the idea, transmit it to the Convenor of the Conference of Heads of Geography Departments,[5] the only organization then in existence concerned solely with University geography. There is no record of the proceedings of a meeting of the London professors and readers, but a letter of Professor Fawcett's mentions that such a meeting was held. In due course the proposal found pride of place on the agenda of the Heads of Departments' Conference, held at the House of the Royal Geographical Society on September 24th, 1931. A parallel meeting of the other British academic geographers was held at the same time, the attendance being greatly helped by the fact that the British Association for the Advancement of Science was holding its centenary meeting in London. No minutes appear to have been kept of either meeting, but a joint committee of ten members[6] was appointed 'to explore the position and to make a report and recommendations to a meeting of university geographers'. This, incidentally, marks the end of the artificial and largely accidental division of academic geographers into heads of departments and the rest.

This committee was the first of three, all engaged on essentially the same task. It sent out a circular, outlining the events leading to its formation, listing the proposals in hand and asking for information on publishable work completed or in preparation. Views and suggestions were invited, especially on the proposal that an annual membership subscription of £3 would be necessary. Of sixty-eight replies received, forty-three approved the formation of an association and promised to become members, fifteen were doubtful but did not give a firm refusal and were, on the whole, sympathetic, while ten declined to have anything to do with such an association if it were formed. This was a very satisfying result so far as general support for a professional organization of geographers was concerned, especially since the arrival of the committee's circular coincided with a notification from the Inland Revenue of heavier income tax imposts, and in some cases with an announcement by university authorities of salary cuts—unpleasant manifestations in academic life of the onset of the great depression of the 1930s. In detail, however, there was a most bewildering variety of views on the aims and organization of the new body. Almost the only point on which there was general agreement was that a membership fee of £3 was too high. The committee, having considered this material, drew up proposals for a constitution and reported them to a general meeting in London in January 1932, but it took two more preliminary committees, one appointed by that January 1932 meeting,[7] one by another general meeting held at York in September 1932,[8] and, finally, a drafting committee[9] of the Inaugural Council to produce a constitution that was acceptable in content and wording to an adequate majority of members. The drafting committee's efforts were considered, and on each occasion amended, at three successive meetings of the Inaugural Council during 1933. They were finally passed by the general meeting in January 1934, but only after more amendments had been made.

Difficulties in the framing of constitutions are a quite normal feature, but here the difficulties were less those of finding the right words to give precise and binding effect to the desires of the people concerned than those of reconciling different views. Perhaps the most widespread obstacle was the tendency to regard the proposal to found a new body as a direct attempt to sabotage the Royal Geographical Society and the Geographical Association. Competition with these senior organizations was never intended by the sponsors, and was explicitly disclaimed, but many of their colleagues found it difficult to see how a direct clash could be avoided. Sir

Halford Mackinder, for instance, forecast in a sympathetic letter to Dr. Wooldridge, which, incidentally, was probably his last direct contribution to the affairs of academic geography, '. . . in the long run you will find your Institute up against the Society, whatever your intentions. . . . You and the Society will sooner or later be competing for the best of the same kind of writing.' Mackinder clearly overestimated the speed with which the Society would or could make such a drastic change in its publication policy, but, even so, he differed profoundly from some of the other critics in using his forecast not as an argument against forming the Institute but merely as a warning that it 'would do well carefully to consider its relations with the R.G.S.' and also to make sure of the adequacy of its financial basis. There were fears, too, of the effect that the formation of the Institute might have on the Geographical Association. University geographers had been active in the Association since its foundation: Herbertson had been one of its editors; Fleure was the current editor; no conference of the Association lacked contributions by university teachers; and *Geography* normally devoted a not inconsiderable proportion of its space to short research papers by university workers. The Association was, indeed, the recognized vehicle for the dissemination of the University stimulus through the teaching body, and it was further claimed that the conferences of the Association provided adequate occasion for academic geographers to meet to discuss common problems and to keep in touch with current research. From our present vantage point it is easy to see that the worst of those fears have not been realized. Relations with the Royal Geographical Society have never been strained and have, indeed, become more cordial as the years have passed. This may have been due in part to the deliberate action of the Institute, in its early years, of publishing only work of monograph length and avoiding competition for short papers. Much more, however, it seems to me, the reason lay in the fact that the Institute was not merely an agency for the publication of geographical work. True, the initial impulse towards its formation had come entirely from the search for a further publishing medium, but even before it was formed other functions had been visualized, and ever

since its formation its character as a professional organization, focusing the professional interests of mainly professional geographers, has been of great significance to members
and has drawn widespread and willing recognition of its
unique position in geography in the United Kingdom. As one
example of this recognition might be mentioned the grant in
1946 by the Royal Society of the right of the Institute to
have a representative on the National Committee for Geography, a representation that was raised to two in 1952,
when the President of the Institute was constituted an *ex
officio* member.

With the Geographical Association the connection of
academic geographers has remained close and warm: academic geographers are active, often prominent, participators
in the central direction of the Association and in the work of
the local branches. There has, however, developed a regrettable clash of interest between the two organizations in
respect of their January meetings. For many years the
Institute carefully dovetailed its meetings with those of the
Association at the London School of Economics, holding
them only at such times as were devoted by the Association
to matters of purely school interest. This was an acknowledg-
ment that the two bodies had much in common, that
practically all Institute members were members also of the
Association, and that 'Be ye members one of another' was a
good professional and practical as well as an ethical com-
mandment. In recent years, as members well know, the touch
on these occasions has been less close, but, regret it as we
may, and most of us do, we have to recognize that it is
inherent in the growth in size and maturity of the Institute,
whose proceedings can no longer be crammed into a few
interstices of the meetings of the older and larger body. A
partial break in the tradition came in January 1948, when the
Institute as the guest of the Royal Geographical Society held
its meetings at the House of the Society. With the Oxford
meeting in January 1949, the first to be held outside
London, the break became, and seems likely to remain,
virtually complete.

This background was one of the main elements conditioning diverse views on publication policy: the other was cost,

the significance of the cost element deriving from the stark expectation of an initial membership of probably not more than fifty–and this at a time when the Royal Geographical Society counted over 6000 and the Geographical Association some 4000 members. One section strove to ensure that the Institute would undertake no direct publication at all. Their plan was to subsidize an increase in the size of the *Geographical Journal* and *Geography* to enable these journals to publish more academic work: this, it was contended, could be done for a modest subscription of not more than £1 per head. Fortunately, this scheme received little support: the practical difficulties in carrying out such a policy and the scope it would give for misunderstanding with both the Society and the Association are sufficiently obvious to need no stressing. Of those who favoured direct publication the more impetuous contended for a regular journal, the more cautious for the publication of longer works, precisely those for which outlets were most conspicuously lacking. The only decision taken, and the only one necessary, at the inaugural meeting in January 1933, was that publication would be undertaken and that obvious competition with the two senior bodies would be avoided. The decision to limit publication to monographs was a decision of the Council. That it was regarded as a sound decision in the circumstances may be deduced from the fact that it was never seriously questioned up to the outbreak of the Second World War in 1939.

At this point it may be appropriate to consider the actual course of publication and the way in which it was managed. The original constitution obliged the Council to appoint an editorial board 'to report upon material submitted for publication and to supervise publications authorized by the Council'. These were somewhat amorphous terms of reference, the only clear point being that authority for publication rested with the Council. The task of refereeing would have to be done by the people most suited to the work concerned, irrespective of whether they were on the editorial board or not, and a report had to be made to Council. Up to the end of 1935 the Board had been able to meet only once, and that was at a joint meeting with Council to discuss principles. At the last Council meeting of 1935 it was decided to cease appointing anyone outside the Council to the Editorial Board, which thus became merely a small committee of Council. The committee remained in practice the three officers, president, secretary and assistant secretary, and from that time the effective editorial duties were part of the responsibility of the Secretary, until an amendment of the Constitution, in 1952, created a single editor responsible directly to the Council.

The joint meeting, mentioned above, of the Editorial Board and the Council no doubt grew in part out of the anomalous position of the Board, but it was precipitated by fears that much of the purpose of the Institute was being thwarted by captious refereeing. It was already (September 1934) on record that four works had been declined before the first one was accepted, and members were at a loss to comprehend the standards that were being demanded. In the replies to the original questionnaire, and at the general meetings, many members had insisted that, if the Institute were to publish at all, it must maintain adequate academic standards. That view was accepted as reasonable, but the publication of only one work in five suggested that standards were being set impossibly high by referees and, further, that they were not being uniformly applied. The joint meeting of Council and Editorial Board, accepting that it was part of the purpose and the policy of the Institute to assist younger members to publish their research, laid down two rules that may well be re-emphasized today: (i) that it was *not* necessary that work should be fully mature or finally authoritative, and (ii) that referees should try to be *helpfully* critical, making suggestions, where desirable, for improvement of content, method or presentation. It would ill-become your president to gird at his colleagues who freely give valuable time and energy to refereeing papers, but I cannot help feeling that our referees are still inclined, on occasion, to set perfection as their standard, and I find myself wondering whether that reflects a certain lack of confidence in the maturity of our subject and a certain inferiority complex vis-á-vis our colleagues in neighbouring disciplines.

III

Meantime, what of the development of the Institute itself? The general meeting at York in September 1932 had agreed that all existing and past members of staff of departments of geography in the United Kingdom should have the right for a limited time to become original members. In all other cases election would be by the Council, and candidature would be welcomed from any geographer, whether university teacher or not. At a Council meeting on April 30th, 1933, the Secretary reported the membership as only thirty-nine, a somewhat disappointing figure when set against the promises and the expressions of sympathy that the joint committee's circular had brought forth; but, by the end of 1934, when the right to claim original membership expired, seventy-three current and former teachers of geography in United Kingdom universities had exercised their right, and several other geographers had been elected to membership. By December 1938, total membership had grown to only eighty-one, of whom all but thirteen were university teachers. The gain in 1939 was small and the outbreak of the Second World War ended the activities of the Institute for six years, but the pre-war period of quiet consolidation had given a firm foundation for the spectacular development of the post-war years. The new growth was directly related to the great expansion of university departments of geography, and the new recruits to membership continued to be mainly university teachers. If we omit student members, for whom a constitutional amendment provided in 1947, the Institute has grown since 1948 by an average of thirty-four new members per annum (in 1949 alone there was sixty-three elections to membership), and its membership now stands at about four times that of 1938. Against average attendances at annual general meetings of between 30 and 50 before the war, we mustered 120 at Oxford in 1949, over 160 at Cambridge in 1950 and Oxford in 1951, while remote Aberystwyth drew 120 in 1952, and Bedford College, London, some 200 in 1953. These numbers suggest some loss of the early intimacy of personal contact and freedom of discussion, a loss, however, which has largely, if not wholly, been offset by the institution of fully residential meetings, with their opportunities for informal contact.

This contrast between pre-war and post-war conditions provokes two lines of thought. In the first place, one is tempted to wonder when, and if, cessation of growth will come. The treasurer, Mr. B. H. Farmer, at the annual general meeting at Bedford College, in January 1953, forecast a measure of stability of membership by 1955. Year by year since 1946 I have myself been making somewhat similar forecasts of stability within a year or two, and every fresh year as it came has proved me wrong. Nevertheless, I still find it difficult to visualize a stable membership of much over 400, and Mr. Farmer's estimate may yet prove right, with a figure of approximately 400. The other reflection concerns the respective amounts of publication actually achieved in the two periods. That the pre-war society, with only about eighty members, and an annual fee income of only some £150, could publish six substantial monographs in five years suggests at first sight a relatively poor performance since the war. It has to be remembered, however, that not a single monograph was published without a grant-in-aid from a university, and some of the grants, notably those from the University of London, lifted a considerable part of the weight from the Institute. Grants have not altogether ceased since the Institute turned from monographs to collections of short papers, but they have been much less prominent, and have usually been limited to some assistance for illustrations. Costs have gone up three- or four-fold, and these heavy costs have been accompanied by exasperating delays at the printers, which in turn have tended to increase costs still further. If I may use a commercial analogy, our capital appreciation in members has offset and masked the uncomfortable fact that for most of the post-war period we have been producing at a loss, and our healthy-looking balances may be not so much proof of prosperity as evidence of a volume of publication distinctly below a desirable minimum.

We have, it will be noticed, come back again to publication, and have thereby remained in tune with the general meetings of the Institute, where publication has always been a major item in discussion. It is appropriate, therefore, to consider post-war publication in a little more detail. The first general meeting after the war, in January 1946, saw a lively discussion on a hope expressed in the secretary's report that the Institute would make its Transactions more representative of its activities by publishing collections of short papers in addition to, or in lieu of, full-scale monographs. The early fears of alienating supporters by following a policy of competition with the older bodies had largely been forgotten in the six years of war, when greater issues had been at stake. The Royal Geographical Society, too, in announcing its decision to revive its Supplementary Papers, seemed to have shouldered the responsibility that the Institute had earlier borne, and to have freed our resources, if we so chose, for use in other ways. The suggestion was adopted with enthusiasm by the meeting, which added a further directive that the publication of papers read by members at the meetings should be regarded as a primary aim of the Institute and a first charge upon its funds. *Transactions and Papers, 1946* was the first fruit of this change of heart, and set the general pattern for succeeding regular publications. The only publication, indeed, since the resumption of our activities, that has not conformed to this pattern is Professor Fleure's *Some problems of society and environment.*[10] The substance of that work was delivered as three public lectures in the University of London, and its issue by the Institute was rendered possible by a grant from the University of London of such proportions that it covered virtually the full cost. Apart from that, an average output of eight papers a year (including three presidential addresses) has been maintained since 1948, and many of these papers have been of quite substantial length.

This achievement does not at first sight look very imposing, but, when it is remembered that it represents a volume of research papers comparable with that published in any one year before the war by the Royal Geographical Society, the Royal Scottish Geographical Society and the Geographical Association put together, it assumes a rather better appearance. On the other hand, measured against the greatly increased number of active workers, this output quite certainly indicated, even when allowance is made for work published in the other journals, an even less effective outlet for research results than the Institute was founded to improve. Clearly, the Institute cannot afford to rest satisfied with the current state of affairs, and it has, indeed, in recent years shown no disposition to do so. Part of the difficulty, possibly a major part, has arisen from conditions in the printing industry for most of the post-war period. Chronic and intolerable delays were encountered in putting through the press every post-war publication up to and including No. 15, and the reflection that authors and editors everywhere else were having the same sort of exasperating experience gave little comfort. No doubt it was good for our short-term financial balances, and on the short-term view we were in a position to support more publication, though whether in the long run our finances would have remained sound in such a case may be another matter. Rate of progress through the press has already been improved, helped by the transference of our printing to the Alden Press of Oxford, a move that has the added advantage of permitting immediate personal contact between editor and printer. This move, too, has done something to reduce costs, but not to the drastic extent demanded on occasion by some of the more vehement critics of Council policy. That policy, while admitting the need for cheaper production, has consistently recognized also the need for maintaining the established format of the publications of the Institute. That format was adopted, largely at the instance of Professor Fawcett, in order to give a page size big enough and a paper quality good enough to permit adequate reproduction of maps and diagrams anywhere in the publication. We may well agree that in that respect we have been well served, and the obvious disadvantages of an alteration of style in a series further point the wisdom of the Council's reluctance to be rushed into a change. Meantime a group of members of the Institute, acting as private individuals and drawing on potential contributors outside, as well as inside, the Institute, has entered on the attempt to supplement the official publications of the Institute by a series of smaller and more cheaply produced journals devoted wholly to academic papers. We shall watch the experiment with interest and sympathy.

IV

The high lights of the career of the Institute have un-questionably been its January meetings. They have always been well attended, on more than one occasion in recent years to the extent of 70 per cent of the total membership. Therein, by the way, lies the justification for the relaxation in 1952 of the rule that required a postal ballot on any motion to alter the constitution—though it may well be thought that this change was not made until the original constitution had suffered so many amendments that it is unlikely to require any more for some considerable time. Amending of the constitution was indeed a favourite form of indoor sport of the Institute, the first proposal for an amendment coming at the very first annual general meeting after the original constitution had been passed. The intention of the founding members in framing their constitution was that the new society should approach as closely to a real working democracy as efficiency in the day-to-day conduct of business would permit. In aiming thus they were con-sciously avoiding the patterns of organization of the Royal Geographical Society and the British Association for the Advancement of Science, which had been founded almost precisely a century earlier and which reflected the concepts of early nineteenth-century England. In the Institute no opportunity was to be allowed for the growth of vested interests in control or for the power of self-perpetuation of a governing oligarchy. To this end they insisted that their Council should be small, that consistent with this small size as many members as possible should have the opportunity of serving on the Council, that the president and the ordinary members of the Council on vacating office should not be eligible for immediate re-election, and that any change of the rules should become effective only if it secured a two-thirds majority of votes cast in a postal ballot held after the change had been approved at an annual general meeting. The general framework of our society has surely given the ordinary member a more intimate touch with the Council and a closer control over its doings than is achieved in either the Royal Geographical Society, the Geographical Association or the

British Association. True, the size of the Council has been raised from nine to eleven members by the addition of a vice-president and an editor, but no single amendment has done anything to make the Council more independent of the views of the general meeting. On several occasions, indeed, the Council has had its ideas reversed by this general meeting and been instructed to take some action that it had previously decided against. Even more important in establishing and maintaining this intimacy has been the relatively small size of the Institute. Even now, with all our growth, we still expect to see at least 50 per cent of our members at our annual general meetings and to be able to find a meeting-place that will accommodate them in reasonable comfort. No doubt we should much like to have available, particularly for publication purposes, the funds that correspond to the membership fee income from several thousand members. If, however, such a membership were the price to be paid for control of such funds, we should have paid too heavily in the complete loss of the happy family character that makes our Institute a unique geographical organization in these islands. That is why, while we have always insisted that the Institute must not be a close preserve for university teachers of geography, we have also insisted that any candidate for membership must be a geographer, sufficiently interested and competent in the work of academic geographers to be able to fit easily and acceptably into the family. It may, perhaps, be all to the good if our membership never succeeds in growing much beyond the four hundred that I earlier suggested as being a likely stabilizing point.

Curiously enough the field meetings have evoked a relatively poor response, and that in spite of some outstandingly successful meetings. The holding of a field meeting was first seriously considered by Council at its meeting on January 3rd, 1936. The immediate impulse was a proposal by Mr. J. N. L. Baker (then secretary) that the Institute should hold a meeting entirely separate from that of any other organization. Mr. J. A. Steers extended that proposal into a motion that there should regularly be two meetings a year. The upshot was the decision to organize a summer field meeting for three days immediately before the meeting of the British

Association at Blackpool. This meeting, organized by Mr. Baker, with Mr. D. L. Linton (then of Edinburgh) as leader, took place in the Lake District, based on Windermere, but it drew only thirteen members. It set a very high standard and was confidently regarded by the participants as marking the beginning of a new and fruitful era in the development of the Institute. It proved to be a somewhat halting beginning. True, in the very next year, 1937, Dr. H. C. K. Henderson and Dr. Alice Garnett led an equally successful meeting in the Derbyshire Pennines, but there was no meeting in 1938, and the meeting arranged to follow the British Association meeting at Dundee in 1939 had to be cancelled on the outbreak of the war. Glasgow in 1947 (conducted by Professor A. Stevens and his staff), Juniper Hall in 1948 (Professor S. W. Wooldridge and Mr. G. E. Hutchings), and Sheffield in 1949 (Professor D. L. Linton and his staff), interesting and enjoyable as they were, attracted an average attendance of under twenty members and were followed by a gap in 1950 and 1951, when the field meetings lapsed for want of support. The Belfast meeting of the British Association in 1952 gave the opportunity for a field meeting in Eire, organized by Dr. D. K. Smee and led by Dr. A. Farrington. Eire was again visited in 1953, when Dr. Farrington shared the leadership with Mr. J. P. Haughton, but, as usual, the party, though enthusiastic, was small. No doubt there are many reasons why such a tiny proportion of the membership musters to the call of what ought to be the most attractive meeting of the year for a geographical body, but time and cost must rank high among them. The University Easter vacations are pre-empted by departmental field classes, the earlier part of the summer vacation is very fully occupied by the labours of examining, and the difficulty of accommodating the competing claims of the Institute, the British Association and family holidays in the later part of the summer becomes acute. While recognizing that, one must still feel that the Institute membership as a whole has not risen to its full opportunities in this matter of pursuing its studies on the ground, and one looks forward to the day when the field meeting will have assumed its rightful place as the outstanding event of the year.

V

Not so well known to the membership, but deserving of mention, are the steps taken on various occasions by the Council to bring to the notice of relevant authorities the views of academic geographers on matters of interest to the subject. Such instances include, for example, an early recommendation to the Director of the British Museum that the notable map collection of the Museum should be housed in an appropriately equipped room of adequate proportions, and supplemented by a comprehensive catalogue. A courteous reply from the Director regretted that funds were not available for this improvement, but that, when the financial situation improved, sympathetic consideration would be given to the recommendation. Perhaps, therefore, the Institute may claim part of the credit for the highly effective housing, staffing and organization now enjoyed by the Museum map collection. Not so fortunate in its outcome was the effort made to obtain a reprieve for the Fifth (Relief) Edition of the Ordnance Survey one-inch map, which it had been decided to discontinue in 1937. The Minister of Agriculture and Fisheries accepted the view of the Institute that for most academic purposes this edition was superior to any other, and for some purposes virtually indispensable. He regretted that disproportionate cost rendered its abandonment necessary, but offered to keep contour and water pulls of the published sheets available and to consider resumption of the full edition when the Fifth Edition came near completion. Resumption did not, in fact, take place. On the other hand the Departmental Committee set up by the Minister of Agriculture and Fisheries in 1936 to consider the revision of Ordnance Survey maps and to review the scales and styles in which they should be issued to the public, did, if we may judge by the results, adopt several of the recommendations put forward by the President (Professor Fawcett) in his evidence. Thus a 1:25,000 map for civilian use was adopted, as was also the establishment of a rectangular grid and the coincidence of sheet lines with grid lines, measures that aided considerably convenience of reference to, and use of, Ordnance Survey series. It is pertinent to note in this connection that the evidence tendered by the president was not merely his own personal contribution: the secretary had circularized the whole membership and had received a mass of correspondence on the subject. It was this material, carefully assessed, that provided the authority for designating the president's evidence the views of the Institute.

On the credit side, too, in a different context, was the agreement reached with the Association of American Geographers, an agreement that was its own tribute to the patience and good-will in negotiation of Professor Derwent Whittlesey on the American side and of Mr. J. N. L. Baker on our side. By it every member of each organization received without further payment the publications of both. This mutually beneficial arrangement came to an end all too soon. When war broke out in 1939, many of the male members of the Institute, including the secretary and the assistant secretary, who were already on the strength of auxiliary or reserve formations of the armed forces, left for active service, and others enlisted or entered various spheres of essential national service. Even those who were left on the staffs of university geography departments engaged in part-time service of various kinds, in addition to maintaining the programme of departments that were stripped to a bare skeleton strength of teaching personnel. It soon became clear that Institute activities would have to be suspended till the end of the war. Even a council meeting could not be arranged, but the president (Mr. J. N. L. Baker) obtained Council approval by correspondence to reducing the war-time subscription to one guinea, which would permit members to continue to receive the Annals of the Association of American Geographers in default of Institute publications to exchange for them. That expedient served its purpose for only a very limited time: it was ended by the inability of the American post office in war conditions to continue to accept the Annals for transmission to Britain. When the Institute resumed operations after the war, negotiations for the renewal of the agreement were reopened from this end, but conditions had radically changed on the other side of the Atlantic, where the A.A.G. was in process of negotiating a merger with the Society of Professional Geographers. This merger was achieved in 1949 and gave the new A.A.G. an initial membership of over 1,400. The institute obviously could not afford to supply 1,400 copies of its publications in return for 200-300 copies of those of the A.A.G., and a scheme for associate membership of the Institute for an appropriate number of A.A.G. members failed through lack of interest in America. Meanwhile, the necessary amendment to our constitution to institute associate membership had been passed in such comprehensive terms that it can be used, if opportunity offers, to provide similar exchange facilities with other geographical organizations. It may be that our nearer continental neighbours can provide such opportunities, and it is to be hoped that the contacts now being made with our French friends may lead among other things to an investigation of this particular possibility.

I have attempted no review of the publications of the Institute and no assessment of the contribution of Institute members to the war effort. On the former topic I would direct your attention to a recent interesting survey by one of our members, Dr. Karl A. Sinnhuber,[11] which reflects a measure of objectivity that I should be quite incapable of achieving. On the latter I wish I had sufficient material to compile an adequate record. Suffice it to say that while many served in fields quite alien to their professional expertise (notably as fighting sailors, soldiers or airmen), others quickly proved their value in closely related services (meteorology, survey and cartography, for example), while, increasingly, the intelligence services of the fighting forces availed themselves directly of the trained ability of geographers, whose contributions ranged from such durable productions as the Geographical Handbooks of the Naval Intelligence Division, to such ephemeral but vital items as split-second operational interpretations of air-photographs. There seems little reason to doubt that the enhanced reputation of the subject at the end of the war owed much to the recognition of the value of geographers' contributions to the war effort. I could wish that a suggestion made in 1946 by the president (Mr. J. N. L. Baker) that a record be compiled of the war service of our members had been followed up: it would have provided a most valuable document for the future historian of the Institute and indeed of the development of the subject in this country.

VI

In what I have said I have tried to give you a glimpse in perspective of some of the facets of our Institute as I see it. Created to serve the interests of the subject and of its practitioners it has, I firmly believe, made a not unworthy effort to fulfil that aim, but if the hopes of the founders are to be fully realized there is still scope for much work. The most immediate practical service the Institute can render to its members is probably the improvement of its publication facilities, and in that context regularity of issue is almost as much to be desired as expansion. Regularity, we may hope, is indeed just around the corner. For expansion the great desideratum is the possession of a solid publication fund additional to, and independent of, our annual fee income, for which, however, the main source will have to be donations. Much more important in the long run is the maintenance and strengthening of our esprit de corps, based on the common interests and personal contacts of all our members and nourished by the intimacy of our annual meetings. Given that, the Institute, having survived the stresses of childhood and adolescence, will go forward in the confidence of its adult strength.

REFERENCES

[1] *Transactions and Papers, 1947*, No. 13, Institute of British Geographers (1948), 1-15

[2] *Transactions and Papers, 1948*, No. 14, Institute of British Geographers (1949), 1-13

[3] The death of Dr. Matthews in 1943, while he was on active service with the R.A.F., was a very severe blow to the Institute and to academic geography in Great Britain.

[4] It was already explicit that the term 'geographers' was not to be limited to University geographers.

[5] Mr. (later Professor) A. V. Williamson (University of Leeds).

[6] J. N. L. Baker, Professor R. N. Rudmose Brown, R. O. Buchanan, Professors C. B. Fawcett, H. J. Fleure and Ll. Rodwell Jones, A. Austin

Miller, Professor O. H. T. Rishbeth, Professor P. M. Roxby and Dr. S. W. Wooldridge.

[7] J. N. L. Baker, Professors C. B. Fawcett and H. J. Fleure, Miss A. Garnett, Professor A. G. Ogilvie, Professor P. M. Roxby, J. A. Steers and Dr. S. W. Wooldridge.

[8] This was the Inaugural Committee, consisting of: Dr. P. W. Bryan, Professors H. J. Fleure, C. D. Forde and Ll. R. Jones, Dr. H. A. Matthews, Professor A. G. Ogilvie, Dr. S. W. Wooldridge. Professor Ogilvie was chairman of the committee.

[9] Professors C. B. Fawcett and Ll. R. Jones, and Dr. S. W. Wooldridge.

[10] No. 12, Institute of British Geographers (1947).

[11] 'Geographische Forschung an der Britischen Hochschulen: Das Institute of British Geographers und seine Publications', *Erdkunde*, Band VII, 3 Lfg. 1953, 225-9

XII

Geography & the Community *

Geography has existed as a subject of study at least back to the time of classical Greece. Indeed it was Aristotle who christened it *'the mother of the Sciences'*. Nor has interest in it only been confined to its professional practitioners. The ideas of the layman about the nature and the limits of the subject may lack precision, he may be indifferent to the more technical problems and philosophical implications, but he never quite loses sight of the facts that the raw materials of the subject are the facts of earth and man with which he is in daily contact as a large, if not a dominant, part of his total environment. Yet the systematic study of the subject in the institutions of higher learning has suffered periods of eclipse, amounting almost to oblivion. The most recent of such periods, the later nineteenth century and earlier twentieth, came in the train of the nineteenth century outburst of activity in the biological and the physical sciences, which opened up great vistas of advance in the individual natural sciences, but which also had the unfortunate effect of reducing the prestige of those scientific studies that did not proceed by way of rigidly controlled experiment in ever narrowing specialisms.

Early Academic Status in Britain

In Britain the revival of academic interest in the subject came relatively late. In Germany the impetus given by Ritter

*A lecture delivered in the University of Hong Kong on May 21st 1957 and printed by the Hong Kong University Press, 1958.

and Humboldt, both of them university professors in the earlier part of the nineteenth century, was never lost. The first comparable appointment in England did not come till 1887, with the appointment of the great Mackinder to a lectureship, later raised to a readership, at Oxford. This appointment, be it noted, derived from the investigation, carried out by Scott Keltie for the Royal Geographical Society, of the state of the teaching of geography in Europe and Britain. That Society whose initiative, indeed pressure, in this matter was to have such vital effects, was then, and still is, an essentially amateur body, organized as an independent, voluntary organ of interested laymen throughout the land. Cambridge soon followed Oxford with an appointment and a limited amount of teaching. There was no honours' degree, but the Oxford Diploma took the form and served the purpose of such a training.

Mackinder migrated at the turn of the century to the London School of Economics, where he was for a time both Reader in Geography and Director of the School. There he was instrumental in having geography incorporated as a compulsory subject in the Intermediate examination in the Faculty of Economics and as an optional special subject in the Final examination. This was the first degree qualification in geography available in the United Kingdom. It was Mackinder, too, who as Principal of the University College of Reading induced H. N. Dickson to accept a lectureship in geography. In 1907 this lectureship was converted into a chair and Dickson's became the first chair of geography in the England of the 20th century, though Herbertson at Oxford was given the personal title of professor while holding the readership.

Meantime Lyde had commenced his work at University College, London, and George Chisholm had pioneered at Birkbeck College, London, prior to going to Edinburgh in 1908 to initiate the university study of the subject in Scotland. By 1914, therefore, we find that geography had got a firm foothold in nine universities or university colleges, though there was only one full chair in the subject. Two chairs, Aberystwyth and Liverpool, were created in 1917 during World War I.

After 1918 advance was rapid. Honours' degrees in the Faculties of Arts and of Science were instituted in London and in several provincial universities, and new departments were created as rapidly as efficient staffing would permit. By 1929 the subject was established in every university in the United Kingdom, and there were seven chairs. In the 1930's in spite of the shattering economic depression, six more chairs were created, including those at Oxford and Cambridge.

The Second World War & Recognition

If that short account implies that geography had completely established itself by 1939, it is none the less true that the recognition was only partial and limited, and the outbreak of the Second World War did not immediately change the position. The Royal Society had included university geographers in the register it had compiled of British scientific workers, but for geographers that register remained a dead letter. So, in the early days of the war keen young geographers, with no fully professional outlet in their own subject, joined the armed forces as fighting soldiers, sailors or airmen. However well they did, this was inefficient use of skilled man-power. Others turned to neighbouring subjects in which they had already some competence, as for instance to survey, especially the Survey Service of the Royal Engineers, and to meteorology, especially the meteorological services of the Royal Air Force and the Royal Navy, as the best available channels of service for their acquired skills. In all these services they did noteworthy work.

Only slowly did the fighting services and the ministries more directly concerned with the conduct of the war come to appreciate the appropriateness of the trained geographer to intelligence work of various kinds, but once this was appreciated the demand for the services of geographers was almost insatiable. Whether it was the interpretation of enemy-held ground in relation to the needs of fighting vehicles, especially for the landings in Sicily and Normandy, and the expression of these interpretations in map form; whether it was the great series of model terrain reports covering much of the operational area of the British and American armies in Northern France and Western Germany; whether it was that most valuable series, *Geographical Handbooks*, produced for Admiralty purposes by a civilian team of geographers based on Oxford and Cambridge; or whether it was the interpretation of air photos by the R.A.F. organization, the work was proper to the peculiar skill of the geographer, and by the end of the war his reputation stood high for what he could do and how he could do it.

In the universities, then, the post-war years in Britain opened with a climate favourable to the development of the subject, and geography has had its fair share of the expansion the universities have achieved. Sixteen more chairs of geography have been created, so that now there exists only one university that has no chair. On the other hand, my own college, the London School of Economics, has lived up to its reputation for progressiveness by being the first institution to found a second chair of geography.

The Proper Perspective of Geography

Let me now try to put this short account of the growth of University geography in Britain into its proper perspective in the context of this lecture. As I see my topic, *Geography and the Community* the university teacher is the key figure, with a pivotal position that derives from the two-fold nature of his work. As researcher he is concerned with the discovery and assessment of new material, with the invention of new techniques and the refining of old ones, and with the formulation of new interpretations and the critical reappraisal of accepted views. It is in the performance of this function that he nurtures the growing points of his subject and keeps it living and vigorous.

The effect may be seen either in the direct professional value of the conclusions he reaches in the problems he investigates, or in the stream of ideas he sends flowing out to the community beyond the university wall. In his capacity as teacher, however, he is concerned not merely with the purveying of facts or even of ideas. His real task is the guidance of the students in the acquisition of techniques and in the development of powers of discernment and judgment, a much more exacting, if also a much more satisfying, business. To the extent that he succeeds in this aspect of his work he is constructing and maintaining channels capable of carrying his influence out to the lay public. It remains pretty certain, however, that only so far as his teaching is kept fresh and stimulating through the interest of his own original work will these channels carry a full flow of fertilizing ideas.

The Nature of Geography

What I have just said of the position of the geographer conveys nothing about the nature of the subject in which he does his work, and the assumption that the nature of the subject requires no explanation is perhaps unsafe. It may, therefore, be advisable to state a few simple propositions that will form the basis of the argument to be developed later. The first is that geography is concerned with the face of the earth, of which the visible part may be called the landscape. The second is that the landscape contains both natural elements and also man and his works—if I may be permitted the very convenient, though logically indefensible, separation of man and nature. The third is that the picture presented by the landscape at any time is a momentary still from a film of continuous change. The fourth is that the aim of the geographer is the understanding of this complex entity.

If these four propositions are agreed upon, there will be no difficulty, in accepting the corollary that the study itself is an evolutionary study, and that real understanding can come only from a knowledge of how the landscape in question acquired its existing characteristics—how it came to get like that. It follows, too, that an essential part of the work must be done in the field, though I should be the last to deny that library material, as e.g. the primary historical document or the official statistics, are also indispensable on occasion. It is in the field that the mature geographer must look for the crucial characteristics of his area. It is in the field that the student sees demonstrated the application of tested methods, and learns to develop his powers of observation and what may be called, for want of a better name, his eye for country.

In parenthesis let me note that in this context *field* and *country* should be interpreted to apply to townscapes as well as to rural landscapes. Towns, no less than regions, cover a significant amount of area (Greater London, for example covers not far short of 900 square miles) and have constituent zones, districts, *quartiers* of distinctive characteristics. Towns in short are geographical entities, and the recent rapid growth of *urban geography* emphasizes that the geography of towns is far more than merely those features of the site that at a particular time were favourable to the growth of a town.

Intellectual Interest

This eye for country, this almost automatic noting of landscape features and seeing them in an explanatory context, can to a greater or lesser extent be diffused among the non-professional community, and to the degree that it is acquired by an individual it adds a new and stimulating intellectual interest to his view of the phenomena of landscape around him. To most of us that, perforce, means the bit or those bits of our own country to which we have access. In total it will be a tiny fraction of the area of the world, but, narrow as it may be, this first-hand experience is the foundation on which must be built our concepts and judgments of other lands. The task is supremely difficult. Even in the best circumstances, when ample literature is supplemented by good pictures and maps, interpretation of other lands is apt to be a caricature of reality unless it is informed by an intimate knowledge of some actual area and the forces at work upon it.

In the large areas for which literature is scanty or partial, photographs few, and reliable maps non-existent, the difficulty is intensified. Yet the attempt must be made. In these days when the international tension that followed World War II has hardly emerged from the cold war stage, and when the peace of the world would seem to depend on the realization of a common attitude to common problems, it is surely vital that public understanding everywhere of the bases, physical and human, of national life and power should be as wide and well-informed as possible.

Professor Eva G. R. Taylor was surely right in her sub-mission to the British Association some few years ago that the precise assessment of the geographies of the United States and the Union of Soviet Socialist Republics is at least as important as the assessment of their ideologies. To those two we should now certainly add communist China, a great power for which, acute as the difficulties are, this neighbouring university seems to have a special responsibility and a special opportunity to interpret to the West. Certainly in the differences that exist between the communist bloc and the western democracies, especially in the presence of such detonators as the explosive Middle East, we can have no such certainty of peace on earth as to render responsible people indifferent to the general ignorance of the relative resources and organization of the three great nation powers of our day.

The Need for Maps

It has been argued earlier that *real* geographical knowledge and appreciation must be based on field study, and that for any individual the areal scope for field-work is limited. It is this limitation that sharpens the need for maps, particularly topographic and geological maps on a wide range of scales. Such maps are pre-eminently the tools of the geographer. They are the shorthand expression of the form and the nature of the area represented, giving the student a précis and a bird's-eye view of country he knows, and providing the best possible substitute for first hand experience of areas he cannot himself reach. They provide, too, the most appropri-ate base for the recording of his own observations, and they are an aid to the formulation of ideas and the making of inductions. This is particularly the case where the small scale map permits the user to visualize enormously greater areas than he can on the ground, and so to arrive at generalizations that would almost certainly escape any investigator working on the full scale of the ground itself. The geographer is of course not alone in being a map user, nor is it his business to provide standard cover of general purpose maps, which demand a separate specialist skill and which are normally the concern of governments, the central executives of their national communities.

Broadly, effective mapping has resulted essentially to meet one of two needs. Firstly there is the need military forces have for adequate maps to permit efficient military organization and action. This was first recognized in England in and following the 1745 Rebellion against the Hanoverian Dynasty, but it should be noted that the Ordnance Survey, which derived from the events of that rebellion, despite its name and its origin and despite the fact that it is still directed by serving officers of the Royal Engineers, is administered by the Ministry of Agriculture and Fisheries and exists to provide maps of the United Kingdom to the civil population of that country for their proper civilian purposes—a typical piece of illogical British organization, which yet works at least as well as its opposite number in any other country. The corresponding military organization in the United Kingdom is the Directorate of Military Survey, a new and more accurate name for what used to be called the Geographical Section of the General Staff, whose initial letters, G.S.G.S., still continue to be used as the index letters of the map series published by the Directorate.

Secondly there is the need of government in lands of new colonization to ensure orderly settlement and accurate boundaries. In such countries, of which the United States is no doubt the chief representative, but of which Australia, Argentina and Brazil are also good examples, cadastral maps come first, topographic maps later, sometimes so much later that they have not arrived yet! It is not surprising, therefore, that great differences in adequacy of mapping exist from one part of the world to another, especially when one remembers that accurate topographic surveying still has relatively few practitioners and that large scale survey on the ground is a very slow and costly business. Difficult, too, is adequate map making from survey data, and reproduction of the maps so made. Great Britain is unique in being completely covered by accurate maps at scales of 6″ to the mile or bigger. Hardly anywhere else in the world are such scales available except for cadastral maps of city properties; comparatively little of the world is mapped at scales of one inch or 1:50,000; and over much of the lightly populated parts only reconnaissance maps of small scale and less accuracy are available. Here, then, is a field in which the community must help the geographer if it hopes to get full value from him.

Professional Training in Geography

What has been argued so far seems to amount in summary to this: Geography can be a source of real intellectual interest to the individual, and it can be a help, perhaps an indispensable help, towards giving the citizens in general a sound basis for the appreciation of regional and international differences. Little has been said of the practical value of a professional training in geography. I should not myself subscribe to the thesis that only those subjects that have an immediately practical application are worthy of study. The prominence of the spirit that prompts a potential student to ask 'What good is it?' meaning 'Can it help me to get better paid employment?' is not surprising in these days of economic pressure; but understanding for its own sake, no less than virtue for its own sake, brings its own reward. There is still something to be said for the attitude of the Cambridge don of a bygone day, who, after a long and concentrated struggle with an intractable mathematics problem regarded his solution with satisfaction and remarked with gusto 'Thank Heaven no one will ever be able to make the slightest use of that!' The central fact is that geography can have value in the community only through the enrichment it produces in the mental experience of the individual, and this enrichment reflects developed systems of valid thinking on the appropriate range of phenomena.

If, however, the trained abilities of the professional geographer can in fact be used for the practical benefit of the community at large, that should not lessen the appeal of the subject. In Britain before 1939 the value to be got from the geographer as a geographer was very imperfectly realized. Indeed for the geography graduates of British Universities there was little hope of appointment to any position that would give scope for their professional competence other than in teaching. This was perhaps hardly so much to be regretted as might at first sight appear, since, for virtually the whole of the inter-war period, the schools, technical colleges, teachers' training colleges and university departments of geography could absorb the whole output of geography graduates and still leave the demand unsatisfied.

The Civil Service Commissioners made tacit admission of the value of geography as a background training for administration by giving the subject very high marks in the Civil Service Examination, and an increasing trickle of geography graduates entered the administrative grade of the Civil Service. For certain technical appointments, too, notably in the Hydrographic Department of the Admiralty and in the Meteorological Office of the Air Ministry a university degree in geography was an accepted qualification for entry, though some further professional training was necessary after admission. In none of these cases was the geographer being used as a geographer after appointment, and in none was the training in geography a necessary preliminary.

Land Utilisation Surveys

One very striking development there was, outside the sphere of official action. This was the Land Utilisation Survey of Great Britain, which from small, experimental beginnings in the field work of some University of London students was built by my colleague, Dr. L. Dudley Stamp, into a co-operative effort of universities and schools working to a common plan over the whole of Great Britain. It took advantage of the fact that the boundary of every field, where there are fields, is shown on the O.S. 6" map. Local field parties recorded on sheets of the 6" map the utilization of every field, with standard symbols for arable land, permanent pasture, rotation grass, orchards, built-up area and so on and so on. The completed sheets were sent to London headquarters, where a small team of geographers, the first professionally employed geographers in Britain, apart from teachers, reduced them to the one-inch scale and prepared them for printing in colour by the Ordnance Survey in sheets corresponding to the Popular Edition of the O.S. one-inch map. The result is a permanent record in map form for the whole of Great Britain of the use of the land in the last few years before World War II, and that map record has been supplemented by a series of county reports under the series title, *The Land of Britain*. The Land Utilisation Survey has been compared with the Domesday Survey, that unique source of information about the land of England in the eleventh century, but the differences are perhaps more striking than the resemblances. Domesday did not touch Scotland, and covered only that part of England where ran the royal writ of William I, and it was essentially a tax-gatherer's survey, a census of production, compiled from oral testimony and entered up as a series of ledger items. It was concerned, that is to say, more directly with the crops, livestock, capital equipment and markets, than with the land itself; and the task of giving it precise areal definition in map form, now being undertaken for the first time, is one of exceptional difficulty. This precise areal mapping was the problem that the Land Utilisation Survey completely solved, and if the essential basis of intelligent planning is accurate knowledge of what already exists, this survey has an important place as part of the foundation on which regional planning in British rests.

National Planning

The Land Utilisation Survey programme was nearing completion when the Second World War broke out. The six long years of that conflict changed not merely the face of the world map, but changed also the economic and social habits of both the warring and the neutral countries. In Britain the outstanding immediate effect of the war from our present point of view was the abrupt and unprecedented extension of government control over almost every aspect of the life of the community. Rationing of food and raw materials, conscription for the armed forces, direction of the labour of the civilian population, selection of imports, discrimination between one productive enterprise and another brought most of the normal activities of the population under the sway of a government suddenly become omnipotent and endeavouring to become omnicompetent. True, the inter-war period had already seen some government encroachment on the traditional English liberty of the subject, backed by widespread agreement that the hardships of the great depression of the 1930's and particularly the plight of the hard-hit areas of heavy industry, especially the North East Coast and South Wales, demanded the whole-hearted efforts of central government for their cure. Those were the days of the definition and delimitation of the depressed areas, later to be rechristened the *development areas*, and of the initiation of the trading estates with government financing and government planning. So Planning (with a capital P!) was already something of a nostrum before 1939, but the scale of the direction of the daily life of the man in the street during the time the war lasted was something entirely new. Six years, however, proved to be a long enough period to get people more or less habituated to the grooves within which they were compelled to move, and the post-war period opened with the victory at the polls of the Labour Party, the party explicitly committed by its underlying philosophy and its specific programme to the policy of expanding the active participation of the government in the business of life. Nationalization of the means of production had been a main plank in the party doctrine almost from the foundation of the party, and a heavy programme of nationalization covered the Bank of England, the railways, the coal industry, road transport. Such acts of nationalization constituted a measure of national reorganization of functional activities, but in the new intellectual climate of the post-war years this could be seen as simply one aspect of national planning, of which another, and equally important facet was the planning of the land itself of Britain.

It is this aspect which touches directly and intimately the interest and the professional skill of the geographer and which has therefore peculiar relevance to my present topic.

There was already in existence before the advent to power of the Labour Government a somewhat cumbrously named Ministry of Town and Country Planning, but the new government gave it wider scope and fuller powers, seeing in it a prime instrument for recreating in a national way the man-made surface of Britain. Such a ministry and such a purpose, be it noted, imply a view of the country as country

in area, and not merely as a collection of people or functions;
It implies, too, that there is a relation between the people
and the land they occupy, and that this relation may in any
particular case depart to a smaller or wider extent from a
conceptual ideal. Further it implies that the face of the
country and the associated relationships with population
change from place to place. Finally it assumes that area, the
face of the land itself, can, no less than function or activity,
be rationally planned so as to secure the optimum use of the
resources of the country at the minimum social cost. In other
words what this really means is that the view behind the
forming and the functioning of a ministry of Town and
Country Planning is a geographical view, quite irrespective of
the soundness of the assumption or of the wisdom of the
administrative action flowing from it. This indeed was recognised by Lord Justice Scott, Chairman of the committee on
Land Utilization in Rural Areas, who said *Town Planning is
the art of which geography is the science*', and, while one
might prefer to substitute 'Regional Planning' for 'Town
Planning', the quotation comes near to expressing the heart
of the matter. Another version of the same kind of appreciation of the situation is to be found in the dictum of Sir
William Holford, Professor of Town Planning, University of
London, *The most fundamental approach to the problems of
town and country planning is that of the geographer*'—and Sir
William Holford was trained as an architect.

The Geographer as a Specialist

If, then, the problem is a geographical problem, the
information on which political and administrative action is
taken must be largely geographical, and the consequences of
the action taken will be writ large in the rural and the urban
landscape of the country. The essential research, indeed,
cannot be confined entirely to the geographers' field: there is
room and need for such other specialists as geologists,
statisticians and economists, but much of the primary research and of the co-ordination of the results of the other
specialized enquiries, with the object of making the real
nature and the critical features of the area available to the

administrators in text, map and diagram, is precisely the kind of work that the geographer and no one else is trained to do.

Let us, then, have a brief look at the organization that was set up to implement the provisions of the Act of 1947. The Ministry itself was charged with various responsibilities, mainly for the stimulation, guidance and co-ordination of the work of the local authorities, but the actual production of plans and the putting of them into effect once they have been approved is the responsibility of the Local Authority. In every case the Local Authority plan has been based on the local survey, which, as I have already suggested, is in effect a regional geography prepared by the research geographers with the help of some specialist contributors. The survey gives a treatment of the physical nature of the area, the relief; the soils; the geology in so far as it is significant for drainage, mineral resources (including such relatively humble minerals as gravel or building stone), water supply and so on; and the climate. In Britain all these features are well known in their general features, but one of the discoveries is that the minor features were often critical. For instance, resources of *sand* and *gravel* in S.E. England capable of meeting the immense demands of building, road and airfield construction were very imperfectly understood, either in their location, the nature of their occurrence or the relative cost of their working. Mean monthly temperatures and mean monthly precipitation are available for numerous stations, wind data exist for selected stations, but the *microclimate*, the local variations of temperature, e.g. with degree of slope and amount of air drainage may be so sharp as to render monthly means from the Stevenson screen all but useless for the guidance of, say, a market gardener in locating his strawberry beds. If one is considering the siting of a noxious industry with a view to reducing the unpleasant effects to the community as a whole, it is customary to assume that the lee side of the town with respect to the prevailing winds is the only acceptable area. Actually when winds are blowing from any direction atmospheric turbulence is normally sufficient to dissipate the smoke or other unpleasant constituent. Much more important are the local conditions leading to concentrations when atmospheric conditions are stable and updraughts are missing.

Major diffusion near ground level may well be in a direction that is not that of the prevailing wind.

Surveys & Research

The other great preoccupation of the survey team is population, with which is closely associated the buildings and, more especially, the built-up areas. Statistical work is required to forecast populations and densities for any particular time in the future, nor is 'it the job of the geographer as such to rule on what is an optimum density of population or a maximum acceptable density. What he can do is to map the location of the existing population and the distribution of densities. In so far as census figures are adequate he can map ten-yearly conditions to show the kind and the rate of change, and especially to highlight the areas of really dense population. Communications and land use can also be mapped and evaluated in relation to internal and external needs.

All of this means that geographers occupied the key research posts both in the ministry itself and also in the planning departments of the local authorities. The administrators who had, or still have, the fateful decisions to take, had access to competent geographical appreciations on which to base their decisions. That, however, (and here I revert to a very personal comment) by no means necessarily gives approval to the operations of local authorities and an overriding ministry directed to the nation-wide control of the landscape of Britain. If 'regional' implies area, 'planning' no less implies time, and time in this case of the order of two generations or more—long enough, surely, to strain the foresight of even the ablest planners. Planning on a national scale, too, seems to carry with it the implication of undesirable rigidity. Nevertheless the official recognition that regional differences exist, that these differences can be analysed, that their implications for society at any given moment can be evaluated and that such analysis and evaluation demand the special expert knowledge of the geographer, is a great step forward, conceding both the reality of the discipline and the value of the product.

The Geographer's Place in the Community

One final criticism remains. The need for the geographer's contribution to the making of adequate plans was recognized somewhat late. Parliament, in passing the act, clearly had no conception of the basic problems, and it was only when the Ministry and the Local Authorities commenced working out their salvation that they realized that geographers were essential. So the first and most important geographical problem of all was neither visualized nor solved. This was the differentiating of appropriate areas for which competent planning authorities could be set up and in which they could work satisfactorily. In fact the Act constituted the Local Authority the planning authority, and so not merely was a chance thrown away, but in addition a whole series of positive snags was introduced into the national organization. Within ten miles' radius of the centre of Manchester, for example, there are ten planning authorities, and the same thing is found within ten miles of Charing Cross, London. Tyneside, Merseyside and Clydeside are other obvious examples of conurbations cursed by division into various arbitrary Local Authority areas, across the boundaries of which, despite the usual joint committees for co-ordinating purposes, agreed plans that fit exactly are almost impossible to achieve. Whether this regrettable state of affairs is to be debited to the haste of a government bent on quickly presenting completed reforms to an expectant public, or whether the authors of the Town and Country Planning Act were just not capable of foreseeing the essential means to its successful implementation, the result has been some quite unnecessary and very frustrating weaknesses.

You may have forgotten by now that this lecture was entitled *Geography and the Community*. I have confined myself perhaps too strictly to U.K. conditions and experience and dwelt perhaps too much on the role of geography in the sphere of planning, central and local. I need not have done so. A whole lecture could have been given for instance, on the kind and amount of geographical work now being done for the American Armed Forces not only by geographers in full-time service employment but also by University geographers throughout the United States and Canada whose research is financed by direct grants from the U.S. Navy and Air Force. Numerous lectures, too, could be devoted to the work of geographers in diagnosing causes of soil erosion in many countries, from the United States to New Zealand, and in indicating the nature of the cure.

If, however, I have left the impression that since the beginning of the Second World War the geographer has come into his own as a valuable and valued servant of the community wherever the community has provided the appropriate conditions for his work, I shall rest content.

The Published Work of R. Ogilvie Buchanan

1930   'Hydro-Electric Power Development in New Zealand', *Geo-graphical Journal*, 75, 1930, pp. 444-461.
'Geographical Influences on the Dairying Industry of New Zealand', *Geography*, XV, December 1930, pp. 630-640.

1931   'Some Grumbles', *Geography*, XVI, December 1931, pp. 308-310.
'Sheep Rearing in New Zealand', *Economic Geography*, VII, 1931, pp. 365-379.

1935   *The Pastoral Industries of New Zealand*, Publications of the Institute of British Geographers, 2, 1935.
An Economic Geography of the British Empire, University of London Press, London, 1935.

1936   'Some Features of World Wheat Production', *Scottish Geographical Magazine*, 52, 1936, pp. 313-324.

1938   'A Note on Labour Requirements in Plantation Agriculture', *Geography*, XXIII, Sept. 1938, pp. 156-164.

1947   'The Empire and World Trade' in Mark Abrams (Ed.), *Britain and her export trade*, Pilot Press, London 1947.

1948   'Geography and the Community', *New Zealand Geographer*, 4, Oct. 1948, pp. 115-126.

1951   'Air Transport: Some Preliminary Considerations', (Chapter 4 in L. D. Stamp and S. W. Wooldridge (eds.), *London Essays in Geography*, The London School of Economics and Longman's Green & Co., 1951.
'Approach to Economic Geography', in Indian Geographical Journal, *Silver Jubilee Souvenir Volume and N. Subrahmanyam Memorial Volume*, 1951.

1952   'Some Aspects of Settlement in the Overseas Dominions', Presidential address to Section E of the British Association, *The Advancement of Science*, 34, 1952.

1954   *Sheep Farming in New Zealand*, The Wool Education Society, London, 1954.
'The I.B.G.: Retrospéct and Prospect', *Transactions and Papers of the Institute of British Geographers*, 20, 1954, pp. 1-14.

1958   *Geography and the Community*, Hong Kong University Press, 1958.

1959   'Some Reflections on Agricultural Geography', Presidential Address to the Geographical Association, *Geography*, XLIV, Jan. 1959, pp. 1-13.
'Australasia', 'Auckland', 'New Zealand' (part), 'Wellington', and other contributions to *Chambers's Encyclopedia*, 1959 edition.

1961   (with R. C. Estall), *Industrial Activity and Economic Geography*, Hutchinson University Library, London, 1961. (revised edition, 1966).

1968   'The Man and his Work', Chapter I in *Land Use and Resources: A memorial volume to Sir Dudley Stamp*, Institute of British Geographers, Special Publication No.1.

1973   (editor) 'An Illustrated Dictionary of Geography' McGraw-Hill Far Eastern Publishers (S), Singapore.

(editor) Bell's Advanced Economic Geographies, London, G. Bell and Sons Ltd., 1963—in progress.